Volume Seven
Inspired learning through great books.

Ages 10-12

Second Edition

By Becky Jane Lambert

Introduction by Jane Claire Lambert

Five in a Row Volume Seven

ISBN 978-1-888659-29-0

Copyright © 1997, 2022 by Becky Jane Lambert

Published by:
Five in a Row Publishing
312 SW Greenwich Dr.
Suite 220
Lee's Summit, MO 64082
816-866-8500

Send all requests for information to the above address.

The units for *Helen Keller*, *Skylark*, and *George Washington Carver* were originally published in *Beyond Five in a Row, Volume 2*; the unit for *The Cricket in Times Square* was originally published in *Beyond Five in a Row, Volume 3*. All of these units have been revised for inclusion in Volume 7.

Many Five in a Row units contain go-along titles that complement the FIAR book selection. Since every family and every child is different, it's important to preview these additional titles before reading aloud or giving to your child to read.

All rights reserved. No part of this publication may be reproduced, stored in a retrieval system, or transmitted in any form or by any means—electronic, mechanical, photocopy, recording, or any other—except for brief quotations in printed reviews, without prior permission of the publisher. The activity sheets following each unit may be reproduced for use by the purchaser's own family.

For Troy
The man of my dreams
and the love of my life.

Contents

Introduction 6
Tips and Advice for Five in a Row Chapter Book Studies 8
How to Use *Five in a Row Volume 7* 10

Helen Keller by Margaret Davidson 14
Skylark by Patricia MacLachlan 54
The Story of George Washington Carver by Eva Moore 126
The Cricket in Times Square by George Selden 190

Sample Lesson Planning Sheets 266
Blank Lesson Planning Sheets (Reproducible) 270
Index 272
Supplemental Book List 276
Scope of Topics 278

Introduction

Good books have always been the doorway to learning. That doorway leads to growth and an appreciation for the wonders around us. The *Five in a Row* curriculum was created to bring excitement and fun to learning and to enrich children's lives through wonderful children's literature. This foundation is evident in every volume, beginning with *Before Five in a Row*.

Continuing this unique and effective way of learning, **Five in a Row Volume 7** contains **complete units for four chapter books and accompanying lessons** (selections that were formerly published in *Beyond Five in a Row Volumes 2* and *3*). These units are designed for students aged 10 through 12; many of these students will have used earlier *Five in a Row* volumes and both teacher and student will be familiar with the very similar approach to learning in Volume 7.

Just as in previous FIAR volumes, the chapter book units in Volume 7 are intended to be extremely flexible, allowing you the option to do any combination of the lessons for each chapter. You may elect to skip over certain lessons which do not fit the needs of your student and you may place additional emphasis on certain ones which seem appropriate. You will find more exercises than you can use, so enjoy choosing just the right lesson elements for your students.

You can adjust school time to fit your needs as well. By using only one lesson element each day, you can work through *Five in a Row* in as little as 30-60 minutes daily, including the time to read the chapter. If you choose to use all or most of the lesson elements, field trips and follow-up exercises, you could easily spend several hours daily. Use *Five in a Row* however it best suits your needs and the needs of your students. The more lessons you do together, or that your student does independently, the more skills that will be acquired—skills which will benefit them through high school, college and throughout life!

Five in a Row chapter book units are complete studies that cover Social Studies (including History, Geography, and Career Paths), Science, Language Arts (including Writing and Discussion Questions and Vocabulary), Fine Arts, and Life Skills. You'll also find Teacher's Notes pages for every title, providing a place to record lessons, go-along resources, favorite memories, and more; and Activity Sheets for every chapter that support and add to the lessons.

As with all volumes of *Five in a Row*, the purpose and mission remain the same: to provide students with "inspired learning through great books." You are the leader for this adventure, so gather the children around you and have a great time!

Jane Claire Lambert, author and creator of *Five in a Row*
July 2022

Tips and Advice for Five in a Row Chapter Book Studies

- There is **no right or wrong order** for covering the material or ordering the books. You will find that throughout the Five in a Row curriculum, some subjects are revisited once, and some several times! This repetition is intentional to remind your student of other books' lessons that have a similar theme or lesson topic. Covering the same topic in new ways or in greater depth at an older age is of great benefit to students.

- Following the individual units in this manual, you'll find **Sample Lesson Planning Sheets** (and a blank sheet for your use). These sample sheets demonstrate how you might organize your studies for two weeks of a sample unit. You can also make your own planning sheets or simply work directly from the manual.

- Keep in mind that there are **more lessons in the manual than you can use**. For each chapter, you'll be choosing the lessons that are especially suited to your student. You might choose topics you've never covered, topics you want to cover again, topics of particular interest to your student, etc.

- You'll occasionally be using **other resources such as your library or the internet** for further information or research. You may want "go-along" titles that match up with a particular lesson, a video that explains or illustrates a certain principle, or a website or book where your student can research additional information. Many times you'll find suggestions for other resources right in the lessons, but you may also desire additional resources depending on the needs of your particular student.

- These chapter book units do not include math; therefore, **you'll need to provide a separate math curriculum** for your child (this is true of all levels of Five in a Row). You'll also want to **add in the narrower language arts subjects** of grammar, spelling, and possibly continue with handwriting (printing and/or cursive) at some point (the timing on language arts may be different for different students). These subjects don't lend themselves to a unit study approach and you'll want to be sure to include them each week.

- Five in a Row was created to be gender-neutral and you'll find a wide variety of **fascinating lessons that appeal to both boys and girls**. Don't assume that a boy may not enjoy a book that has a girl as the main character, or vice versa! And, please note that we've referred to "teacher and student" in the singular. Many of you will have more than one student.

How to Use Five in a Row Volume 7

In Five in a Row chapter book units, you'll no longer be studying certain **academic subjects** on particular days of the week, as you did in early volumes of the FIAR curriculum. Instead, you'll be guiding your student into **a variety of areas each week**; some weeks will have a heavier emphasis on science while others may have a greater emphasis on fine arts, for example. What you study each week derives directly from what chapter you have just read at the time. Overall, your student will receive a comprehensive education in five principal areas:

- **Social Studies** (includes history, geography, and career paths)
- **Science**
- **Language Arts** (includes writing and discussion questions and vocabulary, among other topics)
- **Fine Arts**
- **Life Skills** (includes human relationships, problem solving, and personal development, among other topics)

If you have previously studied picture books in Five in a Row, you're already familiar with many of these subject areas. The following are areas that are new or unique to the chapter book units:

Career Paths are lessons that allow your student to explore and learn about various professions that tie in to the chapter. Use these in a way that fits the needs of your student. You may choose to skip some career paths, while others you may choose to investigate in depth, including a field trip to meet and interview someone in the profession.

Writing and Discussion Questions are found in every chapter, and can be used in different ways. You may choose to simply discuss the question together, or you may assign it as a writing topic. The length is dependent upon your student's age and ability; it may range from a few sentences to several paragraphs or a couple of pages. You can adjust the assignment length depending on your academic goals and what works best for your student.

Fine Arts lessons include such diverse topics as cooking, visual and performing arts, fabric arts and needlework, design and architecture, drama, and other creative arts.

Life Skills lessons cover a wide variety of topics and can be used as springboards for discussion or as writing assignments. The topics are especially appropriate for students ages 10 and up who are growing in maturity and learning to navigate human relationships, develop critical thinking skills, and practice problem solving for upcoming teen and adult years.

With chapter book units, you'll likely vary in the **number of chapters you read each week and the amount of time you spend each day**. Some chapters are brief and you might finish the chapter and activities in one day, but some are longer or more complex and could take up to a week to explore thoroughly. Many families find that they average about two chapters per week, but again, this is a generalization and some weeks may not follow this pattern. In addition, you'll find that amount of time varies per day with your chapter book activities. Some lessons may take only 30 minutes to complete, while some could take an hour or two, or extend to a long-term study or project.

Because chapter books vary in length and number of lessons, the **amount of time it will take you to complete a chapter book study will vary**, as well (two families could easily spend different amounts of time on the same book, even!). Each Five in a Row chapter book could take you as little as 4 to 5 weeks to finish, or as many as 8 to 9 weeks—it's up to your daily and weekly lesson plans, your student's needs, and your academic calendar. The flexibility of Five in a Row is great in all areas, including length of time spent on each unit!

Should you be reading the chapters to your student or should the student read silently? Either way works! Your student may want to read alone, or may want you to read aloud, and that's a decision you can work out together, depending on your child's reading ability and personal preference. Many children who are perfectly capable of reading to themselves still wish to be *read to*, and this could be a perfect opportunity for you to share that time together. Or, you may have a student who is more than willing to read alone—this is also just fine. A **Teacher Summary** has been provided at the beginning of every chapter for your convenience. You can take turns reading, listen while your student reads, read it aloud, let your student read alone … there's no right or wrong way to do it. You might employ a combination of all these approaches.

Whatever method of reading you choose, you and/or your student will **read each chapter only once**. Unlike the Five in a Row picture book units, no repetitive reading is necessary with the chapter books unless you are simply rereading a small section for a particular lesson, etc. This means that on some days, you'll read a chapter and also do a lesson; on other days, you will only do a lesson (from the same chapter) and not start a new chapter. Be sure to see the **Sample Lesson Planning Sheets** following the unit studies in this manual for a clear picture of how this works.

In each chapter's list of "What we will cover in this chapter," you'll see that one lesson is marked with an **asterisk** (there is an asterisk on the actual lesson, as well). This indicates that there is an **activity sheet** for this lesson at the end of the chapter book unit.

Helen Keller

Title: Helen Keller
Author: Margaret Davidson
Copyright: 1969

Chapter 1—A Strange Fever

Teacher Summary

In chapter 1, we are introduced to Mr. and Mrs. Keller and their baby daughter, Helen. Helen was born as healthy as any other baby. When she was not yet two years old, she was stricken with scarlet fever. Helen was quite sick and nearly died. After a long while, her health began to improve, but her parents soon discovered the severe illness had left their daughter both blind and deaf.

What we will cover in this chapter:

Social Studies: History - The Timeframe of Our Story
Social Studies: History - Scarlet Fever: A Sickness of the Past
Science: Human Anatomy - The Eye*
Language Arts: Mary Ingalls - Another Girl Blinded by Scarlet Fever
Language Arts: Writing and Discussion Question
Fine Arts: Making Toys for Children

Social Studies: History - The Timeframe of Our Story

Our author doesn't tell us in the beginning of the book exactly what year Helen was born. However, if your student flips to the end of the book, he will see that she was born in 1880 and died in 1968. If you are keeping a journal or notebook for this unit, your student may wish to include a timeline of Keller's life, beginning in 1880. What other events were happening during that year or decade? (Examples: Vice President Chester A. Arthur becomes President of the United States after the assassination of President Garfield in 1881; by 1880 commercial food packers begin to use glass containers to package their products; the first electric streetcars began to appear in America in the 1880s.)

Near the beginning of the chapter, our author tells us that Helen was born *almost* 100 years ago. Look with your student at the year our book was written—1969. Do a little math with your student (with a calculator or by hand) and discover exactly how many years it has been since Helen was born. It's now been well *over* 100 years! Encourage your student to always balance any information he reads against the year the book was *written*. He will begin to notice points of view, vernacular and items mentioned that will give him clues for guessing the timeframe of the story.

Social Studies: History - Scarlet Fever: A Sickness of the Past

We learn in this chapter that Helen Keller was probably struck down with a disease called scarlet fever. Has your student ever heard of this illness? Scarlet fever is now extremely rare in the United States and Western Europe because doctors have used penicillin since the 1950s to treat the disease. It is called scarlet fever because of the trademark red rash which develops on the face and torso at the onset of the sickness.

Before the 1950s and particularly in the late 19th century, scarlet fever was a common and feared illness. With symptoms including sore throat, nausea, high fever and achy joints, scarlet fever often resulted in kidney infections, kidney dysfunction and blindness. Use this as an opportunity to explore the history of scarlet fever, or other aspects of infectious disease, epidemics, etc.

Science: Human Anatomy - The Eye*

Helen is blind because of her illness. Her eyes no longer operate normally. But how do eyes really work, anyway? How do we see things? What are the different parts of an eye?

Take this opportunity to share with your student some information about the human eye.

Begin by drawing your student's attention to the main parts of the human eye. For example, the **orbit (eye socket)**, **pupil**, **iris**, **cornea**, **retina**, **tear ducts**, **eyelashes** and **lid**. Each piece serves a specific and vital function for our sight. The human eyeball is about one inch in diameter, yet it can see and focus on objects smaller than the head of a pin, and as far away as the moon. Amazing, isn't it?

Explain to your student that our eye doesn't "see" objects in front of it. Instead, it absorbs light reflected off the objects and transmits that information to our brain. That is why we can't see anything in pitch-black darkness. In order for our eyes to function, some light must be present. As light rays enter our eye, the eye transforms these into electrical signals and sends them to the brain. The brain then interprets these signals as visual images.

Five in Row Volume Seven

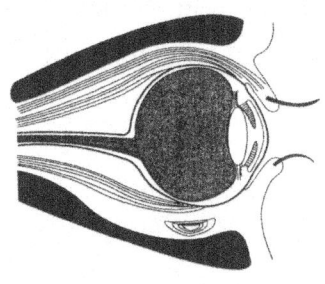

More excellent topics for exploration in this unit might include diseases of the eye, such as glaucoma and cataracts. Why do some people need glasses while others don't? Nearsightedness is a common eye defect, and so is farsightedness. Does your student know that some people (almost exclusively men, although women can carry the color blindness gene) cannot perceive colors properly? This is called color blindness. These individuals will confuse certain colors like red, green, brown and orange. This condition is not correctable; however, it does not worsen.

If your student is interested in learning more about the human eye, you may wish to spend more time exploring this topic together. By building a model of the eye, drawing pictures, dissecting a cow eyeball, looking at websites or videos online, getting books from the library and more, your student can gain a better understanding of this important section of their anatomy studies. If you are interested in doing a cow eye dissection, contact a local butcher or a slaughterhouse in your area. Eyes can be requested and held for you, usually at no charge. Try to arrange to pick up the eye on the day you plan to do the dissection. Fresh eyes are easier to dissect than old ones, because the connective tissues have not had a chance to solidify and toughen.

Enjoy exploring the world of vision and the human eye with your student. This is not only an interesting and fun section to study, but it is an important part of your student's science education.

Language Arts: Mary Ingalls - Another Girl Blinded by Scarlet Fever

Many children have read and loved the classic series written by Laura Ingalls Wilder—the *Little House* series. If your student has not read these books, encourage him to do so, or read them aloud together. Filled with fascinating historical information, family drama and beautiful character sketches, these historical fiction books contain much of the true story of the life of Laura Ingalls Wilder.

If your student has already read and enjoyed these books, he may remember another little girl who was blinded by scarlet fever. Laura's sisters Mary, Carrie and Grace, along with Laura's mother, all contracted the illness, but only Mary was left without her sight. This sad event is related in the opening lines of *By the Shores of Silver Lake*—the fifth book in the series of nine. Here is an excerpt from that book:

The doctor had come every day; Pa did not know how he could pay the bill. Far worst of all, the fever had settled in Mary's eyes, and Mary was blind.... Her blue eyes were still beautiful, but they did not know what was before them, and Mary herself could never look through them again, to tell Laura what she was thinking without saying a word.... Pa had said she [Laura] must be eyes for Mary.

Enjoy making this literary connection with your student!

Language Arts: Writing and Discussion Question

Why do you think Mrs. Keller screamed when she discovered Helen's blindness, and only whispered when she realized her daughter was also deaf?

Fine Arts: Making Toys for Children

Mrs. Keller uses one of Helen's toys to try to capture her daughter's attention. The toy is a can filled with stones. Does your student think this sounds like an enjoyable, or a boring toy? Certainly in our day and age, a rattle made from a can and rocks seems quite crude. But is it? What does your student think of the toys he sees for children today?

Today, we have highly sophisticated toys for children. Toys with lights, moving parts, and even toys that interact with us. Sometimes, however, if you watch children and observe their playtime, the most popular playthings are still the most simple, such as pots and pans, wooden blocks, a large cardboard box or even an old-fashioned teddy bear.

Does your student have younger siblings or know a small child? Encourage him to design and make a toy for that child that is simple, safe and fun. What are things he should consider when designing his toy? The plaything should be safe, have visual appeal, be interesting and age appropriate for the child, be made of non-toxic materials, have no small pieces which could be swallowed and, most of all, should be something which brings delight. Your student may also consider various other factors in his design including shape, color, texture, etc.

There are all types of toys your student can think about—stuffed animals, pull toys, blocks and many more. Have fun inventing and creating an old-fashioned toy today!

Chapter 2—The Dark Silence

Teacher Summary

The doctor confirms Mr. and Mrs. Kellers' realizations—Helen is both deaf and blind. He tells them there is nothing they can do. They go for second and third opinions, only to hear the same response—no hope. As Helen grows, she develops her own "language." Certain gestures mean different things and her parents are able to slowly understand her a bit better—but not much. Most of the time, Helen is in a world of her own. As she grows older, she also grows more frustrated. Why can't she move her lips like other people? What are they doing? Why don't they understand her? The more frustrated Helen gets, the more aggressive and angry she becomes.

The Kellers soon have another baby girl, and this makes Helen even more out of control. Soon, the Kellers are out of ideas. They don't know what to do with Helen. Mrs. Keller reads an article about a school in Boston, the Perkins Institute. They once helped a little deaf and blind girl. As a last resort, Mr.

Keller writes to Perkins, but without much hope of finding any answers.

What we will cover in this chapter:

Social Studies: History - Perkins Institute
Science: Sensory Deprivation Exercise
Language Arts: Archaic Terminology - "Deaf and Dumb"
Language Arts: Writing and Discussion Question
Life Skills: Living with Hope and Determination*

History and Geography: Perkins Institute

Mr. and Mrs. Keller write to Perkins Institute in Boston, hoping the school knows some way they can help Helen. Mrs. Keller has read an article about a little blind and deaf girl who had gone to that school before and she had learned to communicate with others. Interestingly, that little girl was the first student at Perkins who was both blind and deaf. She was the roommate of another little girl who also had vision problems—Anne Sullivan, who will soon become an extremely important person in Helen's life.

Today, Perkins is still in existence, helping the visually impaired and teaching parents and community classes on dealing with blindness. Under its new name, Perkins School for the Blind, people of all ages (birth to the elderly) can enroll in classes and receive training and information. Your student can gather more specific information about Perkins School for the Blind online.

You might also wish to locate Boston, Massachusetts on a map with your student. How far is Boston from Tuscumbia, Alabama?

Science: Sensory Deprivation Exercise

Helen is both blind and deaf. She can't hear any sound, no matter how loud, and she cannot see anything. Can you imagine being in such a dark and silent world? How would it feel? What would you have to rely on for information? How would it change the way you live your life every day? These are all questions you and your student can be thinking about throughout our study of the life of Helen Keller.

To gain a better understanding of how she felt, work with your student on some sensory deprivation exercises. Begin by explaining the exercise to your student. You will take him to an interior room of the house (e.g., bathroom, closet, basement). The darker the room is, the better the exercise will be. If you wish, mask off the cracks around a door jamb or lay a towel at the base of the door to enhance the darkness. Now, place a blindfold over your student's eyes to complete the sight "deprivation." Next, your student will have cotton balls placed in his ears and ear muffs or hearing protection headphones placed over that. The goal is to block out every sound your student might be able to detect.

Now, you and your student can both sit in the room for a pre-determined length of time (the longer your student is willing to sit, the better feel he will get for what it is like to be both blind and deaf). Try setting a goal of at least five minutes—it will feel like longer to your student.

Before the experiment takes place, however, have your student discuss or write down how he thinks it will feel to be "blind and deaf." Will it be much different? What will he have to rely on in order to gain information? Will he be comfortable or uncomfortable?

After the sensory deprivation experiment is complete, talk with your student about his experience. Was it exciting or frustrating? Did he get bored or was he scared? What could he "feel" happening around him? Did he lose his concept of time? Did it seem much longer than he expected or shorter? Can he imagine living in a world like that all the time—like Helen? Does your student have a greater respect for Helen after the experiment?

Language Arts: Archaic Terminology - "Deaf and Dumb"

Draw your student's attention to the sentence near the beginning of the chapter that reads, "Then she became *dumb*—she could not speak at all." Explain to your student, if there is confusion, that in this context, the word "dumb" does not mean stupid or ignorant. Instead, the word "dumb" was often used in the past to denote someone who was unable to speak. Because deaf children cannot hear others speaking, it is extremely difficult for them to imitate and learn speech. Imagine how hard it was for Helen, who could not hear *or* see others speaking! Even though Helen had already learned some words before she was sick with scarlet fever, after she became blind and deaf, she forgot all the words. Deaf children and blind children can be just as bright as any other children. Their disabilities do not in any way affect their intellect or abilities to learn and explore—as the life of Helen Keller certainly demonstrates.

Today, the phrase "deaf and dumb" is considered archaic terminology (used long ago, but no longer used today). The deaf community has worked diligently to eradicate the word "dumb," as well as the term "deaf-mute," from the common vernacular because of the implied negative meaning. Encourage your student to make friends with deaf and blind children. Even if he does not know sign language, deaf people are touched and excited when people want to communicate with them. They will help you learn to speak their language.

Language Arts: Writing and Discussion Question

If you did the "sensory deprivation" exercise, how did it feel? What was the strangest sensation? What did you miss the most? How does it help you to understand deaf and blind children better? Continue your essay, sharing other thoughts that you may have.

Life Skills: Living with Hope and Determination*

Mr. and Mrs. Keller are very frustrated! Their little girl is becoming more and more of a struggle to raise and they don't know how to help her. Would you have thought of giving up? Most people probably would. But Mrs. Keller does not. She begs Helen's father to take one more chance and write to Perkins. Maybe there is someone who can help them with their daughter.

The Kellers are an excellent example of determination. Being determined does not mean you are never discouraged. Instead, it means you don't allow that discouragement to bring you down and frustrate you. It means you have a sense of purpose and you work toward that goal.

Encourage your student today by sharing with him a struggle you have had where you felt like giving up. Did you? How were you able to work the problem out and live with hope and determination?

Chapter 3—The Stranger Comes

Teacher Summary

Mr. Keller's letter to Perkins Institute is soon answered. A teacher named Annie Sullivan is coming to help teach and instruct Helen. When she finally arrives one morning, Helen decides she doesn't like her. She has no idea Miss Sullivan has come to help her. Later on in the day, Helen gets into a fight with Miss Sullivan over a doll she has found. She ends up punching Annie in the face. Miss Sullivan knows the reason Helen is so badly behaved is that the Kellers have let her have her own way for so long. Annie is not sure how she can help change that, but she is going to have to try.

What we will cover in this chapter:

Science: Sound Is Vibration - An Experiment
Science: Exploring the Five Senses*
Language Arts: Creative Writing - What Was Helen Thinking?
Language Arts: Writing and Discussion Question

Fine Arts: Movie Recommendation - *The Miracle Worker*

Science: Sound Is Vibration - An Experiment

In this chapter we see Helen "listening" with her body, not her ears. Our author tells us Helen could feel the "vibrations" coming through the air and ground. Are vibrations the same things as sounds? Take some time to discuss the scientific explanation of sound with your student.

Sounds are made by the vibrations of objects. When an object vibrates, it emits sound vibrations in all directions. When those waves hit our ears, our brain transfers them into sound. Sound travels through water, air and solid objects. Has your student ever read or heard about the Native Americans putting their ears to the ground to hear the hoofbeats of horses in the distance? This practice works because solid ground transfers sound vibrations very well, and you can hear for a long distance.

Is your student still skeptical that sound is actually vibration? Here is a simple experiment to illustrate this principle. Locate a speaker and place it so it is facing up. Place an aluminum foil pie plate or other thin sheet of aluminum on the speaker, then place a few grains of rice on top. Now, select some music and start the volume out very softly. As the volume increases, the rice may begin to move a bit. As the volume gets quite loud, your student will be able to see the rice actually jump and quiver on top of the speaker. Why would this occur? Because sound is vibration! As sound waves are produced and the vibrations move out in all directions, they move the rice.

You can also do this experiment by tightly covering a bowl with plastic wrap (simulating the ear drum). Place a few grains of rice on the plastic wrap. Then take a metal pan and hit sharply with a cooking spoon close to, but not touching, the rice bowl. The rice will vibrate and jump!

Helen couldn't actually hear the sounds like we can, but she certainly felt the sounds! Perhaps you've been to a commercial fireworks display and "felt" the impact of large aerial bombs a second or two prior to hearing them. Helen would have felt them, just like you or me, but would never have heard them a few moments later. If your student is interested in exploring this concept further, encourage him to locate books at the library or look online. Other interesting related topics to explore are the Doppler effect, sound interference, echoes and the human ear.

Science: Exploring the Five Senses*

Ask your student how many senses humans have. What are the basic five? Taste, touch, hearing, sight and smell. Helen, unfortunately, does not have use of two of her senses—hearing and sight. What would it be like to live without one (or more) of your senses? How does your student think it would effect his life? How would he feel? Begin your exploration of this lesson by discussing with your student in brief how each of the basic five senses work. For example, taste is caused by cells on our tongue (taste buds or papillae) responding to molecules in the food or other substance, and transmitting information to the nerves and then to our brains.

Sight involves our eyes collecting light and transmitting the images to our brains. Has your student ever wondered why he can't see in the dark? That is because our ability to see is directly related to the light around us. Our eyes receive the light that is reflected off of images and objects. If there is no light, then our eyes think there is nothing there, even if our brain knows there is. For example, if your bedroom is extremely dark and you're walking through, you might bump into the bed. Your brain knows the bed is there, but if there isn't any light your eyes can't detect the object. If your student wishes to explore sight further, encourage him to learn more about the cornea, iris, light refraction, etc. Also, he may wish to go back and review the anatomy lesson on eyes located in chapter 1 of this unit.

Language Arts: Creative Writing - What Was Helen Thinking?

Reread the section on what Miss Annie and Mrs. Keller are saying and doing during the exchange with the doll. We are not completely sure of what Helen is thinking. Can you imagine? Suddenly some stranger is living in her home, giving her a "gift" and then taking it away?

For a creative writing assignment, have your student write Helen's thoughts throughout this scenario. Who does Helen think Miss Annie is? Why is she there? When Miss Annie grabs the doll, what goes through the young girl's mind? Why does she decide to hit Miss Annie? When Helen runs away for the day, where does she go and what does she do? This creative writing exercise can be as long or short as you wish.

Language Arts: Writing and Discussion Question

Helen slept well that night, but Annie did not. Why do you think this was so? How do you think Mr. and Mrs. Keller slept? Why?

Fine Arts: Movie Recommendation - *The Miracle Worker*

Excellent supporting material for this unit is the film *The Miracle Worker*. Made in 1962, this film adaptation of the play stars Patty Duke. It explores the story of Annie Sullivan and Helen Keller. The movie is superb and makes an excellent family film. If your student is younger, you may wish to preview it first, but be assured that it is a great addition to this study of the life of Helen Keller. Be sure to look for added information not found in the story itself.

Chapter 4—The Worst Fight of All

Teacher Summary

Helen continues to fight with Annie. The little girl can't understand why this stranger has come to her house! Helen gets angrier and Miss Annie doesn't quite know how to handle her. Every time she tries to discipline Helen or explain something, Mr. and Mrs. Keller jump into the conversation and Helen runs to them. After an entire day of battling with Helen over the breakfast table, Miss Annie is at her wits' end. She knows Helen needs to live away from home for a while, but can she convince the Kellers?

What we will cover in this chapter:

Science: How Good Is Your Sense of Smell?*
Language Arts: Writing a Persuasive Argument
Language Arts: Writing and Discussion Question

Science: How Good Is Your Sense of Smell?*

Helen could tell where the last fat sausage was on the table. It was right on Miss Annie's plate! Helen knew because she sniffed and smelled it out.

For a fun activity, let your student try to "sniff" out the last sausage. Prepare some sausages, perhaps for breakfast or brunch and let everyone join in the meal. When the eating is mostly finished, ask everyone to leave the room. Clear away all the sausages but one and leave it on one of the plates. Now, blindfold your student and invite him back into the eating area. No peeking!

Can your student find the one sausage that is left, just by using his sense of smell? What makes it difficult or easy to detect where the sausage is located? Does your student think that Helen's sense of smell might have been sharper than his own because of her disability?

Language Arts: Writing a Persuasive Argument

Miss Annie has a new plan to help Helen, but she's not sure the Kellers will like it. She knows it will take the right words to convince them of her idea. The way in which Miss Annie will need to present her ideas is with **persuasion**. She will need to persuade the Kellers that her idea is valid and workable. Has your student ever needed to persuade someone of something? Of course! Every day, we use persuasion in our conversation and our writing. For example, your student might ask a sibling, "Will you take out the garbage even though it's my turn today? Then I'll do the dishes for you this evening." The first child is trying to persuade the sibling to go along with his plan of swapping chores.

Is persuading someone always easy? No. Sometimes, it takes a lot of thought and pre-planning to present a logical persuasive argument. Take some time and share with your student a few tips on writing a persuasive paper.

When you write a persuasive argument, it is important that you pick a topic that is of great interest to *you*. If you are going to convince someone or change his mind on an issue, then *you* must believe in what you are saying. Persuasive paper topics are often issue debates. For example, your student might write a persuasive paper on: why all students should (or shouldn't) go to college; why it's important to wear a bicycle helmet when you're riding; why increased technology for kids has been beneficial (or not), etc.

As you prepare to write your paper, it is important

that you investigate the topic. Ask other people their opinion. Why do they agree or disagree with your position? If they disagree with you, prompt conversations with them that will help you understand the opponent's side. This, in turn, will tell you what you will need to argue against in your paper. Be open and listen to all sides.

Next, do your research. Find articles, books, television reports and interviews where people discuss the topic you are covering. If it is a local or personal topic (for example, should kids have school year-round, or should soda be offered in school cafeterias), do interviews and ask a lot of questions.

Finally, begin to organize your findings. List the top three or four points you would like to make. Underneath each, list the supporting evidence and facts you have found.

Now you can begin writing your paper, following your outline and choosing your words carefully. When you are trying to persuade someone of your idea, it is never a good idea to offend or bully them. Instead, be logical. Present both sides of the issue and then explain, in concrete detail, why your position is better. Be positive. Don't put their ideas down, but instead show your audience how your ideas can work better for everyone. This is called being "diplomatic." Don't be overly emotional or irrational about your topic, but do let your audience know how you feel.

As you write, build strong images to support your idea. For example, "Every 15 minutes a child is taken to a hospital due to head injuries suffered from a bicycle accident." Encourage your audience by letting them know how agreeing with you will help them. What will they get out of it? How will their lives be changed? And save your most poignant arguments for the end of the paper or speech. Many of your listeners may withhold their decision until the very end—give them something to grab onto.

If your student is interested in trying to write a persuasive paper or speech, encourage him to pick a topic and give it a try. Then, after he has written or presented the completed assignment, find positive things to say about his paper, and also be honest with him. How did you feel after reading or hearing it? Did he convince you? How could it have been better? What really worked?

Language Arts: Writing and Discussion Question

What do you think Miss Annie's idea is going to be? What is she planning to ask Mrs. Keller?

Chapters 5 and 6—W-A-T-E-R! So Much to Learn

Teacher Summary

Miss Annie and Helen take up residence together in the Kellers' garden house. It was Miss Annie's idea to take Helen away from the family for awhile, and it works well. Each day, Helen learns more about Miss Annie, but she still doesn't understand what words are or what all of the "finger" spelling in her hand means. Then one day the connection is made. Helen is playing at a water pump and as she feels the water, Miss Annie spells "water" into her hand. Helen understands! Helen understands that Miss Annie is her teacher and she learns her own name—*Helen*. Things are finally changing for Helen!

What we will cover in these chapters:

Language Arts: Etymology - The Study of Words*
Language Arts: Creative Writing - The Smells of Spring*
Language Arts: Writing and Discussion Questions
Language Arts: Vocabulary
Life Skills: Fostering Anticipation for Each New Day

Language Arts: Etymology - The Study of Words*

Helen now understands that each item in the world has a name—a word that corresponds! We often take that concept for granted, but imagine making that discovery for the first time! Does your student know that there is a science, a study that is entirely devoted to the origins and development of words? It is called **etymology** (eht uh MAHL uh jee).

Share with your student that each word, just like a person, has its own country—its own history. Etymologists work diligently to uncover those facts and stories, as well as to identify changes in words even today. Languages change and go through modifications and additions constantly because societies change.

The primary form of a word, in any given language, is called an etymon. Your student can think of etymons as mother words. For example, the word for father in Italian is "padre," "padre" in Spanish, "pere" in French and "pai" in Portuguese. These words are similar because all these languages branch off of Latin. The Latin word for father is "pater"—pater is the etymon.

Sometimes etymologists work on finding the origins of combination words. For example, the word "smog" is a combination of the words smoke and fog. The word "chortle" was coined by Lewis Carroll in his poem, "Jabberwocky," and is probably a combination of the words chuckle and snort. And what about funny words like "scribble?" That word comes from the Latin word meaning to write—scribere.

And what about the word "etymology?" How did we come up with that word? Like many words, it helps make the word easier to understand to break it into pieces. The suffix "ology" in the word etymology means "the study of." And the root "etym" is Greek for "word" or "truth." Etymology then means "the study of words." Pursue this fascinating field by doing additional study. You might begin with a dictionary,

Five in Row Volume Seven

or with articles or videos online. Learning about our words can be fascinating.

Language Arts: Creative Writing - The Smells of Spring*

Draw your student's attention to the sentence, "The window was open and the smells of spring came pouring in." What does your student think the author means by the "smells of spring?" What does spring smell like?

For a creative writing assignment, ask your student to make a list of the smells he associates with springtime. He might record smells such as flowers, even particular ones such as daffodils, hyacinths, lilacs, etc., rain and fresh-cut grass. For your older student, make this exercise even more challenging by talking through specific descriptions of each item. For example, how would he describe the smell of fresh-cut grass? Make a list of the descriptive words for each item:

newly cut grass
pungent, acidic
lemony, oniony
fresh

If your student is doing this lesson during the summer, fall or winter, encourage him to use his sensory memory. If he can think back to a spring day, he can remember the smells and describe them. Happy spring!

Language Arts: Writing and Discussion Questions

1. When Helen figures out that everything has a name, Miss Annie begins to laugh and sob. Can someone laugh and sob at the same time? Why would those two different emotions go together?

2. Imagine trying to describe subjective feelings to someone who has never known the words—someone like Helen. How would you describe sadness? Love? Joy?

Language Arts: Vocabulary

etymology   The study of words.

etymon   The primary root word.

Life Skills: Fostering Anticipation for Each New Day

The day Helen begins to understand words and the world, April 5th, 1887, began like any other day. Neither Teacher nor Helen knew what an important day it would be. Encourage your student to approach each new day as though something wonderful could happen. By fostering anticipation each morning, we lead more excited, positive lives. Talk with your student about the difference between optimism and pessimism and how those outlooks color both our emotions and our experience.

Chapter 7—A Time to Move On

Teacher Summary

Teacher makes sure that Helen has all the same experiences that any child would at that time. Helen gets to go to the zoo, attend the circus, bake Christmas cookies and enjoy a canary for a pet. Helen is doing very well. Soon, she begins to learn to read braille—the raised symbol language of the blind. In just one year, Helen has learned so much! Teacher knows it's time to learn even more.

What we will cover in this chapter:

Social Studies: History - The Circus
Social Studies: History - Louis Braille*
Science: Primates*
Language Arts: Creative Writing - Frosty Fingertips
Language Arts: Writing and Discussion Questions
Language Arts: Vocabulary
Fine Arts: Juggling

History and Geography: The Circus

Teacher's Note: Several books in the *Five in a Row* curriculum have touched on the topic of the circus—a hugely popular attraction for children and families in years past. As with all "revisited" topics in *Five in a Row*, your student will learn a little something different when covering a topic in a different context and at a later age.

Helen enjoys the circus very much! There are so many new and exciting things for her to smell and touch at the circus—the food, the animals and much more. Today, the circus has changed quite a bit from what it was more than 100 years ago, but there are still circuses in operation today, both in the U.S. and in other countries.

What are the things your student thinks of when he thinks of a circus (either from personal experience or from his FIAR studies)? What comes to mind first? Here are some possibilities: clowns, animals, a man on stilts, a band playing music, trapeze artists, juggling acts, cotton candy, popcorn, and of course, the ringmaster!

Who first thought of the idea for a circus? Where do circuses come from? To answer these questions, first look at the word "circus." Circus comes from the Latin word for circle or oval shape. For more than 2,000 years, circus-type shows have been presented in rings or oval-shaped areas. Today, most circuses are held in arenas or tents, but the acts are still framed within a ring or rings. Has your student ever heard of a "three-ring circus?"

For many years, in many parts of the world, circus groups traveled by train from town to town; later circuses traveled mostly by truck. (The exception to this was the Ringling Bros. Barnum & Bailey circus, which continued traveling by train until its last show in 2017.) Because circuses would travel for months at a time, larger circus groups may have had their own doctor, vet, barber and even school for the young performers.

The people who help set up the circus are known as roustabouts. The performers in any given act are often married or related. That is how many tricks and acts are taught—children learn it from their parents. For example, you might see an act of liberty horses (horses without riders, doing patterns and tricks) being led by a couple. They might be the third or fourth generation of liberty horse trainers.

If your student is interested in learning more about circuses, here are some topic ideas for exploration: train travel and the circus; P.T. Barnum; Circus World Museum in Baraboo, Wisconsin; Circus Flora in St. Louis, Missouri; Lillian Leitzel (aerial performer from the 1930s); Gunther Gebel-Williams (famous wild animal trainer); and the famous circus clown, Emmett Kelly.

History and Geography: Louis Braille*

Your student has probably already noticed, but draw his attention to the back cover of our book—*Helen Keller*. Let him feel the raised dot alphabet. Can he close his eyes and detect the differences between the letters? Does he think reading braille would be easy or difficult? Share with your student some of the fascinating facts regarding the developer of this language—Louis Braille.

Born on January 4, 1809, Louis Braille was much like Helen Keller when she was born—a healthy, seeing, hearing child. It was not until he was three years old that Louis had an accident and became blind. At first, his eyes were just blurry. Before he reached the age of four, Louis became completely blind. Luckily, his parents had a place to turn. In 1819, when Louis Braille was ten years old, he was sent to a special school for the blind—the Royal Institute for Blind Youth in Paris, France. Founded in 1784, this school was the first of its kind. In those days, blind children were left to fend for themselves. Unable to go to regular schools, they never learned to read or write and were often left to beg for money. Not Louis. At the Royal Institute he made friends with other blind children and learned to read, write and do arithmetic.

But Louis was frustrated. The only way for blind people to read books was to follow along with their finger on the pages of embossed books. These books were expensive, heavy and very large. Each letter of each word had to be raised and widely spaced so the students could tell what letter it was. Reading was a slow process and writing was even slower. There had to be an easier way!

When Louis Braille was only 13 years old, he began working on a new system of writing—a code system based on the secret military codes of the French Army. Slowly but surely, Braille worked out the 26-letter alphabet by using raised dots in a 6-dot cluster. Each dot was numbered, and by punching the dots into paper in various combinations, could be felt on the opposite side. Each dot pattern represented a different letter of the alphabet. By the tender age of 15, Louis Braille had developed an entirely new language! Using nothing more than the 6-dot cell, Louis worked out 63 characters—the alphabet, numbers, punctuation symbols and commonly used words.

To write in this new raised-dot system, Braille also developed a special writing tool—a stylus. The paper slipped into a metal frame, and a metal pen (stylus) slid along the paper and was guided by a ruler. The writer could punch holes in the paper and then slide the ruler down to start on the next line. When the paper was flipped over, another person could "read" the writing with his fingers.

Braille was a success! His system made books for the blind affordable, since the dots were easy to reproduce and took up little more space than conventional printed text. The letters and symbols were easy to learn. Imagine developing such an important invention before reaching the age of 16!

By age 20, Louis Braille became a teacher at the Royal Institute. Throughout his remaining years, Braille continued to work diligently as a teacher and advocate for the blind. Although his health began failing at a young age, Braille continued to support his students and friends. He died on January 6, 1852, just two days after his 43rd birthday.

Today, Louis Braille rests in the Pantheon in Paris—the burial place of France's most famous heroes. The house he grew up in, in Coupvray, France, has been preserved as a museum and looks much as it did when little Louis was growing up there. A plaque on the front door reads:

In this house on January 4, 1809, was born Louis Braille, the inventor of the system of writing in raised dots for use by the blind. He opened the doors of knowledge to all those who cannot see.

If your student is interested in learning more about this fascinating inventor and hero, the author strongly encourages you to locate the book by Russell Freedman, entitled *Out of Darkness: The Story of Louis Braille*. Written in lyrical prose, this book is powerful and compelling for adults as well as children. The illustrations by Kate Kiesler are beautiful, too.

Remind your student that like Louis Braille, he is never too young to have a good idea and help change the world!

Science: Primates*

Helen is lucky enough to get to play with the monkeys at the circus! Wouldn't that be fun? If your student has not yet had an opportunity to study monkeys, apes and primates, seize this learning opportunity and spend some time exploring them together. Does your student know that monkeys and apes (gorillas, chimpanzees, or orangutans) are not the same thing?

Orangutan (an ape)

Baboon (a monkey)

Many people use the terms interchangeably. Look at pictures of each. Apes are generally considered smarter than monkeys and don't have tails! Apes are also excellent climbers, while monkeys usually run and jump into the trees.

Monkeys include marmosets, tamarins, capuchins and baboons. When monkeys walk, they usually do so on all fours. Many monkeys can walk upright and even run on two legs, but only for a short time. Baboons groom one another for social activity. Most baboons spend several hours a day either being groomed or grooming another monkey. They seem to bond and enjoy this activity very much.

If your student is interested in learning more about primates, topics to explore might include: how monkeys communicate; the two main types of primates (1) anthropoids—humans and apes, (2) prosimians—lemurs and galagos; the predators of apes and monkeys; how they care for their young, etc. Find a good chart of the Animal Kingdom and see where the primates are located.

Language Arts: Creative Writing - Frosty Fingertips

Helen tells Teacher that some people have "frosty fingertips" while others have hands that "warm my heart." Do you suppose Helen was talking about the character of the person by using the metaphor of fingers and hands? Does your student know a person who is kind and good? A person who warms their heart? And does your student know people who are harder to get along with—quick to argue or take offense? Perhaps Helen would describe this second group as "frosty."

To continue this line of thought, have your student write a creative assignment, describing a person who has "frosty fingertips." What does the person look like? What is he/she wearing? What does the person do for a living? How do they talk to others? Encourage your student to include as many details as he can in the description and narrative. The reader should be able to picture just what the author was thinking.

Language Arts: Writing and Discussion Questions

At the end of this chapter, Teacher decides it is time for Helen to move on. Do you think Helen is ready to go to school with other children? Has she learned enough yet? How would other children relate to her? How would you relate to her?

Language Arts: Vocabulary

braille The special coded raised-dot language of the blind.

Louis Braille The inventor of the language of the blind.

primate Any of the highest ranking order of mammals (including humans, monkeys and apes.)

Fine Arts: Juggling

Helen loved the circus. What is more traditional to the circus than jugglers? Anyone can learn to juggle. Circus camps and clown schools offer classes in the sport. Many bookstores, toy stores or gift shops sell beginning juggling sets or you can easily find them online or make your own. Juggling isn't a modern pastime only. Ancient paintings in Egyptian tombs show people juggling objects. For hundreds of years, court jesters performed juggling acts for kings and queens. Juggling is taken quite seriously by thousands of performers today. There is even an association just for them! The International Jugglers Association was formed in 1947. Juggling provides entertainment, both for the juggler and the person watching. For the juggler, it also develops excellent hand-eye coordination and provides exercise.

With a trio of beanbags or balls and a book explaining the basics, your student can learn this art as well! To make it easier for a beginner, encourage your student to practice standing by the edge of a bed. In this way, when he drops a ball (and everyone drops many when they're learning!), he can quickly pick it up without bending all the way to the ground. He will also find it easier to juggle with a plain, light-colored wall in the background to lessen visual distractions.

Your student can have a wonderful time learning an art as ancient as kings. Juggling is a marvelous vehicle for improving hand-eye coordination and for a surprising number of individuals, juggling becomes a lifelong hobby. Many enjoy learning to juggle with a partner, exchanging clubs and batons. Have fun exploring this fascinating activity.

Chapter 8—"I Am Not Dumb Now!"

Teacher Summary

Teacher enrolls Helen in the Perkins Institute—the same school Teacher went to when she was a girl. The same school that Mr. Keller wrote to when he asked for help for Helen. The teachers and students at Perkins love Helen. Helen loves her classes and the books she's given to read. Helen never knew how much there was available to her. When there are books that are not in braille, Helen asks Teacher to read them to her.

Helen is nine years old now, and she spells so fast with her fingers people have to ask her to slow down. Her brain is faster than her fingers. Helen decides on a way to remedy this. She will learn to talk like a hearing child. At first, Teacher is hesitant, but she finally agrees. Helen works tireless hours trying to get her vocal cords to make the same vibrations she feels other people's throats making. Finally she says her first sentence: "I am not dumb now."

Teacher's Note: Regarding the title of this chapter, ask your student if he remembers this other meaning of "dumb" as it was used several decades ago. You may wish to revisit the lesson from Chapter 2, Language Arts: Archaic Terminology - "Deaf and Dumb," that describes this term that is no longer used today.

What we will cover in this chapter:

Social Studies: History - Robert Fulton and Steamboats
Social Studies: History and Geography - Plymouth Rock
Social Studies: History - Anne Sullivan's Life
Social Studies: Career Path - Speech Therapist*

History: Robert Fulton and Steamboats

In this chapter, we see Helen taking her first steamboat ride. Remember, the year was around 1889. Steamboats had been cruising the waters of the world for nearly 70 years. But who invented the first steamboat? Share with your student some introductory information about this famous invention and the man behind it.

Born in 1765, Robert Fulton lived in Pennsylvania. His father was a farmer, but the young Robert showed more of a penchant for inventing. He made his own lead pencils and designed the fireworks for his town's annual celebration. Before the age of 16, Fulton had designed and built his own rifle, complete with sight and bore of original design.

When he was 21 years old Fulton moved to England to study art, but soon became more enamored with scientific developments. He loved to design new canal plans and explored the use of canal locks. In 1797, Fulton decided to concentrate on designing submarines. He built a diving boat called the *Nautilus* that could descend 24 feet in the water. But Fulton was still looking at new ideas.

In 1802, Fulton began to devote all of his attention to building a steam propulsion boat. In just one year, he set his first steamboat on the water, but it sank. The engine was too heavy. Not to be dissuaded, Fulton kept working on his concept. On August 17, 1807, the first successful steamboat, the *Clermont*, set sail. A statue of Fulton resides in Washington, D.C., in honor of this great inventor.

Teacher's Note: An excellent book to get for your student if he is interested in inventions is *Steven Caney's Invention Book*. As the cover says, "From inspiration to prototype, everything you need to know. Featuring easy at-home projects to start now, plus 35 Great American Invention Stories." This book is so enjoyable to look through. It explores the inventions of things from the zipper to chocolate chip cookies. This book could become a family favorite!

If your student is interested in learning more about this topic, he might explore ship building, ship yards, canals and locks, the War of 1812 and Robert Fulton in greater detail.

History and Geography: Plymouth Rock

Teacher lets Helen stand on Plymouth Rock! If your student has not already studied the Pilgrims and their landing, take this learning opportunity to explore this event together.

According to popular stories, when the Pilgrim explorers aboard the *Mayflower* first set foot on American soil, they stepped on a giant granite boulder. More probably, the large boulder was simply visible and near the place where the Pilgrims came ashore. They christened the stone Plymouth Rock, in honor of their arrival. The rock was moved several times until 1921, when it was finally set permanently by the shore as a tribute to the Pilgrims and their landing in 1620.

You can visit this site today, located in Pilgrim Memorial State Park on the coast of Massachusetts. If you don't live nearby, take a moment with your student to explore this site online and view Plymouth Rock!

Social Studies: History - Anne Sullivan's Life

When Teacher and Helen are reading a story together. Teacher is forced to stop because her eyes get too weak and tired. Why is that? Although our book goes into the reason briefly, take a few moments and share with your student some additional information on the life of Helen Keller's teacher—Anne Mansfield Sullivan.

Born in 1866 in Massachusetts, the young Anne Sullivan had vision problems. In just a short period of time, Anne became almost completely blind, and became a student at the Perkins Institution for the Blind. Interesting to note, Miss Sullivan's roommate for a time was the first blind-deaf child ever educated in the United States—Laura Bridgman. By being around Laura, Anne gained understanding and compassion for those stricken with both deafness and blindness. In 1881 and again in 1887, Anne Sullivan had corrective surgeries done on her eyes that were quite successful. But, although her vision was restored, her eyes would always be weak. Anne Sullivan wore dark glasses most of her life. Toward her later years, her eyes began to worsen again.

Anne Sullivan devoted her entire life to helping Helen Keller. Sullivan married, at age 38, a Harvard professor named John A. Macy. Even after the marriage, she continued to travel with Miss Keller. Anne Sullivan died on October 19, 1936. Helen Keller and Teacher had been together for 50 years.

If your student is interested in learning more about the life of Anne Sullivan, the Scholastic Biography series you're using now also has published a biography on the life of Miss Sullivan. Entitled *Helen Keller's Teacher*, it is written by Margaret Davidson, the author of our book for this study.. You may also want to branch out to study others who have spent a lifetime serving others.

Social Studies: Career Path - Speech Therapist*

Helen is trying to learn to speak. At first, your student may not comprehend how difficult this would be for a person who is both blind and deaf. When we are children, we learn to speak by both hearing our parents and others and by observing the shape of their mouths and lips. Deaf children can learn to speak a little sometimes, by watching people. Blind children don't have much trouble at all because they can hear and imitate. But what if you could do neither?

Many people, not just those who are deaf, have trouble speaking. Sometimes people lisp, or stutter or can't pronounce certain letters or phrases. Sometimes there is a complete or near-complete loss of ability to understand or express language, called aphasia. Sometimes speech and language problems begin early in life, and sometimes they are caused by a traumatic injury— stroke, brain injury or emotionally devastating event. How can people like these be helped? People called speech therapists work diligently with victims of speech impediments and help them learn to speak clearly and gain confidence.

If your student is interested in speech and how it works, and enjoys serving others and helping people overcome problems, a career in speech therapy might be a good job to explore.

Speech therapists work in schools, deaf education centers, hospitals, nursing homes, private practices and public clinics. Students can earn a bachelor's degree and a master's degree in speech pathology/therapy.

The classes you might take in a college program for speech pathology/therapy include phonetics of American English, language development, language disorders in children, audiology, and the neuro-anatomical (brain) functions of speech.

If your student is interested in learning more about speech therapy, contact your local hospital or school. Arrange a visit to a learning center for children or speech pathology office. You may be able to have your student "shadow" a professional for the day, or simply observe them in a classroom setting.

Language Arts: Writing and Discussion Question

Some people in the deaf community (sometimes written as Deaf community or Deaf culture) do not think deaf children should try to speak. They believe that deaf children are special the way they are and shouldn't try to communicate like hearing children. What do you think about this? Do you agree with Helen's attempt at learning to speak? Why or why not?

Chapter 9—College

Teacher Summary

Helen becomes more and more independent. She learns to ride a horse, swim by herself and even rides a tandem bicycle with a friend. Soon, Helen decides she wants to go to college. She and Teacher head off to Radcliffe College for women. Helen is forced to work twice as hard as the other girls. Teacher works hard, too. Both women go to class each day and Helen memorizes all she can. She reads so many braille books her fingertips bleed. But in the fall of 1904, Helen graduates from Radcliffe with honors! She is the best educated deaf-blind person in the world!

What we will cover in this chapter:

Social Studies: History - President Benjamin Harrison*
Social Studies: History - Harvard University and Radcliffe College
Language Arts: Book Recommendation - *Black Beauty*
Language Arts: Writing and Discussion Question
Language Arts: Vocabulary
Fine Arts: Cooking - Helen Keller's Roasted Apples

Social Studies: History - President Benjamin Harrison*

Twelve-year-old Helen is invited to the White House to meet the President of the United States. Who would that have been? If you wish, you might have your student figure out which president it is himself. Helen was born in 1880. If she were 12, then the year would be 1892. Who was president through 1892? By looking in a reference book or online, your student should be able to discover that it was Benjamin Harrison. Here is a great opportunity to explore together with your student some of the history behind this president and a few interesting facts about his life. If you are keeping any kind of timeline or notebook for these units, make an entry for this American leader.

Benjamin Harrison was born in Ohio on August 20, 1833. His father was a congressman and farmer, and his mother was a housewife and mother of thirteen children. Because of his father's political life, Benjamin grew up in the public arena. Even more crucial to his decision to run for President, perhaps, was his grandfather, William Henry Harrison. William was the first Harrison to become President of the United States (ninth president). Sadly, however, President William Harrison caught a severe cold on the day he gave his inaugural speech and died in office just one month later. His grandson, Benjamin, had aspirations to be president from an early age, and in

President Benjamin Harrison

fact, ran under the slogan and song, "Grandfather's Hat Fits Ben."

Benjamin Harrison served as the commander and chief of a regiment of volunteers in the Civil War and moved through the ranks to become a brigadier general. His soldiers were quite fond of him, and affectionately called him "Little Ben" because he was not quite 5' 6" tall.

Benjamin Harrison ran in the presidential elections of 1888 and beat the incumbent, President Grover Cleveland. While in the White House, Harrison worked diligently to strengthen the country. His largest accomplishment was establishing more respect and honor for the flag of the United States. It was President Benjamin Harrison who insisted the flag fly over the White House government buildings and all schools. When you see a flag flying, think of President Benjamin Harrison.

Although he served a productive term, during the election of 1892 he was defeated by his old rival, Grover Cleveland, who then served a second (but not sequential) presidency from 1893-1897. Sadly, just two weeks before this loss at the polls, Benjamin's wife, Caroline, died. He and his daughter were devastated.

After his presidency, Harrison returned to Ohio and practiced law. He married the nurse who took care of his wife during her last days, and had a daughter with her. He authored a book, traveled extensively and died in his home on March 13, 1901.

If your student is interested in learning more about Benjamin Harrison, encourage him to research the president at your library or online. If your student enjoys musicals, there is a Disney film entitled *Family Band* featuring Buddy Ebsen, Richard Crenna, and Leslie Ann Warren. The film centers around a musical family that is politically divided. Most of the family feels allegiance to Benjamin Harrison but the grandfather supports Grover Cleveland. The climax of the film centers around the election. This movie would make an entertaining addition to your study of our 23rd president—Benjamin Harrison!

Social Studies: History - Harvard University and Radcliffe College

Helen wanted to go to Harvard University. Teacher didn't think Helen could do the work in college, but she used the excuse, "Not Harvard, Helen. That's a boys' school."

Later, Helen goes to Radcliffe College. Take this opportunity, if there is interest, and share with your student some information about these famous universities.

Harvard University is the oldest institution of higher learning in the United States of America—established in 1636 under the name "Newtowne." The school was renamed for John Harvard, a Puritan minister, who left the campus half of his estate and over 400 books when he died in 1638. Harvard has maintained a fierce pride and remains one of the top universities in the U.S. today. In fact, the school still operates under a charter written in 1650. With an endowment (money given to a school to maintain costs) of over $4 billion, Harvard is also one of the richest and most prestigious colleges in the country. Some of Harvard's most famous alumni include Presidents John Adams, John Quincy Adams, Rutherford B. Hayes, John F. Kennedy, Franklin Delano Roosevelt, Theodore Roosevelt, George W. Bush and Barack Obama.

Radcliffe College was established in 1879 as the "Harvard Annex." It was, in all respects, a sister campus which provided instruction for women at the level they would have received at Harvard. In 1894 it was renamed Radcliffe College. In 1999, Radcliffe merged with Harvard and was renamed the Radcliffe Institute for Advanced Study, which is open to both women and men (as is Harvard, of course!).

Language Arts: Book Recommendation - *Black Beauty*

Helen's horse was named Black Beauty. Helen may or may not have named her horse after the well-known Anna Sewell novel. Nonetheless, this is an excellent opportunity to make reference to the classic book. If your student has not already read or heard the famous tale of a horse and his masters, then take this time and introduce him to the book.

Written by Anna Sewell in 1877, *Black Beauty* is the fictional autobiography of a horse and his different masters. Because the book is written from the point of view of Black Beauty, your student will gain insight into writing from different perspectives. The book is also a moral tale about the treatment of animals and how we should all strive to be good and loving toward animals who are under our care.

Sewell was born in England in 1820 and only lived to be 58 years old. When she was 14 she suffered a severe sprain to both ankles and remained crippled for the rest of her life. Her favorite times, both as child and adult, were when she was on her horse or in her horse-drawn carriage. She wrote *Black Beauty* over the course of six years while she was confined to her bed with an illness. It was her only book, but gained international renown. Today she is considered to be one of the most beloved childhood writers and her only book is still extremely popular.

The story is masterfully written and lovingly told. Find it, and begin a read-aloud time with your student today!

Language Arts: Writing and Discussion Question

Why do you think Anne Sullivan was so extremely devoted to Helen?

Language Arts: Vocabulary

tandem   Made for two; two people working together; a bike for two; a pair.

Fine Arts: Cooking - Helen Keller's Roasted Apples

Helen loved adventure and new experiences, but she also enjoyed quiet evenings at home. Our book tells us that sometimes she and Teacher made roasted apples and played games in front of the fire. Why not take a break and let your student cook up something special? Here is a recipe for roasted apples the way Helen might have fixed them herself:

Helen Keller's Roasted Apples

4 apples, peeled whole and cored
4 Tbs. butter or margarine
8 Tbs. brown sugar
4 Tbs. raisins
1/4 cup water

Preheat oven to 375° F. Set the 4 cored apples in a shallow glass or ceramic baking dish. Place 1 Tbs. butter, 2 Tbs. brown sugar, and 1 Tbs. raisins in the core of each apple. Then pour the water into the dish and bake, covered, for 35-45 minutes or until the apples are soft. Enjoy!

Chapter 10—The Busy Years

Teacher Summary

After graduating from Radcliffe, Helen begins to do all she can to help other blind and deaf people. She writes papers and then gives speeches. These provide forums where people can ask her questions and she can speak on the issues closest to her heart. On October 19, 1936, Helen suffers her greatest loss when Annie Sullivan dies. Helen finds the times very difficult, but she bravely continues. World War II has begun, and she travels to hospitals in the United States, encouraging the wounded and telling her story. Helen's life is never without adventure. She lives to be 87 years old, and dies on June 1, 1968. She continues to be an inspiration and hero to millions even today.

What we will cover in this chapter:

Social Studies: History - World War II*
Language Arts: Writing and Discussion Question

Teacher's Note: The main lesson opportunity in this chapter is an exploration of World War II. If you have not already done so, put heavy emphasis on this important historical event. Investigate and explore the various topics given below and encourage your student to put together a notebook or poster set of his WWII studies. This major event in American and world history deserves a thorough study.

Social Studies: History - World War II*

Helen Keller spent a great deal of time visiting WWII veterans in hospitals around the United States. She had compassion, particularly for those who were blinded during battle. Franklin D. Roosevelt asked her if she would be willing to help show the soldiers that life was still worth living.

Although there is no way to give a "brief" look at such a major historical event as World War II, this lesson will be an attempt to examine some of the more important points. Specifically, this lesson will present a variety of ideas for your student to explore. Find an interest and then pursue that interest through the lens of World War II.

To begin, World War II is considered by nearly every expert to have been the most destructive global conflict in history. It killed more people, destroyed more property and infrastructure, and had more far-reaching consequences them any war before that time or since. The number of casualties due to the war will never be completely calculated, but according to several sources they are estimated to be between 40 and 50 million people. More than 8 million soldiers from the Soviet Union alone! More than 19 million Soviet Union civilians were killed as a direct result of the fighting and bombing.

World War II began on September 1, 1939, when Germany invaded Poland. Germany's dictator, Adolf Hitler, had been working systematically to make Germany into the most feared and powerful nation in the world. He had, in many ways, succeeded. In only ten months, his armies soundly defeated and conquered Poland, Denmark, Luxembourg, the Netherlands, Belgium, Norway and France! Great Britain stood alone, but strong, against Hitler. Then, forces began to join Germany—Italy and Japan. These three countries formed one side of the war—they became known as the Axis. Together they invaded northern Africa and the Soviet Union.

Japan attacked the United States military base at Pearl Harbor, Hawaii on December 7, 1941. This brought the United States into the war full force, and they soon formed their own alliance. The United States, Great Britain, the Soviet Union and China formed what they called the Allies. By the end of the war, nearly 50 countries would be a part of the Allies.

The bloody battles continued throughout 1944. In the background of all the fighting, the Allies had a trump card, however. In 1939, the scientist Albert Einstein had informed President Roosevelt that he believed he could build a "super bomb"—a nuclear bomb which would be unparalleled in its intensity because the explosion would occur from the splitting of an atom. Einstein was afraid Germany would develop the bomb before the United States. Interestingly, Einstein had been born in Germany. Immediately, the President ordered testing to begin and the "Manhattan Project" was birthed.

On May 7, 1944, Germany, finally broken and penniless, surrendered to the Allies. President Roosevelt died in April of 1945, while the war was still being fought. Harry S. Truman became President. He,

Five in Row Volume Seven 39

along with many Americans, was sickened by the length and devastation of WWII. He wanted the fighting to stop. He, along with Great Britain and China, sent Japan an ultimatum. If they did not surrender, American forces would destroy Japan. Japan refused to back down.

As a result, on August 6, 1945, a large American bomber (the *Enola Gay*) dropped the first atomic bomb ever used in battle on the Japanese city of Hiroshima. The blast killed approximately 100,000 people instantly and completely leveled nearly five square miles of land. Still, the Japanese did not surrender. So, the President ordered a second bomb to be dropped on Nagasaki just three days later. Japan's Emperor Hirohito pleaded with the government to surrender. On September 2, 1945, Japan formally ended the war. That day, as named by Truman, is known as V-J Day, or Victory over Japan Day. World War II had finally ended.

United Nations emblem

From this catastrophic event in our history, the United Nations (UN) was founded. The war had been so horrifying and devastating that no one a wanted a tragedy like that to occur ever again. In October of 1945, a new charter went into effect, signed by delegates from 50 different countries. The United Nations still works today to prevent conflicts and to help nations maintain peaceful relations.

There are innumerable topics for your student to explore when looking at World War II. What were some of the causes of the war? (World War I, the Treaty of Versailles, nationalism, the rise of dictatorships) What were some of the consequences? (casualties, buildings and land destruction, displaced persons) What ships were used? Submarines? Airplanes? The Atomic Bomb. Presidents Roosevelt and Truman. Albert Einstein. The Manhattan Project. Adolf Hitler. Pearl Harbor. The U.S. homefront (the effects on family life, women's issues and the work force). The entertainers and celebrities who traveled to encourage the troops (Bob Hope, Bing Crosby, Dinah Shore, and more). Recall with your student some other things he has learned about WWII during his previous studies in *Five in a Row*, and decide whether to explore new topics or to dig deeper into topics he's covered previously.

For further connections, here are some other things that were happening during the years of WWII:

1939: The movie, *The Wizard of Oz* (Judy Garland) came out. Popular songs were: "God Bless America," "Over the Rainbow," and "I'll Never Smile Again."

1940: Ernest Hemingway wrote *For Whom the Bell Tolls*. Duke Ellington became a popular composer and jazz musician. The population of the United States reached 132 million.

1941: The Panama Canal construction began. New York won the World Series from Brooklyn (4-1). Great Britain began to encourage clothing rationing because of the cloth shortage due to WWII.

1942: The Disney film *Bambi* was released. Enrico Fermi (U.S. scientist with the Manhattan Project) successfully splits the atom. The first automatic computer is developed in the United States.

1943: The movie *Casablanca* won an Academy Award. The Rodgers and Hammerstein musical play *Oklahoma* reached over 2,248 performances. George Washington Carver, a U.S. scientist covered later in this volume, died on January 5.

1944: The Ringling Bros. Barnum & Bailey circus had a fire in Hartford, CT, which killed more than 165 people.

1945: President Truman takes over in office. The Empire State Building was struck by a B-25 bomber on the 78-79th floors on July 28.

Take some time to go on an educational "voyage" with your student as you explore World War II and the times that surrounded it.

Language Arts: Writing and Discussion Question

Helen said many times, "The best and most beautiful things in the world cannot be seen or even touched. They must be felt with the heart." What did Helen mean by this? In your opinion, what are some things which can only be felt with the heart?

Teacher's Notes

Use this page to jot down relevant info you've found for this *Five in a Row* chapter book, including favorite lessons, go-along resources, field trips, and family memories.

HELEN KELLER

Dates studied:

Student:

Favorite Lesson Topics:

Social Studies:

Science:

Language Arts:

Fine Arts:

Life Skills:

Relevant Library Resources: Books, DVDs, Audio Books

Websites or Video Links:

Related Field Trip Opportunities:

Favorite Quote or Memory During Study:

Helen Keller

Helen Keller - Chapter 1

Name:
Date:
Science: **Human Anatomy - The Eye**

After completing the **Science: Human Anatomy - The Eye** lesson, use the illustration below to label the parts of the eye. The parts to label are listed below.

Conjunctiva
Cornea
Pupil
Iris
Lens

Eyelid
Retina
Fovea
Optic Nerve
Sclera

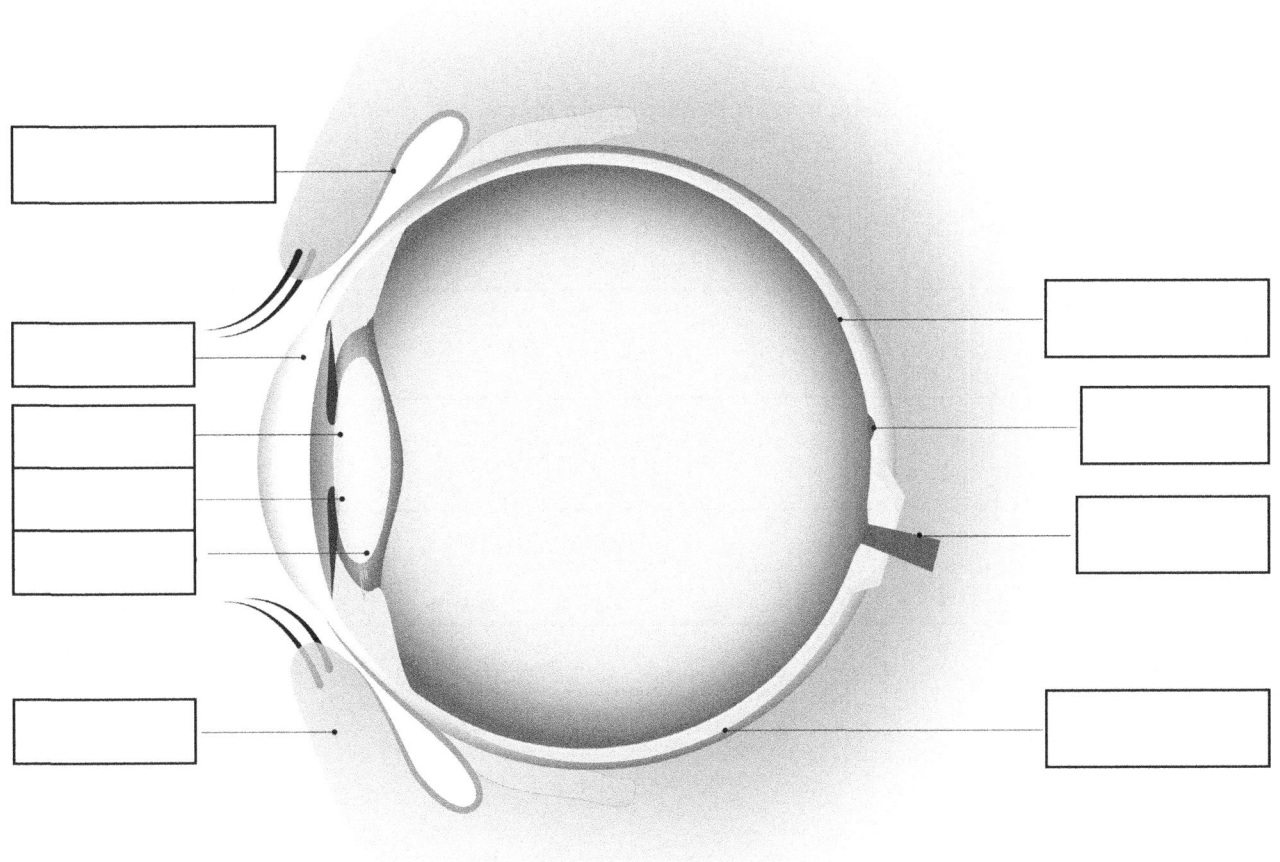

Five in Row Volume Seven

Helen Keller - Chapter 2

Name:
Date:
Life Skills: **Biography - Who Am I?**

After doing the **Life Skills: Living with Hope and Determination** lesson, search "famous people with disabilities" online and choose someone to research and write about. Below are a few options you could choose from using these go-along books from the library:

Stevie Wonder - *Who Is Stevie Wonder?* by Jim Gigliotti
Frida Kahlo - *Who Was Frida Kahlo?* by Sarah Fabiny
Louis Braille - *Who Was Louis Braille?* by Margaret Frith
or, *Six Dots: A Story of Young Louis Braille* by Jen Bryant

Print and paste an image of the person you chose into the frame.
Write information gathered through your research into the spaces below.

Name: _____

Lived: _____

Known for: _____

_____

_____

Connections to story: _____

_____

_____

Helen Keller

Helen Keller - Chapter 3

Name:
Date:
Science: **The Five Senses**

After completing the **Science: Exploring the Five Senses** lesson, reread chapter 3 (The Stranger Comes), slowly, noticing each time that Helen uses one of her three remaining senses to "see" or to "hear" what's happening around her or nearby. Make a note of each instance under the corresponding sense below.

Example: Helen knew her mother was leaving because she "*felt* her mother put on her hat and gloves."

touch

taste

smell

Helen Keller - Chapter 4

Name:

Date:

Science: **Do Other Senses Heighten After the Loss of One Sense?**

After completing the **Science: How Good Is Your Sense of Smell?** lesson, search "do other senses get stronger" online and record information or answers that you find below.

For an older student, a **Language Arts** lesson can be added here that introduces citing the information you find and use in your writing. A citation is created by listing the website(s) used at the end of your writing. Citing your reference is how you tell someone that the information you have in your writing came from another source and gives that source credit. The citation includes specific information so that your reader can find the source again to verify your writing or to draw their own research-based opinions.

As a basic introduction to citation, there are two spaces provided below to write down a couple of short pieces of information you found through your research. Below that are corresponding numbers to place your citation for that information. To learn how to create a proper citation for difference sources and how you would use them in a research paper, search "Middle School MLA Citation Guide" online and follow the instructions.

1. _____
   _____
   _____
   _____

2. _____
   _____
   _____
   _____

1.

2.

Helen Keller - Chapter 5

Name:
Date:
Language Arts: **Learning to Love Words**

The lesson **Language Arts: Etymology - The Study of Words** opens up a whole new way to study and learn about words. Perhaps, before digging deeply into the science and history of words, you could explore and find a *love* of words. Here are three engaging books that might inspire you!

The Word Collector by Peter H. Reynolds (a picture book, enjoyable for all ages)
The Right Word: Roget and His Thesaurus by Jen Bryant
The Word Snoop by Ursula Dubosarsky (for upper elementary or middle school students)

Begin keeping a list of words that inspire you, that spark your curiosity, or, that just sound lovely to your ears. Add definitions to any that you do not already know.

words. inspire. curiosity. lovely.

_____   _____   _____
_____   _____   _____
_____   _____   _____
_____   _____   _____
_____   _____   _____
_____   _____   _____
_____   _____   _____
_____   _____   _____
_____   _____   _____
_____   _____   _____

Helen Keller - Chapter 6

Name:
Date:
Language Arts: **Descriptive Words for the Smells of Each Season**

After finishing the **Language Arts: Creative Writing - The Smells of Spring** lesson, record lists of descriptive words for each smell you associate with the three remaining seasons below (think and *remember* what types of weather and other events happen during those seasons and what they smell like). Add in the list of words you created for the **Language Arts: Creative Writing - The Smells of Spring** lesson as well.

spring	summer	fall	winter
_____	_____	_____	_____
_____	_____	_____	_____
_____	_____	_____	_____
_____	_____	_____	_____
_____	_____	_____	_____
_____	_____	_____	_____
_____	_____	_____	_____
_____	_____	_____	_____
_____	_____	_____	_____
_____	_____	_____	_____

Helen Keller

Helen Keller - Chapter 7

Name:
Date:
History: **Biography - Who Am I?**

After completing the **History: Louis Braille** or **Science: Primates** lessons in chapter 7, choose either Louis Braille or Jane Goodall to study further. (If you chose Louis Braille to study for the chapter 2 activity sheet, then choose Jane Goodall now.)

Go-along books for Louis Braille include:
Who Was Louis Braille? by Margaret Frith
Six Dots: A Story of Young Louis Braille by Jen Bryant

Go-along books for Jane Goodall include:
The Watcher by Jeanette Winter
Who Is Jane Goodall? by Roberta Edwards

Print and paste an image of the person you chose into the frame.
Write information gathered through your research into the spaces below.

Name: _____

Lived: _____

Known for: _____

_____

_____

Connections to story: _____

_____

Five in Row Volume Seven

Helen Keller - Chapter 8

Name:
Date:
Career Path: **Who Needs a Speech Therapist?**

After completing the **Career Path: Speech Therapist** lesson, you might want to explore this career and who needs the help of a speech therapist further. Some questions to ask online include: Who needs a speech therapist? What does a pediatric speech pathologist do? Do elderly people need a speech therapist? Note answers to these questions below.

You could also search online for a "speech therapist video for children," and watch how a speech therapist works with kids to help them form sounds correctly. Please have a parent search for any online video. Most speech therapists that work with children incorporate play-based learning into their therapy sessions—look for examples of this in the videos you find online (it could be that the therapist uses toys or games, bubbles, or even apps on a tablet, etc.).

An excellent go-along book to pair with speech therapy or speech disorders is: *I Talk Like a River* by Jordan Scott

Who needs a speech therapist? _____

_____

What does a pediatric speech pathologist do? _____

_____

Do elderly people need a speech therapist? _____

_____

_____

Helen Keller

Helen Keller - Chapter 9

Name:
Date:
History: **Biography - Who Am I?**

Helen Keller became a human rights advocate and met nearly every president of the United States during her lifetime. After completing the **History: President Benjamin Harrison** lesson, research another U.S. president who held that office during Helen Keller's life (1880-1968). You can search online or use books from the library.

A go-along book that you could use for research is: *The Buck Stops Here: The Presidents of the United States* by Alice Provensen

Print and paste an image of the president you chose into the frame.
Write information gathered through your research into the spaces below.

Name: _____

Lived: _____

Known for: _____

_____

_____

Connections to story: _____

_____

_____

Five in Row Volume Seven   51

Helen Keller - Chapter 10

Name:
Date:
History: **Timeline of Helen Keller's Life**

The lesson **History: World War II** introduces many topics of study for exploring the history of World War II. People, events and dates are mentioned within the lesson and provided as topics for additional research.

The timeline below spans Helen Keller's life (1880-1968). Mark any people or events that you may have already encountered (such as President Benjamin Harrison and other presidents mentioned in this unit). Include the beginning and ending dates of WWII. Search online for specific areas of interest (actors, musicians, scientists, artists, politicians, battles, inventions, etc.) between the dates of WWII (1939-1945). Add several people/events/things to your timeline, including printed images if desired. Use hash marks along the timeline to represent specific dates and mark accordingly.

1880

1968

Skylark

Title: *Skylark*
Author: Patricia MacLachlan
Copyright: 1994

Teacher's Note: *Skylark* is the sequel to *Sarah, Plain and Tall*, which was a unit in Five in a Row Volume 6. If your student hasn't done this previous unit, you may want to take a few days to read *Sarah, Plain and Tall* with your student first, before beginning *Skylark*.

Chapter 1

Teacher Summary

In this sequel to *Sarah, Plain and Tall*, Papa and Sarah are now married, and the four Wittings live together on the prairie.

Our first glimpse at the family is with them getting their photograph taken. Sarah wants to send a wedding/family picture back home to Maine. We also learn from their conversation with the photographer that the prairie is experiencing an intense drought. Some families have been forced to move. Papa tells Sarah and the children that they would never leave the prairie. He says, "We were born here. Our names are written in this land." Caleb and Anna agree but both wonder—what about Sarah? She wasn't born on the prairie. Her name isn't written in the land.

What we will cover in this chapter:

Social Studies: History - Family Portraits
Social Studies: History - A Look Back at Drought*
Science: Film Photography
Language Arts: A Writer's Style - MacLachlan's Use of Nature
Language Arts: MacLachlan's Other Books
Language Arts: Writing and Discussion Question
Language Arts: Vocabulary
Life Skills: Avoiding Hurting Others When You Hurt

Social Studies: History - Family Portraits

Joshua came to take the Wittings' wedding photo. Has your student ever had a family photograph taken? What was it like? Did the photographer meet the family somewhere (park, at their home, outside, etc.)? Did the family go to the studio? How did your student's family dress? Were pictures sent to different family members?

In the late 19th century and early 20th century (the time of our story), photographs were a much larger production than they are today. Today, taking pictures is a common, sometimes daily, occurrence. But back then, a photograph was a major event. For some families (like the Wittings), they may have only had one or two photographs taken of them in their entire lifetimes.

Sarah wanted a wedding picture (including Anna and Caleb—and Nick and Lottie) to send back to Maine for her aunts. Many pioneer families (in the west or out on the prairie) would save their money and hire a photographer to take a picture of them in order to send back to their relatives. But what if you lived on the prairie and wanted a picture of your family—could you get one taken that day? Probably not. Unless you were lucky enough to live in a town where a local photographer worked, you would have to wait until a photographer was traveling near your home and schedule the session then.

It was common in those days, as well, for families to pull some of their prized possessions outside just for the photograph. At that time, flash photography wasn't possible, making interior photos difficult. The families wanted their relatives back home (generally in the East) to see that they were prosperous and doing well. A piano, a beautiful sofa, a prize Victrola, etc.—these things would be moved outside onto the lawn and the family would stand proudly next to their things.

Can your student imagine doing that today? Dragging the piano outside in order to take a photograph next to it?

Today, families still schedule sittings for family photographs, but the cost is much more reasonable and every town or city has many options for professional photography. It is not the event it once was.

Perhaps, if your student is interested, it might be enjoyable to recreate an "old-timey" family photo. Encourage your student to formulate in her mind how she would like it to look. Standing under a tree, perhaps with a few chairs and someone holding a fancy clock, a family photograph from the late 19th century can be recreated. By applying a variety of vintage filters to the pictures, her family can be photographed beautifully.

Or if your student has even more creativity for the project, an "updated" family photo can be taken with the family's current prized possessions pictured with them. Have each family member choose something which represents "modern success" to them (these could be objects they use in daily life that represent up-to-date technology or equipment, or just beloved objects to them at this time in their life). Then take a "here's what's important to us now" photograph with each family member next to, or holding their object.

This can be a great history lesson and planning project for your student. She can even mount the photo and write a little description beneath to hang in her room or in her home.

Social Studies: History - A Look Back at Drought*

The Wittings are experiencing a bad drought on the prairie. If your student has completed Five in a Row Volume 5, refer back to the lesson on Water Cycle and Drought in chapter 2 of *The Boxcar Children*. A brief reminder of what your student studied in that section will help enrich her understanding of *Skylark*. (*Skylark* takes place two decades before the Dust Bowl and the Dirty '30s, but the information in that lesson would still be helpful to understand drought.) If you did not cover this lesson or did not use Volume 5, here is an excerpt from that lesson.

A tragic and scary time in American history occurred during the mid-1930s across the plains of Kansas, Oklahoma, Texas and the adjacent parts of Colorado and New Mexico. This area of the United States became known as the Dust Bowl. The name came from the low annual rainfall and high winds that blew dust and dirt for miles. This time period is also referred to as "The Dirty '30s".

Farmers in this area of the country had previously stripped the land of the natural grasses and planted fields of wheat. Without the aid of the root systems of the natural plants, too much dirt and dust was picked up by the high winds. Soon dust storms formed and buried entire houses. More than half the population was forced to leave the area. Our government replanted the grasses and trees and helped the land return to its natural state. Self-directed research on the Dust Bowl years can make an interesting project for students.

Science: Film Photography

Today, most photography is digital, but from the late 1800s until the very early 21st century, photography was done through the use of film. Your student might want to explore this older way of making photographs through online research or library books. She might be interested in questions like: What goes into the actual development of the film? How does a 35mm film camera work? What is film made of? What happens to the film after it's dropped off at a processing center? How is a picture really made?

There are five basic steps in the process of 35mm film photography: (1) collecting light, (2) focusing, (3) exposing the film, (4) developing and (5) creating the printed picture. Any one of these five areas of photography would be interesting for your student to study. Here are a few more questions your student can research:

What is an aperture? What is a latent image? How is it used in the film process? What chemicals are used to create a print? Why can undeveloped film never be exposed to light? What is a darkroom? What shape is a camera lens? Film photography fully incorporates both science (chemistry and calculations) and creativity (positions, compositions, subject selection, etc.).

Language Arts: A Writer's Style - MacLachlan's Use of Nature

Our author, Patricia MacLachlan, certainly has her own writing style. One of the things you can explore with your student is her use of three specific subjects in her chapters' opening lines. The three subjects are flowers/plants, animals and seasons. For example, draw your student's attention to the first line of *Skylark*, "Papa married Sarah on a summer day."

If you refer back to *Sarah, Plain and Tall*, from FIAR Vol. 6, here are some chapter openers:

Chapter 2 - ...and before the ice and snow had melted from the fields...
Chapter 3 - Sarah came in the spring.
Chapter 4 - The dogs loved Sarah first.
Chapter 5 - The sheep made Sarah smile.
Chapter 6 - The days grew longer...
Chapter 7 - The dandelions in the fields had gone by...
Chapter 8 - The rain came and passed...

Your student, if she is observant, will find the same "nature" motif used by MacLachlan in *Skylark*. Although not in every chapter, the majority of opening lines include the weather/seasons, animals or plants. Certainly, this is not what your student "should always" do in her own writings. Every author chooses different styles for her writing. However, it is interesting to note for your student that as she writes her stories, she can be thinking of different **motifs** to use herself. Perhaps each of her chapters might begin with someone talking or with one particular character's thoughts. Perhaps her chapters could include a description of a different feature of one character. There is a great variety of topics which would make an interesting "through-line" for her writing. Your student's choice of motif can help carry the reader smoothly from chapter to chapter.

Language Arts: MacLachlan's Other Books

If your student is enjoying this study of *Skylark*, perhaps it would be fun to read some other books by Patricia MacLachlan (1938-2022). This is the way many people find new, interesting books. If they enjoy one, they begin to search for other books by the same author. Interesting to note, many of MacLachlan's books also center around the prairie as their subject.

Five in Row Volume Seven

If your student used FIAR Vol. 2, perhaps she studied a MacLachlan picture book, *Three Names*. *Three Names* is the story of a young boy's great-grandfather, his dog and life on the prairie. It is an excellent study in description and even much younger children can appreciate the sweet story.

If your student has already studied this book, you may wish to simply go back and reread it. If you have never read this story, locate a copy and share it with your student. Encourage her to compare the writing (description, style, dialogue) with MacLachlan's work in *Sarah* and *Skylark*.

Other Patricia MacLachlan books you and your student may enjoy are: *Word After Word After Word*, *White Fur Flying*, *Kindred Souls*, *The Poet's Dog*, *Fly Away*, *The True Gift* (a Christmas chapter book), *Cat Talk*, *Once I Ate a Pie*, *Snowflakes Fall* and *All the Places to Love*.

Language Arts: Writing and Discussion Question

How do you think Caleb felt when Anna told him he couldn't spell? Knowing Caleb's character, do you think he would have returned the mean comment with an equally mean reply? What do you think he might have said back to her?

Language Arts: Vocabulary

motif   A recurring idea, feature or theme.

Life Skills: Avoiding Hurting Others When You Hurt

Explore with your student the interchange between Anna and Caleb at the end of the chapter. Both children are nervous about Sarah and Papa and the drought. As Caleb verbalizes, "Sarah wasn't born here." What if the drought forces them to leave? What if Sarah misses the green and rain of Maine?

Caleb decides to solve the problem in his own way. He will write Sarah's name in the land himself. We know, of course, it is just a figure of speech to have "one's name in the land." And Anna understands this too. But she is quick to criticize Caleb and is hurtful when she says, "You can't even spell, Caleb. You can't." The book tells us that Anna was sorry for being cross, but she doesn't apologize to Caleb. Why do people sometimes lash out at others when they are frightened or hurt? Has your student ever hurt someone else's feelings when *she* was the one hurting? Does it really make you feel any better to hurt someone else?

Encourage your student to recognize when she is being "short" with someone, and to monitor her own feelings. Is she simply taking it out on the other person because she is scared or hurting herself? Instead of needlessly hurting the other person, share with your student other ways to cope with her feelings.

If a person is brave, sharing with someone your concerns or fears can be greatly beneficial. But if the hurt is too deep or the fear too great, other activities can take your mind off of your problems (instead of lashing out at others). Exercising, walking, playing an instrument, drawing a picture, reading a book or just hammering on some wood are all good ways to relieve tension and not hurt someone else in the process.

Anna allowed her own fear and worry to hurt Caleb. She was wrong, but we can understand how she was feeling. Learning to direct our emotions in constructive and nondamaging ways is a sign of maturity and growth.

Chapter 2

Teacher Summary

The days grow hotter and hotter, and still no rain comes to the prairie. Papa tells Sarah she'll have to quit washing the floor, in order to save water. She thinks that is a mixed blessing. Other things are changing as well. Seal is pregnant and will have kittens. We also find out Anna is keeping a diary—notes on her life and Papa, Caleb and Sarah.

Teacher's Note: If your student hasn't already noticed, this would be a good time to draw her attention to the italicized portions of writing at the end of each chapter. In this chapter, we find out that Anna keeps a diary. As you continue to read, it becomes obvious the italicized portions are excerpts from her journal. The story is written in first person, so we are already privy to Anna's thoughts and feelings. However, these journal entries give us an even more intimate look at how she perceives her world and her family—a nice addition by Patricia MacLachlan to the already delightful text.

What we will cover in this chapter:

Science: Gestation Periods in Different Animals*
Language Arts: Writing and Discussion Question
Language Arts: Vocabulary
Fine Arts: Watercolor Painting and Color Mixing

Science: Gestation Periods in Different Animals*

Seal isn't just getting fat. She's pregnant! Does your student know how long it takes for a cat to have kittens? What is that period of time called, while the baby is still in the mother? Is a cat's pregnancy time different from other animals? Take this opportunity to share some fascinating animal science information with your student, beginning with some general facts surrounding all animals.

Scientists have classified nearly one million kinds of animals. This amazing figure can be broken down into all the categories of animals, including more than 5,000 kinds of mammals.

A cat is a mammal. To be called a mammal, an animal must be warm-blooded, (generally) covered in hair, whose offspring (babies) are fed by milk from the mother. The period of time during which the baby(ies) are in the mother's womb is called the period of **gestation**. For a human baby, the gestation period is nine months. A baby born earlier than that would be called **premature**. However, the gestation period differs from animal to animal. Here are a few examples of the variety:

Animal	Offspring	Gestation Period
Mouse	Pup or pinkie	19 days
Cat	Kitten	2 months
Beaver	Pup	3 months
Bear	Cub	6-8 months
Cow	Calf	9 months
Horse	Foal	11 months
Giraffe	Calf	14-15 months
Whale	Calf	15-17 months
Elephant	Calf	18-23 months

Imagine a human being pregnant for as long as an elephant—nearly two years! Each animal's gestation period is just long enough for all the necessary developments to take place and for the young to be born healthy. See if your student can find which animal on the chart has the same gestation period as a human. Which animal is pregnant for nearly one year? And how long will it take for Seal's kittens to be born?

Language Arts: Writing and Discussion Question

Sarah tells Caleb and Anna that she loved what was "between the lines" in Papa's letters. What does that saying mean? How would you have described it to Caleb?

Language Arts: Vocabulary

gestation   The act or process of the young developing in the uterus.

premature   A baby who is born earlier than the full gestational period.

primary colors   Red, yellow and blue.

secondary colors   Colors created by blending primaries.

tertiary colors   Colors created by blending a primary and secondary.

analogous   Colors which are similar, close on the color wheel.

complementary   Colors which are opposite in origin.

Fine Arts: Watercolor Painting and Color Mixing

In Anna's journal entry, we read that Sarah teaches Anna how to paint with watercolors. Has your student ever tried this type of painting? Watercolor painting can be simple or complex, and very rewarding.

For just a few dollars, invest in a simple box of watercolors. Prang®, available at any hobby store or art shop, does very well for beginners. A simple brush, a jar of water and some paper, and your student is set.

Allow your student to experiment with the different values of colors. A color value refers to the intensity of the shade—a blue can have a light value (sky blue) or a dark value (midnight blue). Various shades can be achieved depending upon the ratio of water to paint on the brush. If the brush is more "watery" then the value will be lighter. Brushing with very little water is called "dry brushing."

Watercolors can also be an excellent jumping off point for a discussion on color mixing. Most children, at this age, understand the term **primary color**. The three primary colors are red, yellow and blue. All other colors come from a combination of these three. **Secondary (binary) colors** are created by mixing two primaries. For example, orange is made from red and yellow. Green is made from yellow and blue. Purple is made from red and blue. **Tertiary colors** are created by blending a secondary and a primary—red-orange, blue-green, etc.

Two other terms useful for students are **analogous** (a NAL a gus) and **complementary**. Analogous colors are colors that are adjoining or adjacent to any one of the primaries on the color wheel and are obviously similar in nature. For example, red, red-orange and red-violet are analogous because they all contain red. Complementary colors are opposite in their origin (opposite each other on the color wheel)—blue and orange, red and green, yellow and violet.

The color wheel is a concept that has been covered in several volumes of Five in a Row. There is a lesson and make-your-own color wheel activity sheet in Vol. 1 (*Papa Piccolo*) and a lesson an analogous colors in Vol. 5 (*The Bravest of Us All*). You might want to review those lessons, if possible, or you can easily find examples of a color wheel online.

To practically apply this color lesson, share the following example with your student. If she is painting a picture of a house with sunlight on it, she will, no doubt, use yellow/orange shades to bathe her house in "sun." To make shadows, many artists would then choose purple or blue hues. Through the contrast of these complementary colors (yellow and blue), her "sunny" areas will appear that much more brilliant.

Chapter 3

Teacher Summary

On Sunday, the Wittings go to church and talk with their friends about the drought. Still, no rain has come and everyone is worried. The next day, Anna is awakened by Caleb calling to her in a very excited voice. During the night, Mame, their cow, gave birth to her calf. Papa says the calf's face is as pale as the winter moon. Caleb names her Moonbeam and everyone laughs. Anna continues to note in her journal that Sarah is good for Papa. She helps him forget his worries and gets him to laugh again.

What we will cover in this chapter:

Social Studies: History - How the Church Served the Community
Social Studies: Career Paths - Astronaut and Astronomer
Science: Cows - Herbivores*
Language Arts: Writing and Discussion Question
Language Arts: Vocabulary

Social Studies: History - How the Church Served the Community

The Wittings enjoy going to church. Not only because it is their place of worship, but for other reasons as well. They are able to see friends and neighbors they don't see very often, visit and share stories.

Share with your student the place churches had in the past. For communities, particularly communities of pioneers spread far apart, after Sunday morning services was their only time for visiting. Families supported one another and were able to find out what the others needed. Without the aid of technology or quick mail service, communicating with friends was difficult in those days. Therefore, churches became social gatherings for the congregation as well as a source of spiritual refreshment.

Encourage your student to look for old, small churches in and around the place where she lives. These old churches were generally just one or two rooms and often had a graveyard beside or behind them. Families generally attended the same church for generations, and as family members passed away they would be laid to rest in the site directly adjacent to their church.

What does your student think it would have been like to have lived during a time when she only got to see her friends once a week—on Sunday? How important would that gathering be?

Social Studies: Career Paths - Astronaut and Astronomer

Papa likened the new calf's face to a "pale winter moon." Has your student ever enjoyed just gazing at the moon? Has she ever wondered why a winter moon looks more pale than a summer moon? Is she interested in the stars or planets? Does she enjoy science and math? Perhaps a career in astronomy is just the thing she should begin to explore.

Astronomers study the stars, planets and space every day to learn more about our universe. They use massive telescopes (some as big as whole rooms) to see distant celestial sights. Astronomers also use a tool called a radio telescope. Instead of collecting visible light and displaying it to the human eye, a radio telescope collects invisible light in the form of energy. A radio telescope can be used during the day, as easily as at night and can tell the temperature in space! Spectroscopes are used by astronomers to determine the temperature, makeup and density of stars.

But beyond telescopes, astronomers also use a variety of other tools, like cameras and computers. Some astronomers work in observatories, planetariums, or even as teachers in universities all over the world.

Teacher's Note: If your student shows any interest in astronomy, a beneficial field trip would be to your area planetarium. Your student will learn a great deal and the instruction she receives from the tour guide will further deepen and solidify her understanding of this section. Many children have had life-long interests in astronomy sparked by an early trip to a planetarium.

In order to become an astronomer, several years of concentrated study are required. Key subjects for students interested in astronomy are mathematics, physics, life and earth science. Check your local library for children's books on various careers in science. You can also search online for interviews with astronomers made especially for middle grade students.

Here are some names your student might wish to use for research—all are famous American astronomers: Percival Lowell, Edwin Hubble, Carl Sagan, Neil deGrasse Tyson, Williamina Fleming and Maria Mitchell. A book report, imaginary "interview," or poster board depicting the life of an astronomer—all would make good assigned learning projects.

After discussing astronomy with your student, this would also make an excellent time to bring up perhaps the most famous "moon" career choice—an astronaut.

Teacher's Note: Your student may have heard the term "cosmonaut" before in reference to an astronaut. Cosmonaut is the word for astronaut in the former Soviet Union.

The word astronaut comes from the Greek words meaning "sailor among the stars."

Wanting to become an astronaut is a high goal. Astronauts are highly trained, specialized personnel who do a variety of jobs. Being able to control and fix a spacecraft, understand the checklists and goals

Five in Row Volume Seven

of the voyage, successfully maneuver in space in a bulky space suit, conduct scientific experiments regarding the planet Earth, monitor and program the high-tech science laboratory equipment on board, and of course, to have incredible bravery are just a few of the requirements for an astronaut.

When you are an astronaut, you work for a government agency called NASA (National Aeronautics and Space Administration). Many astronauts today, from various countries, spend time at the International Space Station, a modular space station in low Earth orbit.

Astronauts who are mission specialists perform a variety of tasks. Some drop off equipment (like satellites), and others go to those equipment sites to repair them. Working nearly 16-hour workdays, mission specialists are in charge of

performing the experiments, compiling observation logs (information on pollution, atmospheric conditions, weather patterns, etc.), maintaining the spacecraft, and even photo sessions of the planets and space.

Pilot astronauts are generally career officers in the Air Force or Navy and they command and control the flight of the spacecraft.

NASA accepts applications to become an astronaut on a continuing basis. But, there are a few very specific requirements (one of which is not age). First, the applicant must be a U.S. citizen and must have earned a master's degree (or higher) in engineering, biological or physical science, computer science or mathematics. All candidates must prove their physical and mental fitness during a week-long physical exam and interview.

Pilot astronaut candidates are required to have flown at least 1,000 in-command hours in a high-powered jet aircraft. They must also be between 64 and 76 inches in height. Mission specialist candidates don't need any flight experience, but they must be between 60 and 76 inches tall. Why does your student think these height requirements are put in place?

If your student is interested in any aspect of astronomy or becoming an astronaut, you can explore the NASA website together for answers to all of her questions. Your city or state may also have programs designed for aspiring astronauts, space camps, or other STEM-related classes that your student would enjoy. These programs are designed to enhance interest in space science and related career development. Becoming an astronomer or astronaut requires bravery, a keen mind and an interest in the universe and learning all there is to know about it.

Science: Cows—Herbivores*

Mame and her new calf, Moonbeam, are certainly loved by the Wittings. Mame is a cow—cows are female cattle. The male cattle are called bulls. Has your student ever studied cattle? Fascinating from both a scientific and a sociological point of view, cattle are an important section of life science.

Teacher's Note: For simplicity, this lesson will refer to the animal as a "cow." Note for your student that this is the female term.

Cows are very large animals—and there are more than 250 different breeds. Some of the most famous breeds are the Guernsey, Jerseys, Holstein, Angus and Herefords. Weighing between 1,000 and 3,000 pounds, they are impressive creatures. All cows naturally grow horns, but many farmers cut the horns off the cattle when they are young. Cows that have been bred without horns are called polled cattle.

Cows are **herbivores**, meaning that they eat plants, not meat (meat-eating animals are **carnivores**). Cows generally eat grass, hay, clover and corn. They do not have any top front teeth, but instead simply bite, chew a little with top and bottom molars and then swallow large mouthfuls of food. Cows also drink a lot of water—nearly 20 gallons a day! Can your student imagine drinking that much? (Humans are encouraged to consume eight 8-ounce glasses of water a day—how much more do cows drink?) Dairy cattle (cows used for milking) are usually milked twice a day by farmers. One cow can give almost 6 gallons of milk a day—nearly 100 glasses of milk!

Because cows are herbivores, their bodies are set up in a special way to digest all the roughage they consume. Instead of just one stomach, cows have four!

Five in Row Volume Seven

Share with your student some information about this unusual digestive system.

When a cow chews its food for the first time, it isn't able to break the fibers down very much. After the cow swallows, the partially chewed food travels to the first stomach called the **rumen**. The rumen can hold nearly 50 gallons of food! In the rumen there are also vital enzymes and bacteria which help break down the food for the cow. Without these bacterium, the cow would not be able to digest any of its food.

The food is then **regurgitated** (or spit back up) in the cow's mouth and the cow again chews on it for awhile. This partially digested food is called the **cud**. Has your student ever heard of a "cow chewing her cud?"

When the cow has successfully chewed the food a second time, it is swallowed a second time and it now passes to a stomach called the **reticulum**. Then it passes to a third stomach called the **omasum**. Both of these stomachs provide nearly the same function—to rid the food of all its moisture—allowing the cow to fully absorb the water.

Finally, the food travels to the fourth stomach called the **abomasum**, where it meets acid and enzymes to fully digest the proteins. The abomasum is the only one of the four stomachs much like our own.

From there, the food (like the food we eat) goes through the small intestine and then large intestine.

If your student is interested, it might be helpful to make a drawing, somewhat like a flowchart, of the different digestive stages in a cow.

Besides providing the people of the world with milk and meat, cows are fascinating animals to study!

Language Arts: Writing and Discussion Question

Early in the chapter, Sarah says, "I'm surrounded by motherhood." Anna thinks her voice sounds "sad and thoughtful." Do you think Sarah would like to have a baby of her own? Give some reasons from the story (examples from both *Skylark* and *Sarah, Plain and Tall* are appropriate) to support your answer.

Language Arts: Vocabulary

rumen The first stomach of an animal; food lands almost immediately after being swallowed.

regurgitate To spit back up after being swallowed.

cud The partially digested food the animal chews again.

reticulum Second stomach of an animal which continues the digestive process.

omasum Third stomach, continues to digest the food.

abomasum A fourth stomach where the food meets acids and enzymes to fully digest the proteins.

Chapter 4

Teacher Summary

One day Papa comes home from town with letters for Sarah from her three aunts in Maine—Harriet, Mattie and Lou. Sarah sits and reads from the letters to the whole family by lamplight that night. Unlike the Wittings' experience on the prairie with the drought, Maine is getting a lot of rain. Two inches by the glass measure, Aunt Mattie's letter says. Caleb immediately asks what a "glass measure" is, but no one explains. Everyone is thinking about the rain and how much it is needed on the prairie. Sarah feels bad about reading the letters to Papa. She doesn't want him to feel worse about the drought.

That night, Caleb sets a small glass on a fence post out in the yard. He tells Sarah he did it for Papa—the glass is waiting for rain.

What we will cover in this chapter:

Social Studies: History and Geography - Droughts and Floods: Your State's History
Science: Building Your Own Weather Station
Language Arts: Writing and Discussion Question
Life Skills: Optimism and Hope
Activity Sheet: Vocabulary Words*

Social Studies: History and Geography - Droughts and Floods: Your State's History

The Wittings' home and the surrounding land is experiencing a terrible drought. Where does your student live? Chances are, even if not in her lifetime, wherever she lives your student's state has had periods of flooding and/or drought. Why not do some research and find out when those times were?

At your local library, your student can ask a librarian for assistance in locating this information, perhaps in an almanac. Almanacs typically contain hundreds of tables of information graphing and calculating the high temperatures, low temperatures, and average rainfall (or lack of) for a particular area or region. Your student can also look online for this information, either at home or with a librarian's assistance.

After she has compiled a few interesting facts about her area (perhaps the longest period of time without rain, the most rainfall in a given 24-hour period, etc.), your student can create a poster or drawing to depict her findings. By drawing an outline of her city or state, she can pinpoint and identify specific regions or areas where floods or droughts have occurred. She can even create a timeline at the bottom or around the sides of the poster, giving comparisons of weather events with other major events. Find library books on weather, droughts and floods, or similar information online, to supplement your student's research.

Science: Building Your Own Weather Station

Caleb is very interested in this "glass for rain" concept. Does your student understand how this works? In very simple terms, a glass set out for a period of time will collect the rainfall, and then each morning you can measure how much has fallen—one inch, two inches, etc. Your student can create a rain measuring device (called a rain gauge) as easily as Caleb did, by simply setting a glass outside on a tabletop or deck. However, why not take this idea a step further?

Quite easily, using everyday materials, your student can create her own "weather station." She can build instruments that will measure temperature, air pressure, rainfall, wind direction and speed, and humidity.

First, have your student create a **record-keeping chart**. There should be a column for the date and then subsequent columns with the categories she wishes to track: temperature, dew point, clouds, wind, rain, etc. Using this chart each day or week will allow your student to compare her findings to local meteorologists', and can assist her in making predictions of her own.

The first piece of equipment your student will probably want to include in her weather station is a **thermometer**. Although these can be made at home, it is much easier (and will provide more accuracy) to simply buy an inexpensive indoor/outdoor thermometer at any hardware store.

Next, a **rain gauge** can be created by using a clear plastic bowl or glass, some masking tape and a permanent marker. Have your student place a vertical strip of masking tape on the side of the container. Then, with a permanent marker, she can mark off a measuring scale by the inch, quarter-inch or eighths. Remind your student, if she is comparing her records to that of the meteorologist's and finds they differ, that rainfall can differ greatly from one area to the next—even from one side of a street to the next! What the meteorologist generally reports is the *average* rainfall—the entire area's measurements averaged to one figure.

Your student can create her own **barometer** to measure air pressure. This is what she will need: a saucer or bowl, water, masking tape, a pen and an empty, clean, plastic soda bottle.

First, fill the saucer or bowl halfway with water. Fill the bottle with water until it is almost full. With your help and supervision (and maybe outdoors), your student should put her thumb over the mouth of the bottle and invert it onto the saucer. When it is in place, upside down, have her remove her thumb quickly and steady the bottle. (Strips of tape from the bottom of the bottle to the sides of the saucer can help secure it.) Now, have your student place a strip of masking tape to the side of the bottle and have her mark the water level and the date.

Why doesn't the water in the bottle pour out? The air pressure inside the bottle is pressing down and prevents the water from running out. When the air pressure changes, so will the water level. An increase in air pressure sends the water level inside the bottle up. A decrease in air pressure allows it to drop down. When the water in the bottle drops down (low air pressure), you can usually predict warmer, wetter weather. When the water is high (high pressure), you can usually predict less humid, drier weather. (There are several other ways to make a simple homemade barometer. Look online for videos or explore science experiment books at your library for more ideas!)

The dew point is the temperature at which the surrounding air can no longer hold all the water vapor it contains. Then, some of that vapor begins to change back to liquid form (condensation) and form droplets. The closer the dew point temperature is to the air temperature, the more likely it is that you will have rain or snow. (Your student may have previously done the Dew Point and Frost lesson in FIAR Vol. 6, *Thomas Edison* unit, chapter 3 lesson activities.)

Here are the things your student will need to create her **dew point thermometer**: a metal soup can (washed and label removed), water, ice cubes and a thermometer.

First, have your student record the current temperature. Next, fill the can with water and then make sure the outside of the can is very dry. Place the thermometer in the water and begin adding ice cubes, one at a time. Carefully stir it with the thermometer. Watch both the sides of the can and the thermometer. As the temperature goes down, liquid beads begin to form on the outside of the can. The temperature the thermometer reads, at the point at which liquid begins to form on the can is at, or near, the dew point.

There are more science weather measuring devices your student can build and add to her weather station, but these are enough to get her started. Encourage her to record each day, or week, her findings and to compare those to the professionals. Encourage her to make her own predictions and to do further research on her own (if there is interest) on weather at the library or online. You might even wish to call your local television station and see if you can arrange a tour and a visit with the meteorologist.

Language Arts: Writing and Discussion Question

MacLachlan writes, "There was more that Sarah hadn't read..." Why didn't Sarah read all of the letters to Jacob? What was her motive in concealing parts of the letter? Why does Anna cry when she reads the part in the letters that Sarah skipped?

Life Skills: Optimism and Hope

Caleb demonstrates his optimism by placing his rain glass on the fence post. Had there been any rain in their area recently? Was there any prospect? No. But, Caleb isn't going to be discouraged. He has hope.

Each of us has a choice. We can choose to embrace hope and faith, believing the best in every situation, or we can choose not to believe, expecting nothing positive in life. The choice we make will impact our own life and the lives of those around us. Encourage your student to cultivate an attitude of optimism, embracing hope and faith in her daily life. By believing the best about others, and by not allowing ourselves to develop a negative attitude, we can encourage those around us and make the most of our own life.

Chapter 5

Teacher Summary

The water level in the Wittings' well drops lower and lower, and Papa decides they will have to go to town to haul water for the animals. When they get there, Sarah runs into Maggie who is comforting another friend, Caroline. Caroline and her husband Joseph are being forced to move because of the drought. Their well is completely dry. Sarah is forced to see the painful, very real result of a drought. She is frustrated and overcome with sadness.

What we will cover in this chapter:

Social Studies: History - People Follow Food and Water
Science: Moving in the Heat - Heat Exhaustion
Language Arts: Writing and Discussion Question
Language Arts: Vocabulary
Fine Arts: The Colors of Drought*

Social Studies: History - People Follow Food and Water

Caroline and Joseph are being forced to move. Their well has gone dry, and they have no choice. People, just like animals, must have water to survive. During times of drought (as in times of famine), people tend to follow food and water.

Teacher's Note: If you did the unit study on *The Boxcar Children* from FIAR Vol. 5 (chapter 10), you may have covered the lesson on potatoes, which mentioned the Great Potato Famine in Ireland. Here is an excerpt from that lesson: Because of the lack of industry, the Irish relied mainly on agriculture for both their livelihood and their food. Potatoes became the main staple for most of the impoverished Irish people. A plant disease attacked the potato plants in 1845, and for the next three years people began dying from lack of food. Approximately one million people lost their lives due to what is now known as the

"Great Potato Famine." Further study on this tragic time in Ireland's history could serve as an excellent research or speech project for your student, as you discuss the concept of famine and drought.

Certain regions of land in the world are in constant water shortage, because they never get enough rain. However, drought can even strike areas that normally have average rainfall, and can do so quite suddenly. In the 1960s, regions of the Northeastern United States, as well as parts of China, Brazil and Portugal were stricken with drought, while simultaneously, flood waters drenched and damaged massive areas in the Midwestern United States and in Mexico.

In the United States, we have a great diversity of land types—prairies, mountains, bays and deserts. Several of these land types are difficult for people to live in, due to either lack of water or too much water. **Land reclamation** and irrigation methods have been used to convert unusable land to farmland and usable housing, commercial, or industrial areas. Your student may want to research various ways to irrigate crop fields and to build and make use of aqueducts and water sources.

For example, desert soil can become quite rich and fertile soil for farming (or for growing a lawn), because there is no rain to wash away chemicals the plants need. Water reuse and drip irrigation systems are common ways to irrigate farm fields. Water trickle hoses are used on many lawns and golf courses.

Wet, marshy land can be reclaimed by draining it of excess water, building retaining walls or filling and raising it to be dry and useful. There are many methods of land reclamation, as well as drawbacks to each. Your student may want to learn about ways that land is reclaimed, as well as the environmental challenges and conservation guidelines involved. Learning about water conservation, land reclamation and caring for our environment are all ways even young people can take part in managing our land and water supplies.

Science: Moving in the Heat— Heat Exhaustion

Read with your student the following sentence: "Everything seemed to move slow in town, as if the heat had taken over." Take this time to discuss with your student heat exhaustion and other ways heat affects the human body.

Has your student ever noticed when the weather is very hot she often doesn't feel like running or playing? Why is that? The human body has an internal thermometer. Our temperature, when it is normal, should read about 98.6° F. As in many areas, our bodies somewhat self-monitor themselves. Your body knows when it is losing heat, as well as gaining heat. When we are outdoors and the sun is beating down, we may feel a bit sluggish or slow moving. Our brains are telling us we shouldn't be moving too quickly, or we could overheat. If we ignore our body's warning and exert a great deal of energy, we can overheat. When this happens it is called heat exhaustion or heatstroke. Either of these conditions can be quite serious.

Your body helps itself maintain the right temperature through several means, one of which is sweating. Does your student know that sweating is a positive, healthy thing? When you sweat, the beads of water form all over your body, and as they evaporate, your skin cools slightly. That drop in temperature, caused by evaporation, helps keep you cool and your internal thermometer happy. But what happens if you get too hot, too quickly?

Five in Row Volume Seven

Heatstroke sometimes affects people when they have been working in excessive heat for a very long time. Scientists have found that the longer you are in hot temperatures, the less you sweat. And remember, the less you sweat, the hotter you are going to become. Unfortunately, people often don't even notice when they quit sweating. If left unchecked, a heatstroke victim's temperature can easily exceed 110° F, and require immediate hospitalization.

Heatstroke victims can also experience pulse weakening, irregular breathing, and lightheadedness, as well as the lack of perspiration. First aid recommendations for heatstroke are fairly simple. The most important thing is to quickly lower the person's temperature. This can be done by submerging her in a cool bathtub of water and/or applying cold compresses to her forehead, pulse points and the back of her neck.

A slightly less serious heat condition, and even more common, is called heat exhaustion. Heat exhaustion occurs when people work or play in areas of high heat and high humidity. Although the person may continue to sweat freely, her body temperature may begin falling below normal (unlike heatstroke where the temperature escalates). A heat exhaustion patient may become weak and dizzy, and may even vomit. Someone experiencing heat exhaustion must be taken to a cooler area. People who suffer from heat exhaustion sometimes take salt tablets under a doctor's care to compensate for the salt loss in their sweat.

It is both interesting and important that your student understand the ways heat affects our bodies—and how to help someone in need.

Language Arts: Writing and Discussion Question

In the first line of chapter 5 we read, "Each day Papa dropped a rope with a stone down the well to measure the water level." By writing an informative or technical paragraph, describe how this would work—think through the process. How did Papa use a rope and stone to measure the water level? You may even wish to draw a diagram to accompany your explanation.

Language Arts: Vocabulary

land reclamation   The process of converting lands to make them more suitable for a different use.

heatstroke Collapse or sudden illness with fever and dry skin, caused by overexposure to excessive heat.

heat exhaustion A condition caused by excessive exposure to heat and characterized by cold, clammy hands and general symptoms of shock.

Fine Arts: The Colors of Drought*

In this chapter, MacLachlan offers us an unusual description of the prairie. Because of the drought, the land has become dry and dusty. We read, "...as far as I could see the fields were brown...There was no green." What does your student think that would look like? Land stretched out as far as you could see without a blade or spot of green?

Taking MacLachlan's description, encourage your student to paint or draw a picture reflecting the words—"There was no green." Perhaps she would use only shades of blue for the sky, and shades of sienna, brown and tan for the earth and trees. Or she could sketch a picture of the prairie, drawn completely in shades of brown. If your student created a picture of the prairie for *Sarah, Plain and Tall*, compare these two pictures and note the differences in the colors chosen to represent the *same* prairie under very different circumstances.

Chapter 6

Teacher Summary

On their way home from town, the Wittings see a fire in their meadow. Quickly, they work together to soak down sacks and beat the fire back. The fire is soon out, but Papa warns the family they must be on constant alert for fire from now on—the drought is causing everything to be dry and a fire hazard.

What we will cover in this chapter:

Teacher's Note: This particular chapter is rich with lesson ideas surrounding the topic of fire. It might be interesting for your student to complete the following lessons and keep her notes and research in a separate folder or journal, thus compiling a complete unit study on fire and related topics. Your student may also recall studying (and possibly creating instructions for) building a campfire, found in FIAR Vol. 5, *The Boxcar Children*, chapter 5.

Social Studies: History - The Great Chicago Fire
Social Studies: Geography - Areas Where Fire Is a Constant Risk*
Social Studies: Career Path - Firefighter
Science: The Chemical and Scientific Background of Fire
Language Arts: Learning to Interview
Language Arts: Writing and Discussion Question
Language Arts: Vocabulary
Fine Arts: How to Create your Own "Fire" - Tips from the Stage
Fine Arts: A Famous "Fire" Poem by William Blake - "The Tyger"
Life Skills: Health and Safety - Fire Precautions
Life Skills: Health and Safety - First Aid for Burns
Life Skills: Being a Person of Commitment

Social Studies: History - The Great Chicago Fire

The Wittings' fire was relatively easy to stop. With hard work and wet sacks, the family is able to beat it back and control the flames. Sometimes, however, fires cannot be put out so easily. Throughout history, famous fires have occurred which changed people's lives and destroyed entire cities. One of the most famous fires in the United States was the Great Chicago Fire of October 8, 1871. Share with your student the story and the surrounding myths of this famous disaster.

In the late 19th century, most buildings were built of wood. Those that were not (constructed mostly of brick or stone) certainly weren't equipped with modern-day fire protection, i.e., fire walls, fire retardant curtains, fire extinguishers, etc.

Most of Chicago, a booming metropolis of that day, was constructed of wood (a few building were made of brick, iron or stone). The population at that time had soared to nearly 350,000 people and was rapidly growing. Just like the Wittings experienced, during that summer of 1871 Chicago had suffered a great drought. According to legend, late on the night of October 7, a Mrs. O'Leary was milking her cow out in her barn. Mrs. O'Leary made her living selling milk to her working class, Irish neighborhood. Supposedly, that evening her cow got riled and kicked over Mrs. O'Leary's lantern. The straw and barn caught fire almost immediately and with the dry grasses and the strong winds, the fire spread rapidly north and northeast. Nearly 30 buildings were consumed before the fire department could even arrive at the scene.

Throughout the night, 90 firefighters (nearly half of the city's department) worked tirelessly to fight the flames. The fire reached the waterworks of the city sometime around midnight, and the pumps were ruined. There was now no way to fight the fire. Miraculously, rain began to fall around the same time and by 3:00 a.m. on October 8, the fire was finally out. The new day revealed more than 20 acres of Chicago's West Side burned to the ground. Thirty firefighters died, 300 people lost their lives and one-third of the city was utterly destroyed. More than 18,000 homes were destroyed, leaving tens of thousands homeless. The city was virtually wiped out.

The story of Mrs. O'Leary and her cow has become more than a legend as the years have passed. Although many believe that is actually the way the fire started, other critics and lawyers have continued to search for more answers. Another culprit recently cited is a Mr. Daniel Sullivan, a one-legged horse-cart driver who was a neighbor of Mrs. O'Leary's—and who may have, in fact, been in her barn lighting a lantern or smoking a pipe on that night, October 7. Whether or not it's true will probably never be known. In any event, the story of Mrs. O'Leary has become an historic legend, a part of Chicago's mythology. It has been said, "This is the city a cow kicked over." Songs have been written about the event. The first verse to one of these goes like this:

Late last night, when we were all in bed
Old Lady Leary left a lantern in the shed
When the cow kicked it over, she winked her eye and said,
"There'll be a hot time in the old town tonight."

A movie about the fire, entitled *In Old Chicago*, came out in 1938 starring Don Ameche and Alice Brady (who, incidentally, won an Oscar for the role).

If there is interest, encourage your student to do more of her own research into this famous American disaster. Perhaps she can uncover clues regarding the real story of the Great Chicago Fire. There have also been many other famous urban fires in such famous cities as ancient Rome, London, San Francisco, New York City, Boston, Mexico City, and more.

The Wittings were certainly lucky they were able to control their fire, weren't they?

Social Studies: Geography - Areas Where Fire is a Constant Risk*

Fires can be dangerous and risky no matter where you live. However, there are certain areas of the United States where fires are much more of a problem. Certainly, where the Wittings live on the prairie, it is a risk. With low rainfall and fields of hay and crops, fire can spread quickly.

Generally, in the United States the highest risk areas are in California and other western states such as Texas, Colorado, Arizona, Idaho, and Washington. Each year, fires rage through various areas in these regions, often consuming many acres.

Interesting to note for your student, not only do fires consume people's homes and businesses and destroy forests and parks, they also cost a great deal of money. The monetary losses from fires can be astounding, often with property losses and damages in the hundreds of millions or even billions of dollars. In some states, there are laws to bill all people responsible for forest fires.

Where does your student live? Has she ever seen or been near a large forest fire or prairie fire? What was it like? If your student lives in a high-risk fire area, she is probably already aware of the dangers and the precautions your area takes. If not, why not take some time to research and study a specific region of the country and the fires which have occurred there.

Social Studies: Career Path - Firefighter

Papa, Sarah and the children were forced to fight their fire alone, weren't they? They were able to beat it out. But what if it had been a larger fire? Anna would not be able to simply call 911 as we can today. How lucky we are to have firefighters who are willing to serve and protect us.

If your student is interested in helping people, enjoys being a part of emergency situations, and likes working on a team, then explore the career of a professional firefighter.

Firefighters are men and women who are expertly trained to assist and save lives in emergency situations. Firefighters never know what each workday will bring. A burning home with four people to help, a car accident, a kitchen fire, a warehouse fire, a heart attack victim—each could happen at any moment. Firefighter shifts are very long, including overnight, weekends and holidays. They must be prepared to handle all emergency calls any time during the day or night.

Five in Row Volume Seven

When firefighters are on duty, they live together and work together for the entire shift. Generally, the same team of fighters is on call together. Teamwork and sharing responsibilities are vital to make the station run smoothly.

It takes a good deal of courage to be a firefighter. These men and women risk their health and lives every day to help others. It takes a consistently positive attitude, creative problem solving skills, physical strength and endurance, and emotional maturity (to handle intense emergency situations). It also requires a good deal of compassion for people.

Different communities have different requirements for becoming a firefighter. Your student can search online for requirements in her area. Some programs require an associate's degree in fire science, some require a few months of academy training, and many firefighters are also required to be paramedics or EMTs.

If your student is interested in researching this career path further, there are several things you can do to help. First, call and arrange a tour of a fire station in your area. This will give her more insight into the job, as well as increase her knowledge of fire safety. The Exploring club, affiliated with the Boy Scouts of America, is another hands-on resource that teens and youth (both boys and girls) can participate in.

If your student is extremely interested and motivated to explore this career path further, she can obtain and browse through a sample firefighter's exam at the library, or check online for more information. This sample exam will give your student an idea of the questions and requirements a firefighting program will ask and demand.

Science: The Chemical and Scientific Background of Fire

Teacher's Note: Before doing this lesson, it might be beneficial and fun to light a candle and observe the flame with your student. See what questions she has—or how much she already knows.

As we have seen in this chapter, fire can be a dangerous and destructive thing. But what exactly is it? Does your student know the chemical make-up of fire? What makes the flame look blue at the base, then red, then orange and sometimes yellow at the top? What makes it hot?

Fire is the word used to describe the combination of heat and light that come from burning substances. A famous French chemist, Antoine Lavoisier, proved in 1777 that burning (and therefore sometimes fire) is the chemical result of oxygen combining with other substances. When, for example, iron is combined with oxygen (which is present in the air), a slow change develops called rust. This is known as **oxidation**. When the same process occurs more quickly, for example, oxygen combining with gasoline, the action causes heat to be given off quickly. The process is called **combustion**.

For fire to occur, three things must be present. First, a fuel or substance that will burn is necessary (solids: examples are wood or coal; liquids: oil or gasoline; and gases: natural gas or hydrogen). There must also be heat—enough heat to raise the temperature of the air (and oxygen) to a combustible point. This temperature is called the **kindling temperature**. Finally, there must be oxygen present—usually from the air.

For a fire to start, it is often necessary for the proportions of flame to substance to be fairly equal. For example, it might be difficult for your student to get a giant log burning from a single match. On the other hand, a small stick or twig might burn quite easily. This is because there is more oxygen surrounding the twig in relation to the burning match than there is around the large log. Sometimes, when people build campfires, you'll notice them fanning the flames. Why? Because the slight wind brings more air (and therefore more oxygen) into contact with the beginning flame. The fire is, therefore, more likely to continue burning brightly.

Teacher's Note: If you covered the unit on *Thomas Edison* in FIAR Vol. 6, you may have done the lesson on the chemical element phosphorus, located in chapter 13 of that unit. Phosphorus must be kept wet (even submerged in water). It is extremely flammable. Its kindling temperature is so low, it can become combustible in normal air temperatures. If you already did this lesson, you may wish to take this time to go back and review it with your student.

Ask your student whether or not she thinks fire can totally consume a piece of wood. Is there anything left? Actually, although the flames will destroy most of it, fire cannot entirely burn a piece of wood. What about the ashes? What are they? When you see ashes and bits of charred black pieces left in the bottom of a fireplace or fire pit, what you are seeing are the remains of a log. Ashes are a mixture of minerals present in the wood that are not flammable. Different fuels produce different amounts of ash—this ratio is known as the ash content.

If your student shows interest in this topic, other fascinating related subjects for study are: matches, spontaneous combustion and smoke.

Language Arts: Learning to Interview

Imagine how frightened and tired Papa and Sarah were after they beat out the fire! What a story they would have to tell. Does your student know anyone who has been in some kind of natural disaster such as a fire, flood, tornado, earthquake, etc.? If she knows someone who is willing to share his or her story, take this opportunity to help your student develop interviewing skills, as well as work on writing techniques.

Interviewing someone for a writing project can be a fascinating and rewarding venture. It might seem simple to some students, but there are several key guidelines you should always follow.

First, call or contact the person you're interested in interviewing and share with them your ideas for the project. If the person is willing to participate, it is appropriate to set up an interview time. It is also wise to share with the interviewee a few of the questions you will be asking. In this way, she can be prepared for you.

Next, it is important to do your own research on the topics beforehand. This will help give you background on the situation and will help you formulate intelligent questions. For example, if you are interviewing someone who was in an earthquake, it would be advantageous to look up some information on earthquakes and possibly some other people's stories concerning their experiences.

When you are at the interview itself, be sure to take a means of recording your session, whether by taking notes, making an audio recording, or both. Your questions should already be written out, but never limit yourself to only these ideas. If something arises in conversation and you have a new question, go with your instinct. Sometimes the best ideas, quotes and stories come from within the interview itself. An audio recording will help you get accurate quotes when you are writing the article, but it is important to make brief hand-written notes throughout the interview. These notes will remind you of key questions or responses that you'll want to go back to later.

When you are ready to write your article, using the quotes and story from the interview, remember—it is vital you quote accurately. If you have any doubts about something that was said—a date or time, a person's name, etc.—always double check! Now you're ready to write!

Language Arts: Writing and Discussion Question

In our chapter, when Sarah asks Papa, "Do you really think I would leave?" Papa remains silent. If he had responded right away, what do you think he would have said? Does Jacob believe she might leave, or is he just frightened and stressed? What do you think Sarah will do?

Language Arts: Vocabulary

oxidation   The chemical result of oxygen combined with other substances.

combustion   A rapid oxidation accompanied by heat and light.

kindling temperature The temperature of the air required to create combustion.

Fine Arts: How to Create Your Own "Fire" - Tips from the Stage

The flames and heat the Wittings fought in their field were not fake, but quite real. However sometimes, in old movies and on the stage, technicians create "fake" fire. Has your student ever been interested in special effects or technical theatre work? Here is a simple project your student can create which will teach her a little about both.

To create your own "fire" you will need: sticks and twigs, a small fan, a flashlight, scissors and cellophane paper (yellow, red or orange are preferred).

First, have your student cut flame-shaped strips from the cellophane paper. She can cut as many as she thinks are needed, in whatever shape she thinks looks realistic. If she has a choice in colors, she may wish to experiment with several different combinations of red, orange, yellow or even blue.

Next, have your student (in a room which can be made fairly dark) arrange the twigs and sticks in whatever pattern she wants for her "fire"—perhaps in a circle like a campfire or a pyramid shape like a bonfire. When she has the wood arranged, she should take the fire strips and in some way attach them to the underneath section of the twigs. Hot glue (used with supervision), super glue, or strong duct tape all work fairly well. The logs can be taped together, too, so they will stay in their pattern. However, enough of the cellophane strips should be left free in the middle of the wood (where the flames would be in an actual fire).

Now, she needs to set up a practice session. By placing a flashlight against or under the wood and turning it on, your student should be able to achieve a glowing effect. By positioning a small fan behind the logs and the strips of paper, she can make the flames "come alive" and flicker, like real flames.

Finally, with the lights turned off and everything set, your student can sit back and marvel at her special effects. Imagine! With paper, light and wind she has created fire! For even more effect, your student can play fire sounds from a real campfire or fireplace blaze during her demonstration. This type of exercise is an avenue for creativity. It also builds problem solving skills as your student tries to see what will work best.

Fine Arts: A Famous "Fire" Poem by William Blake - "The Tyger"

Fire is a fascinating topic. A poet named William Blake wrote a now-famous poem using flame as a main image. Share with your student some information about this poet and the poem.

William Blake (1757-1827) was a painter and poet. All of his artistic endeavors showed a great sense of imagination and creativity. His colors, his word choices, and his philosophies were unconventional and astounding. Blake was born in London, England and lived most of his life there. He was, by profession, an illustrator and engraver.

Perhaps one of his most beautiful poems is entitled "The Tyger." Share this famous poem with your student. It is well suited for memorization and recitation. If your student is willing and interested, assign the poem and then have her recite it for a parent or grandparent. This sharpens memorization and public speaking skills. Perhaps your student would like to draw or paint a picture to correspond with the poem. You may also use it as a practice piece for your student's penmanship practice, or have your student type it out and illustrate it on the computer.

The Tyger

Tyger! Tyger! burning bright
In the forests of the night,
What immortal hand or eye
Could frame thy fearful symmetry?

In what distant deeps or skies
Burnt the fire of thine eyes?
On what wings dare he aspire?
What the hand dare seize the fire?

And what shoulder, and what art,
Could twist the sinews of thy heart?
And when thy heart began to beat,
What dread hand? And what dread feet?

What the hammer? What the chain?
In what furnace was thy brain?
What the anvil? What the grasp
Dare its deadly terrors clasp?

When the stars threw down their spears,
And watered heaven with their tears,
Did he smile his work to see?
Did he who made the Lamb make thee?

Tyger! Tyger! burning bright
In the forests of the night,
What immortal hand or eye
Dare frame thy fearful symmetry?

What does your student think Blake is trying to understand by writing this poem? Is it just about a tiger? Examine this poem with your student and allow the metaphors and images to ignite more discussion.

Life Skills: Health and Safety - Fire Precautions

Sometimes fires just start—like the Wittings' fire in their field. The grass is dry and accidents happen. But is it possible to take precautions and prevent fires? Yes! Ask your student if she has ever heard of a fire escape map or the words: stop, drop and roll? Does she know how to operate a fire extinguisher and remember where it is located in her house? All of these things are ways your student and her family can protect themselves and prevent many dangerous fires.

Remind your student of the main protections she should always have in place: smoke detectors on each floor of her house (perhaps several detectors, depending upon the layout), fire extinguishers in at least the kitchen, basement and garage, and a fire escape map charted and practiced for her family.

A fire escape map is basically a plan of action, in case of emergency. Each family member should have a clear understanding of what doors or windows from which they can exit and how to do so quickly! Always remember: if there is a fire in your home, DO NOT STOP for pets or special items or anything else, just GET OUT! That is the *number one* rule for safety. The second rule is once out, never go back in for anything and hold all little children so they do not run back into a burning building. Once a fire escape map has been charted and discussed, it is always good to practice a few times. If there were a real fire, the smoke and heat would be confusing enough. It would be better if the escape route had been rehearsed in advance.

Here is a list of other **Fire Safety Do's and Don'ts:**

Don't leave electrical appliances (coffee makers, irons, hot plates, portable heaters, etc.) on and unattended.

Don't overload your electrical circuits.

Don't allow furniture to sit on top of an electrical cord (be careful especially when moving furniture such as couches or chairs).

Don't leave bare or splintered wires and cords out. Wrap them or dispose of them. Don't leave candles or other open flames unattended.

Don't try to move or carry a contained fire.

Don't use an elevator to escape a fire.

Don't open a door that is hot to the touch.

Don't re-enter a burning building for any reason.

Do clean and maintain your fireplaces and chimneys.

Do properly dispose of burnable trash.

Do teach fire safety to your friends and family.

Do teach the dangers of fireworks.

Do close your doors at night for added protection.

Do store and use any flammable liquids safely.

Remind your student of perhaps the most important tip of all: If she ever finds herself in the situation where her hair or clothes have caught on fire, STOP, DROP and ROLL! This will smother the flames and could save her life.

Life Skills: Health and Safety - First Aid for Burns

If your student has ever had a burn (even a small one) she knows how painful they can be. Some people argue a burn is worse than a laceration, because of the slow healing process.

To treat a burn properly, care should be taken to cool the area immediately. By using water or cold compresses, the pain should subside somewhat. Never put butter or oil on a burn—this can hold in heat, causing further damage. Next, loosely bandage the burn with some gauze. The tighter the weave, the less likely it is the gauze will stick to the burn. Of course, for more serious third degree burns, professional help should be sought immediately.

If you have any questions about helping someone or treating yourself in a genuine emergency situation, always call 911 and seek more assistance.

Life Skills: Being a Person of Commitment

Draw your student's attention to this conversation between Papa and Sarah:

"Travel? Where would I go, Jacob?"
"Somewhere green," said Papa. "Somewhere cool."
Sarah looked at Papa.
"Do you think I would leave?" asked Sarah softly.
Papa was silent.

We see this same conversation arise a few pages later, when Sarah reiterates the question. What does your student think about this exchange? What do we know about Sarah thus far in our story? Is she a person of commitment? From what we have come to learn about Sarah, one could easily argue that she is, in fact, such a person. She left her only home and friends to come to the prairie in the first place. She obviously loves Jacob and the children very much. She has helped out during the squall, helped fix a roof, and she has also brought a lot of good times and memories to the Wittings. Sarah is a person of commitment. She's not likely to leave because things get difficult.

Learning to be a person of commitment is an important character journey. It doesn't take much to tell someone you'll help them out, but following through is different—particularly if you're extra tired or the day is filled with other activities. Keeping your word and staying with situations even when they are difficult is part of being mature and strong.

Encourage your student today by sharing with her a time when perhaps you were struggling to keep a commitment. How did you deal with that struggle? What have you learned about promises and character that you could share?

Being committed to people and tasks is a positive and productive way to live!

Chapter 7

Teacher Summary

Every day the drought worsens. The children aren't taking baths anymore to conserve water and each day requires the family to haul water for the animals. One day, as the Wittings near the river's edge, they see Matthew and Maggie's wagon already parked there. Maggie is very sad. Soon the truth comes out. Matthew, Maggie, Rose and Violet are being forced to move because of the drought. They have no choice. Sarah is angry and doesn't understand why anyone would choose to live on the prairie. She tells Maggie (and Anna overhears) she hates the prairie—that she hates the land. Maggie tells her in order to survive here, you must love the land. She tells Sarah that Jacob was right. You have to write your name in the land to live here.

What we will cover in this chapter:

Social Studies: History - Hauling Water: How Much Work It Really Takes
Language Arts: Analogies*
Language Arts: Imagery - Sarah's Voice
Language Arts: Writing and Discussion Question
Language Arts: Vocabulary
Fine Arts: Cooking - Biscuits

Social Studies: History - Hauling Water: How Much Work It Really Takes

Papa, Sarah and the children must go every day to haul water in wooden barrels for the animals and themselves. How difficult a task is that? How much water do you think the Wittings had to haul?

Remind your student of the lesson on cattle located in the chapter 3 lessons of *Skylark*. In that reading, we learn that cattle drink nearly 20 gallons of water daily! That is just enough water for one cow or bull, and the Wittings have Mame, her calf and maybe a couple of others—not to mention the horses, the three chickens, Nick, Lottie and Seal. And those are just the animals we know of! In other words, they must have needed to haul a great deal of water.

But how difficult is it to haul water? Bring realism to this lesson by allowing your student to try her own hand at hauling water.

Teacher's Note: This part of the lesson would probably be done best outside.

Let your student select a "barrel" of sorts to fill with water. (10-20 gallon plastic trash buckets work the best.) It must be large enough to hold a significant amount of water. Now, have your student fill it nearly full. Can she lift it? How many gallons does she have in the bucket? How many must she take out in order to carry it? Then work some calculations with her. If she can carry five gallons, and one cow drinks twenty in a day, that one animal will require four trips. Multiply that times 4 and you have sixteen back-breaking loads for only the cattle!

Five in Row Volume Seven 83

The story tells us the Wittings have ceased taking baths in order to save water, but what about washing dishes? Drinking water? Scrubbing their clothes? Cooking? When you stop and think about it, the amount of water a family needs from day to day is astounding.

If your water company sends you an itemized bill showing how many gallons of water your family used in the past month or quarter, this would be a great time to show it to your student. Many bills include month-to-month usage graphs. If your water usage is higher in the summer, for example, ask your student why she thinks that would be? (Perhaps from watering plants or gardens, irrigating a lawn, filling a swimming pool, etc.)

Learning to conserve water and take care of our resources is one way we can help prevent water shortages and help our environment. Aren't you thankful you don't have to haul water like Papa and Sarah? Remind your student to be thankful the next time she takes a bath or shower!

Language Arts: Analogies*

Sarah is angry and sad that her neighbors have to move away. Maggie tries to explain, but doesn't get far. Then she tells Sarah she reminds her of a prairie lark—"You are like a prairie lark, you know. It sings its song above the land to let all the birds know it's there before it plunges down to earth to make its home. But you have not come to earth, Sarah."

Why does Maggie offer this kind of explanation to Sarah? Why does she use a story of a bird? Sometimes when people are trying to explain a difficult concept or feeling they use what is known as an **analogy**. An analogy is a comparison of two things—often one complex example and one simpler example. Analogies help provide clarity. Maggie knew Sarah loved wildlife and would know what a prairie lark was and how it lived. She knew Sarah would understand.

Language Arts: Imagery - Sarah's Voice

At the end of our chapter, in Anna's journal entry, we read her description of Sarah's words, "...even her words were like a song." What does your student think that means? Does she think Sarah's voice actually lilts when she speaks, like a song?

For discussion, your student might examine this possibility. Often, song lyrics use a lot of imagery. Imagery is a literary term meaning words or phrases which include comparisons and vivid description. For example, "the sunset as red as a robin's breast." Or, "her eyes spoke a thousand words, like throngs of angry people." Imagery is used in poetry and literature of all sorts, and sometimes people employ beautiful imagery in their speech.

When Sarah speaks, her words are full of images. Look back on just a few of her phrases from *Sarah, Plain and Tall* and *Skylark*:

"But I've touched seals. Real seals. They are cool and slippery and they slide through the water like fish." (*Sarah*)

"The sea is salt. It stretches out as far as you can see. It gleams like the sun on glass. There are waves." (*Sarah*)

"What was between the lines?" Caleb asked... "His life," she said simply. (*Skylark*)

So, perhaps when Anna described Sarah's words as a song, this is what she meant—the use of imagery and poetic devices.

Language Arts: Writing and Discussion Question

Sarah and Caleb discussed the difference between a daydream and a night dream. How would you describe the difference? What is a daydream you have often?

Language Arts: Vocabulary

analogy   A story or example which helps simplify a more complex idea.

Fine Arts: Cooking: Biscuits

The beginning of our chapter finds Sarah mixing up biscuit batter. Biscuits were a staple during pioneer times. These bread products were easy and quick to make, not requiring any time for rising like yeast breads.

If your student likes to cook, perhaps this would be a good opportunity to take some time and bake. Here is one recipe for biscuits, but if you have a favorite, by all means, use that.

Biscuits Like Sarah Might Have Made

1 3/4 cups all-purpose flour
1 tsp. salt
2 tsp. baking powder
1 tsp. sugar
1/2 tsp. baking soda
1/4 cup cold butter
2/3 cup buttermilk

Sift together flour, salt, baking powder, sugar and baking soda. Cut in butter or margarine. Add buttermilk. After very lightly mixing, turn the dough onto a floured board. Knead it very lightly for 1 minute. Pat the dough into a flat circle approximately 2" thick. Pushing straight down without twisting, cut into circles with either a biscuit cutter or the floured rim of a drinking glass. Bake at 450° F. for 10-12 minutes. Enjoy!

Chapter 8

Teacher Summary

A lone, starved coyote comes to drink from the Wittings' well and Papa must shoot it. Sarah, completely devastated by seeing the animal put down, retreats to be alone. Fortunately, Sarah's birthday arrives and the festivities cheer everyone up. Her aunts from Maine send her a phonograph. Papa and Sarah dance. By the end of the day, Sarah is feeling much happier.

What we will cover in this chapter:

Social Studies: History - The Phonograph: An Edison Invention
Science: Shade - A Scarce Commodity on the Prairie
Language Arts: Book Recommendation - *What You Know First*
Language Arts: Author's License - Breaking the Rules on Purpose*
Language Arts: Writing and Discussion Question
Language Arts: Vocabulary
Life Skills: Making Instead of Buying - Giving Precious Gifts

Social Studies: History - The Phonograph: An Edison Invention

Sarah's aunts from Maine are very kind to send her such a thoughtful birthday present—a phonograph! Imagine being isolated on the prairie and suddenly having the gift of music. If your student studied Thomas Alva Edison in FIAR Vol. 6, she might remember that Edison developed the first working phonograph in 1877.

Edison's first model of the phonograph, although somewhat crude, is still quite similar to the more modern record player. They all operate by the principle of sound being a vibration. Edison had someone speak (or sing) into a funnel-like mouthpiece and the person's voice vibrations were then recorded by a needle on a piece of tin foil. To replay the speech or song, Edison placed another needle on the same piece of grooved tin, which had been wrapped around a cylinder tube. When the tube was turned and the needle passed along the grooves and was amplified, the sounds could be heard.

Later on, in 1887, Emile Berliner, a German inventor living in America, improved the invention further. Instead of tin or metal cylinders, he created discs coated in **shellac** (sha LACK—a varnish made from alcohol and secretions from the lac insect which gives a very smooth and shiny finish to wood, metal or plastic). Not only did Berliner's new "records" provide clearer sound, but they were easier to mass-produce for sale. The earliest models of phonographs became available by 1925.

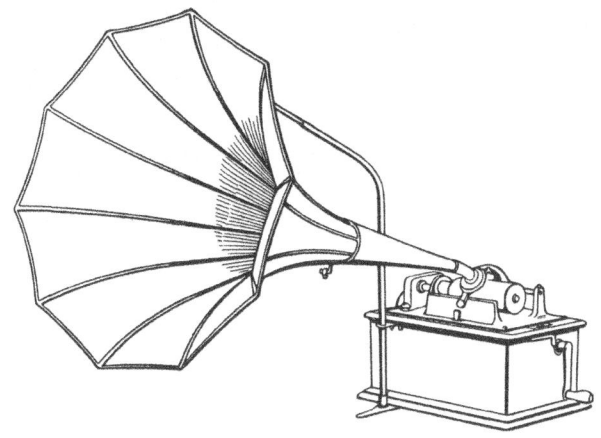

If there is interest, more study can be done on the history of the phonograph. Your student might also be interested in learning the terms record player, turntable, and vinyl player. If you have a record player in your house, be sure to show your student how it works, or look online for a video.

Science: Shade - A Scarce Commodity on the Prairie

Draw your student's attention to the following line: "Outside there was a table in the shade of the house, set with food and lemonade." This is similar to a sentence from *Sarah, Plain and Tall*: "...then they set up a big table in the shade of the barn..."

If your student were going to give a picnic outside on tables, where would she think to put the tables and chairs? One common response might be under the trees. Certainly, if it were summertime and hot, shade would be what you were looking for and trees do seem like the logical spot, don't they? However, remind your student of where our story takes place. Sarah, Papa and the children live on the prairie. Generally, prairies do not have many trees, if any (unless a windbreak has been planted). For the Wittings and their guests, the only spot for shade is under the eaves or in the shade of the house or barn.

For very similar reasons, due to the heat, drought and lack of shade, having a nice, green grass lawn was obviously difficult as well. In this chapter we read, "Everyone danced, then, in the dirt yard..." Does your student have a lawn? What would it be like to have a front yard of only dust and soil? It would certainly be different.

If possible, discuss this lesson with your student outdoors, in the shade of a tree or building!

Language Arts: Book Recommendation - *What You Know First*

Patricia MacLachlan, our author, is an outstanding writer. Many of the things she remembered from her childhood influenced her books, and if you read them carefully, you'll see similar themes used again and again. For example, look with your student at the final lines from Anna's journal—Sarah's birthday gift.

"My mother, Sarah, doesn't love the prairie. She tries, but she can't help remembering what she knew first."

MacLachlan used this same sentiment as a title and theme for a different book, published a year after *Skylark*. If your student is enjoying *Sarah, Plain and Tall* and *Skylark*, try to locate another MacLachlan title, *What You Know First*.

Written with the same creativity and integrity MacLachlan is known for, this book is a delightful supplement to your Sarah studies. The illustrations are breathtaking. Barry Moser, an American Book Award-winning artist, selected (with the help of MacLachlan) old family photographs. Then, by using a synthetic wood medium, he created engravings of the photographs, made blocks and then printed them. The result is magnificent.

This book is highly recommended for anyone, young or old. It is another MacLachlan treasure.

Language Arts: Author's License - Breaking the Rules on Purpose*

If you feel your student has a firm enough comprehension of basic grammar and sentence structure, this lesson offers an interesting introduction to author's **license**. Sometimes writers (particularly in poetry and fiction) make exceptions to basic grammatical rules. In this chapter, MacLachlan writes, "For a while, everyone was happy again. Even Sarah. Even Papa."

Ask your student if the last two sentences are really sentences? No, they are not. To be complete and grammatically correct, a sentence must include a subject and a verb.

These sentences are lacking a verb. Ask your student why she thinks MacLachlan uses these odd, short sentences at the end of her paragraph?

Perhaps she wanted to draw attention to those two characters—Sarah and Papa. When you read that section, an emphasis is obviously on those two phrases.

Authors and poets sometimes break other grammatical rules on purpose. For example, the famous American poet, e. e. cummings (1894-1962), often did not make use of capital letters or standard punctuation. Cummings' full name was Edward Estlin Cummings. His poetry is famous for its lack of traditional sentence structure, his abandonment of proper syntax, his purposeful disregard for punctuation and capitalization, and his wild and fanciful experiments with typography (the arrangement of the words on the page).

Here is an example of e. e. cummings' work:

In Just -

in Just -
spring   when the world is mud-
luscious the little
lame balloonman

whistles   far   and wee

and eddieandbill come
running from marbles and
piracies and it's
spring

when the world is puddle-wonderful

the queer
old balloonman whistles
far   and   wee
and bettyandisbel come dancing

from hop-scotch and jump-rope and

it's
spring
and
          the
                    goat-footed
balloonMan   whistles
far
and
wee

Another striking example of cummings' creativity with letters and shapes is found in the first line of another poem, which is:

"mOOn Over tOwns mOOn"

cummings has made the observation that the letter "o" resembles the moon. To emphasize this point, he breaks the rules of punctuation and exaggerates the letters "o" by placing them in capital form.

If your student enjoys creative writing, either in fiction, journal writing, or poetry, perhaps she would like to experiment with her own creative "license" by making simple changes, as subtle as MacLachlan, or wild changes like that of e. e. cummings.

Language Arts: Writing and Discussion Question

Caleb's glass disappears from its resting spot on the fence post. Sarah notices this and asks Jacob to put it back. Why do you think Caleb's rain glass was gone? Who took it down? Why?

Language Arts: Vocabulary

shellac   A resinous substance (obtained from the lac insect) melted into thin flakes, used for making varnish.

license   Freedom of action, speech or thought.

Life Skills: Making Instead of Buying - Giving Precious Gifts

Anna gave Sarah a precious birthday gift—something she had written herself. Anna's journal for her mother includes her own thoughts and feelings—

her*self*. Sometimes, the gifts we make for others mean more to them than those we buy. Has your student ever made her own present for someone? What was it? What gave her the idea? Did it take more work than buying something? Was it worth it? Did the recipient appreciate the extra time and love? Or has your student ever received a gift which was hand-created just for her?

Often the value of a gift is not dependent upon how much it cost. Instead, it is based more in the love it took to make it. Encourage your student to try to make a gift for a friend or family member soon. Just like Anna, she too can give precious gifts.

Chapter 9

Teacher Summary

Just as things were beginning to get a little brighter, Maggie and Matthew's well runs dry. They are forced to move. Having her neighbors and only close woman friend leaving is difficult for Sarah. That night, Anna is awakened by a clap of thunder. Lightning strikes the barn and a fire begins to rage. No matter how many buckets of water they collect and pour on the flames, the Wittings cannot stop it. The family stands and watches their barn burn to the ground. The next day a major decision is reached. The drought has become too severe. Sarah, Anna and Caleb will move back to Maine and stay with the aunts until it is over. Papa will not go with them because he must watch over the land.

What we will cover in this chapter:

Social Studies: History and Geography - Wells
Science: Watertable - What It Is and How to Create Your Own*
Language Arts: Writing and Discussion Question
Language Arts: Vocabulary
Life Skills: Dealing With Hard Choices

Social Studies: History and Geography - Wells

Maggie and Matthew are being forced to move from their home on the prairie. Their well has run dry. The Wittings and their neighbors obviously rely on their wells as the primary source of water. Does your student live in a rural area where people still use wells? Has she ever thought about where her own water comes from?

Take some time and explore with your student the topic of wells. Throughout history, wells have been gathering places of the community. For centuries, in many parts of the world, the town well was not only the place for collecting the family's water supply each day, but it was also the "information post"—the place where the men and women in the village discussed civic matters, family life and social events.

A **well** is a hole in the ground from which water (or oil or natural gases) can be withdrawn. The water that is taken from a well (just like Sarah and Jacob's) is known as **groundwater**. This water is present in the ground generally from rain soaking down through the crust of the earth. The water is contained in the soil and the permeable and semi-permeable bedrock.

But how does a person find the area in the ground where a well can be dug? Highly trained geologists and engineers make this their careers. They can find where the water is located and then, through the use of special equipment, they are able to determine where to drill or dig, how much water can be removed without destroying the natural resources, and at what rate.

In pioneer days, men and women simply observed their surroundings and attempted to determine where water would be most likely found. At times this was a matter of guesswork—a matter of trial and error.

If your student is interested in learning more about wells, additional topics suitable for study are: artesian wells, oil and gas wells, seismographs and mineral wells.

Science: Watertable - What It Is and How to Create Your Own*

Matthew and Maggie's well ran dry. Why? Where did the water go? When someone digs a well, won't there always be water in it? To answer these questions and to develop a better understanding of geology, discuss with your student the subject of watertables.

A **watertable** is the scientific term for the surface of groundwater—the top level. Below the watertable is the water source and above it is the earth. In certain areas (flood plains are a good example), the soil is so highly saturated (soaked) in water, the watertable is very close to the surface. When heavy rains fall, the watertable rises (sometimes above the level of the ground) and floods occur. The soil cannot absorb or hold any more water. Conversely, in drier areas (much like that of the prairie where the Wittings live) the watertable is low and then in times of drought, drops even further down. This is what causes wells to run dry.

To illustrate this point for your student, help her create her own mini-watertable. Take a clear drinking glass or Mason jar and have her fill it 2/3 full, with small stones, gravel, or even marbles.

Teacher's Note: Sand or soil may be used for this experiment, but the rate of evaporation will be much slower. If pebbles or marbles are used, the results can be seen in just a day or two.

After the glass is filled with your student's "earth," fill the jar with water. Your student can observe how the water filters down and surrounds the pebbles, and then begins to fill above them and creates a clear water reservoir. A **reservoir** is a place where water (or another substance) is collected and stored for use.

Now, have your student mark on the side of the jar where the watertable (or surface) is located.

Help your student place a small straw (or one cut in half) on the inside of the jar and tape it to the side (place it where you can see the bottom of the straw easily). Don't put the straw all the way to the bottom of the jar and marbles—instead, only about a third of the way down. This straw is now your student's well. What does she think will happen? If every time a little water evaporated, she continued to replenish the supply (in the way rain and rivers would under normal conditions) then her straw would always be submerged in the water. But what if a drought occurred? To illustrated this, encourage your student to leave the jar in a sunny window (or even outside) overnight. Has the water level gone down at all? How about in one day? In two days? How long does it take before the watertable is below the bottom of the straw? What happens then? If no more water is put into the "earth," no water can be drawn out. Sure, you could dig the well deeper. But then what? This is the dilemma which faces Maggie and Matthew. When a well runs dry, people begin to panic. Without water, people and animals will die.

When people like the Wittings dug a well, they would generally dig a good number of feet down past the watertable. Then, in case of a dry spell, they would have some leverage and still be able to access water. But when a drought occurs and the watertable drops below where the well can reach, that is when you say, the well has "run dry."

Understanding watertables and the way ground saturation affects our supply of water is fundamental to understanding flood plains and droughts. Nature has a delicate balance of resources and it is important to learn how to conserve and share those resources to our best advantage.

If your student is interested in learning more about watertables, good topics of discussion are dams, geology, water conservation and water pollution.

Language Arts: Writing and Discussion Question

Jacob and Sarah have their discussion about leaving the prairie in private. Anna watches them talking, but she doesn't hear anything they are saying. How do you think that conversation went? What do you think Papa might have said to convince Sarah to go? What do you think Sarah might have said in disagreement?

Language Arts: Vocabulary

well   A hole in the ground from which water (or oil or natural gases) can be withdrawn.

groundwater   Water held beneath the earth's surface.

reservoir   A place where water is stored and collected for use.

watertable   The level below which the ground is saturated with water.

Life Skills: Dealing With Hard Choices

Reread with your student these sentences:

"I saw her shake her head, no. I saw Papa take her hand. She shook her head again. Then Papa put his arms around her. I knew we would have to go away."

Sarah and the children don't want to leave Papa and go to Maine. Leaving the prairie, leaving Nick and Lottie and Seal, and most of all, leaving Papa will be difficult and sad. Certainly watching Maggie, Matthew and the children being forced to leave their home was an incentive for Jacob to come up with a plan. The Wittings don't want to lose their home entirely. If Sarah and the children can live in Maine for awhile, then there will probably be enough water for Jacob and the animals alone. He can also keep an eye on his land and watch for any more fires.

Sometimes it is necessary in life to deal with hard choices. Has your student ever had to make a difficult decision? What were the circumstances? What did she decide? There is an old saying, "You're between a rock and a hard place." Ask your student what she thinks that means. It is a play on words—rocks *are* hard places. Using this phrase is like saying you are between a hard place and a hard place. It's a way of describing a tough situation. It means there is no easy answer.

For Sarah, staying on the farm with Anna and Caleb could be dangerous for all of them. But leaving Jacob and returning to her former home for a season is going to be painful, too. How does a person decide what's best? In the end, Sarah probably had to rely on two things. First, she understands that going back to Maine is the safest thing for the children. Secondly, she trusts Jacob. He thinks they should leave and so she listens.

Learning to weigh issues and compare pros and cons is one way people deal with difficult decisions. Sometimes it results in picking the option that's the least painful—but hard, nonetheless. Sometimes, being in tough situations means we may need to listen to others and what they say—people we trust to steer us in the right direction.

Encourage your student to think about what making a difficult choice involves— how people think and what they can do to arrive at a decision. It is a sign of maturity when people are able to face tough problems with grace and commitment to a solution, instead of folding under the pressure.

Chapter 10

Teacher Summary

Sarah, Anna, and Caleb travel for three days by train to Maine. They travel the same route Sarah had taken to come out to the prairie to live with them. When they arrive at the train station in Maine, they are met

Five in Row Volume Seven

by an old friend who takes them by car to Sarah's aunts' home. Aunts Mattie, Harriet, and Lou love the children and are thrilled to have Sarah back. By the end of the evening, Anna begins to cry as she remembers how much she's already missing her father.

What we will cover in this chapter:

Social Studies: Geography - Maine*
Social Studies: History - A Clue to *Skylark's* Timeframe: The Automobile
Science: Tides and Oceans
Language Arts: Writing and Discussion Question
Language Arts: Vocabulary
Fine Arts: Julius Caesar and Aunt Lou's Dog
Life Skills: Being a Part of a Family - Understanding More About Sarah

Social Studies: Geography - Maine*

Anna and Caleb are in Maine—Sarah's birthplace and home. It must be very different from the prairie. The first observation of this new place we see is that "Maine was *green*."

If you did an introductory lesson on the state of Maine in *Sarah, Plain and Tall* (FIAR Vol. 6, chapter 1), your student may already have a basic understanding of this interesting northeastern region. However, for more detailed information on Maine, you might wish to take some time and do more in-depth research with your student.

Your local library may have good books about Maine. Try to locate video online about this state and look for additional tourism information. You might even locate a Maine newspaper online for additional study.

To make it more interesting, give your student an imaginary mission of some kind. For example, tell her you need to find an area to live in Maine where you will get the best view of the ocean or the most forest behind your house, or the quickest access to Boston or New York. Perhaps she enjoys snow skiing or snowmobiling—where would she go for these activities? What's Maine's southernmost city? What's the northernmost city?

By setting goals for research, your student will learn a great deal about this state and will have fun at the same time.

Social Studies: History - A Clue to *Skylark's* Timeframe: The Automobile

Up to this point in our story, we could only guess at a general timeframe for our tale. MacLachlan never gives us a year or date for our characters. When does your student think this story takes place? What clues can we gather? How do we determine a timeframe?

One good way to judge roughly when a story takes place is to look at the technology and industry mentioned. Sarah and Jacob do not drive an automobile, but instead, a horse and buggy. However, Sarah did arrive on the prairie via train. In *Skylark*, chapter 10, we see Chub arriving to pick the Wittings up in a car. Caleb comments, "I've never been in a car before." If cars were already in the east, but not much in the west, then it must have been a fairly new invention.

Henry Ford, born in 1863 in Dearborn, Michigan, invented the first gasoline powered engine in 1893, and his first automobile in 1896. After working for several years at the Detroit Electric Company, Ford (at the age of 40) organized the Ford Motor Company. The company developed the first car for family consumers and called it the Model T. These affordable and surprisingly reliable cars were available for sale in 1908. By 1913, they were fairly common on the east coast.

From this information, we can deduce that our story of the Wittings probably took place not long after the turn of the 20th century—perhaps between 1905 and 1915. Caleb didn't seem shocked by the *concept* of an automobile—he didn't say he had never heard of or seen one. He just said he had never *ridden* in one.

For more study and enriched lessons, your student can now take this approximate timeframe and begin doing outside research into the life and times of the Wittings. Who was President? (William Howard Taft served as President from 1909-1913. President Taft is the only U.S. president to serve first as President and then as Chief Justice.) What was the favorite sport? (Baseball, which had been introduced by Northern soldiers to the South during the Civil War [1861-65], was now so popular it became known as the national pastime.) What was the music of the time? (The most popular music was called ragtime, evolving from old-time military marches. This highly syncopated music became the rage from 1895-1915. The most famous ragtime piece was written by Scott Joplin in 1899 and was called "Maple Leaf Rag." Joplin himself was called the "King of Ragtime.") Find some examples of ragtime music and listen.

Share these bits of information with your student and encourage her to find many more. This time in history was fascinating. Understanding more about it helps us to flesh out our understanding of the Wittings and their life. Remind your student that it is from these kinds of clues that we are often able to decipher the timeframe of a story.

Science: Tides and Oceans

In this chapter, Caleb and Anna get their first peek at the great Atlantic Ocean. Caleb's first remark is an excellent description. He merely says, "All that water!" Can you imagine how amazed the children must have been to see the ocean, after living on the prairie all their lives? And after being in a drought? What a shock it must have been. In Anna's journal entry we read her observations, "... the tide going in and going out, the moon rising above the water."

Why not take this opportunity to share with your student more information on the oceans of the world? You can even do some exploration into ocean tides and how they are patterned.

To begin, the word "ocean" is used to describe the single massive body of water that covers 70% of the earth's surface. This body of water is often referred to as the **global ocean** or world ocean. To make it more specific, however, scientists have broken this body of water into five smaller oceans. They are, from largest to smallest: Pacific Ocean, Atlantic Ocean, Indian Ocean, Southern Ocean and Arctic Ocean (occasionally called the Arctic Sea). The average depth of the ocean is 12,000 feet, but many areas are much deeper.

Using an up-to-date map, globe, or the internet as your resource, locate these bodies of water with your student and compare each. As we learned from Sarah in *Sarah, Plain and Tall*, the sea is salt water. Seawater, on average, contains 3 1/2% salt. The wildlife found in an ocean is different from the animal life anywhere else in the world. If there is interest, take some time and let your student explore one or two interesting sea creatures (for example: anemones, jellyfish, manta rays or starfish).

The water in an ocean moves in tides. These rising and falling movements in the water are on a very specific time schedule. Some cultures that live along an ocean coast tell time by the tides. Tides follow the motion of the moon as it orbits the earth. According to researchers, the tides rise and fall twice in the time between two rising moons, 24 hours and 50 minutes. As the earth turns on its axis, the moon appears to move across the sky about once a day. The gravity of the moon's rotation pulls the water in each ocean away from the solid ground on one side of the earth, and on the opposite side of the planet, the gravity of the moon is pulling the earth away from the waters. These two pulls from opposite sides of the earth produce a hump of water, and these are the positions of high tide.

If you are fortunate enough to live near the ocean, take your student for a day trip soon. Examine wildlife and fascinating plants, and observe low and high tide. This field trip can provide your student with hands-on exploration and enrich her studies.

If you do not live near an ocean, find some books or videos that depict marine life and the oceans of the world. If you can't see something in person, a beautiful full-color photograph or video can be the next best thing!

Language Arts: Writing and Discussion Question

In this chapter we read, "When we got off the train, Sarah stood still. She looked at the train station, and at the trees, and at the people… 'It's all right, Anna,' said Sarah. 'It's just what you wrote in your book. I've come back to what I knew first.'"

What do you think Sarah was thinking about as she looked around her? Does she miss Maine, or is she thinking of Papa back on the prairie? Is she sad, happy, or a combination? Describe what you think Sarah's thoughts are like.

Language Arts: Vocabulary

global ocean   The ocean waters as a single body of water, worldwide.

tides   The rise and fall of the ocean, approximately every twelve hours, due to the movement of the sun and moon in relation to the earth.

Fine Arts: Julius Caesar and Aunt Lou's Dog

Does your student remember what Aunt Lou's dog is called? Brutus is an interesting name! Take some time and explore with your student Marcus Brutus, Julius Caesar and even some information about Shakespeare's interpretation of the historic assassination involving these two figures.

Julius Caesar (100?-44 B.C.) was one of the most famous and powerful Roman statesmen and leaders of ancient times. He was a renowned orator (a speech giver) and philosopher whom many compared to Cicero (SIS-er-oh, the most recognized orator, writer and philosopher of the day). Caesar won many battles and was appointed the dictator (ruler) of Rome. He was a charismatic and fearless man, and his people loved him as much as his enemies hated him.

One of Caesar's chief administrators and generals was a man named Marcus Brutus (BROO tuhs). In a fascinating turn of events, Brutus, who had been fighting on behalf of Pompey (Caesar's political rival—the last man who stood in the way of Caesar's rise to power), was appointed by Caesar to align with Rome. Pompey was defeated mercilessly and killed, and Brutus came to fight for Caesar. However, Brutus never truly trusted Caesar and was frightened by the love of power that he displayed. Brutus did not want Caesar to be king.

Caesar considered Brutus a friend. He worked and spent social time with Brutus every day. He trusted him. Brutus was jealous of the power Caesar was gaining. On March 15, 44 B.C. (a date known as "the ides of March"), with the encouragement and help of the Roman General Cassius, Brutus led a march to kill Caesar. Brutus, along with several other men, stabbed their leader to death on his way to a Roman Senate building. The great Julius Caesar was dead.

Throughout history, since this terrible event, the name Brutus has been used much like the name of Benedict Arnold—as a term for a traitor. William Shakespeare wrote of this famous event in one of his plays. The now-famous literary line, synonymous with friends turning on friends and political overthrow "Et tu, Brute?" is Latin for "And you, Brutus?"

If your student is interested in great historical events, politics, military stories or Shakespeare, take some time to read or watch the play *Julius Caesar* by William Shakespeare (the scene where Caesar is killed is in Act 3, Scene 1). It might prove to be a great enrichment lesson. The beauty of the language and the story are both stunning.

Julius Caesar

Life Skills: Being a Part of a Family - Understanding More About Sarah

From our story, we understand that Sarah is not a very "conventional" woman of the early 1900s. Ask your student what she can remember from our first book, *Sarah, Plain and Tall*, that would give her any clues. Sarah wore Papa's overalls. She helped him fix the roof. She let her chickens run around in the house. Remember what Jacob said? "Sarah is Sarah. She does things her way, you know."

Then, in this story, we are allowed to meet her aunts from Maine—Mattie, Harriet and Lou. Just as Sarah mentioned before, the aunts wear silk dresses around the house and no shoes. That's unconventional! And her Aunt Lou wears overalls and high boots, and works with animals—she doesn't like silk and pearls.

What can we learn from these delightful character sketches? When we grow up, we will never be "just like" our parents or a grandparents. We are a product of our mother, father and our ancestors. However, sometimes, the way we are raised dictates to a degree the way we turn out. Sarah is unconventional, but now we see her aunts are as well. Meeting her family helps us understand Sarah better, doesn't it?

Teacher's Note: Remind your student that when she writes her own stories, she can develop her characters by showing how both people and events have influenced their lives.

What does your student see in herself that reminds her of a parent? What does she notice about her interests or characteristics that are different?

Chapter 11

Teacher Summary

The days stretch into weeks as Anna, Caleb and Sarah stay in Maine. The children miss their father more and more, and the letter writing grows more frequent. One day, Sarah has her brother take her to see the doctor. She won't tell the children what the doctor said, but she assures them she's not sick.

Papa writes and tells them that Seal had her kittens—three gray and one orange. Caleb and Anna begin to wonder if the drought will ever end—will they ever go back to Papa and the prairie?

What we will cover in this chapter:

Language Arts: Developing Symmetry in Your Writing
Language Arts: Writing and Discussion Question
Language Arts: Vocabulary*
Fine Arts: Lullaby - "Hush, Little Baby"

Language Arts: Developing Symmetry in Your Writing

In *Sarah, Plain and Tall*, the story is framed by letters from Sarah to the Wittings. In that book, we learned information about Sarah and the other characters and were able to follow the story through the letters, just as Anna, Caleb and Papa did.

Now, in *Skylark*, we find Anna, Caleb and Sarah in Maine, writing letters back and forth to Papa. Through the use of these letters, our author, Patricia MacLachlan, has created symmetry within her story. **Symmetry** means balance or equality—to arrange two things evenly and opposite one another.

When we write stories, it is interesting to try to achieve symmetry in a variety of ways within the story. Perhaps at the beginning of your story a character makes a specific statement, and then that same sentiment is repeated at the end of the story. Here, in the *Sarah* books, we can observe a subtle, but effective symmetry in the way MacLachlan uses the postal letters.

Noticing symmetry or balance in stories allows us to more fully appreciate the thought and skill the author used when writing them. Encourage your student to try developing symmetry today in one of her own stories.

Language Arts: Writing and Discussion Question

Why do you think Sarah went to see the doctor? What's going on?

Language Arts: Vocabulary*

symmetry   Balanced; opposite sides which are equal.

Fine Arts: Lullaby - "Hush, Little Baby"

Sarah comforts Anna and Caleb with a song. It is an old lullaby, originating in the Southern U.S., entitled "Hush, Little Baby." The song centers around presents being offered by the parent to the baby, one by one. Even if the presents don't last, the song seems to say the love of the parent will always be there.

If you remember the song's tune, sing it along with your student today, or find a version online to listen to. Here are the full lyrics (either "Papa" or "Mama" can be used, depending on which parent is singing it):

"Hush, Little Baby"

Hush, little baby, don't say a word.
Papa's gonna buy you a mockingbird.

And if that mockingbird don't sing,
Papa's gonna buy you a diamond ring.

And if that diamond ring turns brass
Papa's gonna buy you a looking glass.

And if that looking glass gets broke,
Papa's gonna buy you a billy goat.

And if that billy goat won't pull,
Papa's gonna buy you a cart and bull.

And if that cart and bull turn over,
Papa's gonna buy you a dog named Rover.

And if that dog named Rover won't bark,
Papa's gonna buy you a horse and cart.

And if that horse and cart fall down,
You'll still be the sweetest little baby in town.

Chapter 12

Teacher Summary

Anna and Caleb wake up to the sound of rain beating down. They haven't heard that sound in a long time. Sarah, Anna, Caleb and even William dance and jump and laugh in the rain. When Anna writes her father a letter that night, she does not tell him about the rain.

Later that evening, the three aunts drink tea under the moon. Caleb gets to know Aunt Harriet better, and Aunt Lou goes skinny-dipping. Anna sits and wonders if Sarah is missing Maine even more, now that she's back. The children hope they can return home soon.

What we will cover in this chapter:

Science: Water Safety
Science: Loon - An Interesting Bird
Language Arts: Writing and Discussion Question
Language Arts: Vocabulary
Fine Arts: Special Occasions - Setting Up a Moonlight Tea*

Science: Water Safety

Draw your student's attention to the following sentence: "The bell buoy made a lonely, sad sound." Does your student know what a buoy is? Why is it called a bell buoy? A **buoy** is just one device people employ to make coastal and lake waters safe. Take this learning opportunity to share with your student some of the fascinating technology and equipment people use to guide their ships and their crews.

A buoy (pronounced either BOY or BOO ee) is an anchored object which floats on top of the water and helps guide ships. Buoys work a little like lines on a road—showing the captain and crew where the safe area of water is located, in order to dock or pass through a narrow inlet. Buoys are designed in different colors and shapes. For example, in the United States, red buoys are used to designate the right side of a channel when facing upstream. In other countries the color green is used. Buoys with an orange diamond on a white background means "boats keep out", showing ships where dangerous waters are located. Some buoys are cone-shaped, cylindrical or even spherical.

Like the buoy in our story, some buoys have bells, lights, whistles or other sounding/sighting devices. The sounding buoys help ships during fog, when they cannot see colors or lights.

Buoys are only one means ships use to navigate through the water. Maps are essential tools for captains and their crews. A map for a ship or boat is called a **chart** or nautical chart. Oceanographers and cartographers (people who create maps) use tools and special equipment to create the charts. Nautical charts are often updated every year, making note of changes in reefs, sandbars, underwater mountains, islands, etc. Charts are vital for a ship's safe passage. You and your student might enjoy reading *We Didn't Mean to Go to Sea* by Arthur Ransome, part of his Swallows and Amazons series.

Lighthouses are another way ships are able to navigate safely. Throughout history, lighthouses were depended upon heavily by navigators because they allowed them to see the edges of piers, ports and shore. As technology has advanced, however, new electronic navigation systems have been developed—using radio signals to determine the ship's course. In the early 1900s (the time of our story), there were over 1,500 lighthouses operating in the United States. Today, there are about 700. These lighthouses used to be operated and maintained by people— they even lived in the lighthouse all the time. They checked the lamps, cleaned the glass and prevented vandalism. Today, however, the lighthouses left are operated automatically, with no need of human assistance.

If your student is interested in this discussion, she may wish to do additional research on any of the

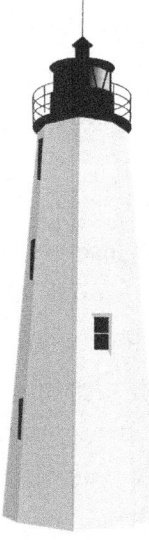

topics mentioned above. Another excellent subject for research is electronic navigation methods. LORAN for example, is the name of the method that was used in the United States for nearly 60 years, since the days of World War II. **LORAN** stands for long range navigation. LORAN-C was the system used in Canada. These two systems used highly technical transmitting devices and radio signals. Today, LORAN has been replaced by GPS (global positioning system), but there is a possibility that an upgraded version of LORAN could be used again. Although this topic is complex, your student may want to explore it.

Another great way to enrich your student's understanding of ship navigation is to look at a ship navigation chart (search for images online). Let her look at the legend, the directional signals and the complex nature of the chart. To guide a ship safely to dock, sailors must have a grounded understanding of charts and the waters that they navigate. (Again, an enjoyable way to learn about charts, navigation and lighthouses is to read the beloved stories of Arthur Ransome.)

Science: Loon - An Interesting Bird

In this chapter, Anna hears the cry of a loon. Does your student know what a loon is? Has she ever seen one? Take some time to explore this interesting animal with your student.

The loon is a water bird that swims and dives. It has a long, sleek body and a sharp, pointed bill that is used to catch fish for food. When the loon swims in the water, it looks like a very large duck. Unlike ducks, however, instead of just bobbing beneath the water's surface for food, the loon can dive to deep depths in search of food.

The loon is the state bird of Minnesota, but can be seen all along the Northern United States. Common loons have black bodies with white spots, and striking red eyes. There are also the yellow-billed loon, the Arctic loon and the red-throated loon.

The loon's call is quite unusual. They have a slightly maniacal, raucous laughing voice. Their bizarre "laughter" is the basis for the old saying, "crazy as a loon." The Canadian dollar coin has a loon engraved on one side. Canadians call them "loonies." And the two-dollar coins are called "twoonies."

Find a color photograph of a loon for your student—and share with her the beautiful bird Anna and Caleb were able to see. Also find a video or recording of a loon call so your student can hear this distinctive sound. If you have a student who loves drawing, have her draw or paint a picture of this interesting bird!

Fine Arts: Special Occasions - Setting Up a Moonlight Tea*

Sarah's aunts serve tea under the moonlight. What a fun idea! If your student would enjoy it, why not plan a late night tea time? If your student likes to cook this could be an opportunity to let her bake some special cookies, biscuits or sandwiches. And, of course, tea is only necessary if that is something everyone likes. Aunt Harriet, Mattie and Lou preferred tea, but you could serve lemonade, soda pop or cocoa if that would be more to your student's liking. Allow your student to help with as much of the preparations as she wishes—this can be an enjoyable exercise in planning as well.

Spread a big blanket on a grassy patch, and make sure you have a nice view of the moon. Pillows can be taken out, if you want to lie back and look at the sky. Then, under the stars, chat with your student about whatever comes to mind. Make this a special, sparkling event—something to be remembered for a lifetime!

Language Arts: Writing and Discussion Question

Anna describes the fireworks they see from far away: "They're like the dandelions that bloom in the fields at home in summer." How would you describe the designs of fireworks against a night sky? What would you compare them to?

Language Arts: Vocabulary

buoy   An object in water which is anchored and then floats; may have bells, whistles, or lights attached.

chart   A map used on ships.

LORAN/LORAN-C   The names of the previously used long range navigational devices in the United States and Canada.

Chapters 13-15

Teacher's Note: Due to the brevity of the last three chapters in *Skylark*, the lessons have been combined as a single lesson plan. Each of the three chapters, however, has its own activity sheet.

Teacher Summary

Caleb and Sarah begin to doubt whether or not they will return to the prairie. Even Sarah doesn't seem to know when. Caleb loses interest in fishing and Brutus and begins to become very sad. Anna finds him one night crying near a cove by the house. He wants to go home.

The following day, Papa arrives in Maine! He has surprised everyone. It rained on the prairie and he has come for them. The children cry and laugh, and Sarah is happy. That night Papa and Sarah tell the children they are expecting a new baby—this is why Sarah had made that trip to the doctor. Sarah assures Anna she is healthy and the baby will be okay. She knows Anna is frightened because of what happened to her first mother, when she gave birth to Caleb.

Five in Row Volume Seven

Finally, after many long weeks, the Wittings arrive home on the prairie. Caleb runs and greets the dogs. The children laugh at Seal's new kittens. The family enjoys being together again. In the spring, they will have a new baby to call their own.

What we will cover in these chapters:

Social Studies: Adding to the Sea and Prairie Notebooks
Science: Genetics*
Language Arts: Creative Writing - The Wittings One Year Later*
Language Arts: Writing and Discussion Question
Language Arts: Vocabulary*
Life Skills: Working Through Fears

Social Studies: Adding to the Sea and Prairie Notebooks

Did your student create Sea and Prairie Notebooks during her study of *Sarah, Plain and Tall*? If so, now would be a great time to finish that project. This chapter offers a few more ideas for the journals—lobster traps, coves and buoys, and don't forget previous new topics in *Skylark* like lighthouses, wells, and loons.

If your student hasn't already done so, she could also decorate the outside of her notebooks. Quotes from the story, drawn or painted pictures of sea or prairie scenes, even a picture of her favorite character would make excellent cover art.

When your student has finished her project, she can show and discuss it with her family, grandparents or friends. She may even wish to keep adding to one or both if she is interested in continued study on a specific topic. For example, prairie grasses, fishing, ships or droughts.

Encourage your student to file her notebooks away carefully. They will provide excellent review materials later on in her school year, and will be an enjoyable reminder of her time spent with these two Patricia MacLachlan books.

Science: Genetics*

Seal is a gray cat and Sam, Maggie's cat, is orange. Draw your student's attention to the description of Seal's new kittens: "three colored gray and one with an orange coat." Does your student know why that happens? If a parent has blue eyes, will all of his/her children have blue eyes? What determines which characteristics are passed on?

Share with your student a simple introduction to the world of **genetics**. A characteristic such as blue eyes, small ears or gray fur, is called a **trait**. Traits are revealed in our bodies through our genes. It is from the word "gene" that we get the word "genetics." Traits can be things we see (like hair color and foot size) or they can be things inside our bodies (like allergies or mental capacities). When we talk about traits, two words are used to describe them: **dominant** and **recessive**.

A dominant trait is one which, when put up against any other, will always show itself. It is the "stronger" trait. A recessive trait will be masked, unless the genes it is represented by are all recessive. For example, three of Seal's kittens were gray. Gray is obviously the dominant color trait. The kittens that have gray fur either had all dominant genes, or an equal number of each—dominant and recessive. Only the kitten that had two recessive "orange" genes became orange.

This is obviously a very elementary look at genetics, but it might spark interest in your student to study the subject further. For more interesting topics and explanation, encourage your student to explore Gregor Mendel (the great Austrian botanist), Punnett squares, and other related subjects. Many books from your library will have interesting explanations of genes or you can search online for articles or videos.

Language Arts: Creative Writing - The Wittings One Year Later*

Look with your student at the last page of our story—Anna's journal entry. She writes, "There will be flowers in the spring, and the river will run again. And in the spring there will be the new baby, Papa and Sarah's baby." Who does your student think the baby will look like? Will it be a boy or a girl? What will its name be? Will it rain enough to fill the cow pond for swimming?

Encourage your student to take these questions and more and write a short story of what life is like for the Wittings one year later. The baby would be a few months old and surely many things will have changed. What does your student think it will be like? This assignment can be as brief or lengthy as you deem appropriate. Remind your student to keep her characters consistent with how they have acted before. If the characters have changed, be sure to explain what happened that has caused their behavioral change. For instance, if Caleb becomes difficult or mean, perhaps he's jealous of the new baby or maybe no one is spending enough time with him, etc. Teach your student how to let her reader in on what's happening to her characters.

Language Arts: Writing and Discussion Question

Sarah is going to have a new baby. Take a moment and think about what you know of Sarah and Jacob's physical and emotional characteristics. What do they enjoy doing? What are they like? Now write a paragraph or page describing what you think the new baby will be like. Will he/she be plain like Sarah? Will he/she love the prairie like Papa? Will he/she be good with words, or will he/she speak "between the lines"? Be as creative as you can and bring in as many clues from the stories as you were able to find to help you.

Language Arts: Vocabulary*

trait   A distinguishing characteristic.

genetics   The branch of biology dealing with heredity.

dominant   A gene which expresses itself most often.

recessive   A gene which is expressed less often.

Life Skills: Working Through Fears

Caleb is extremely frightened by the thought of staying in Maine. He wishes to go home to the prairie and he misses his father a great deal. He even wonders if Sarah has forgotten about going home. Has your student ever been afraid of a situation or person and tried to keep his feelings to herself? What happened? Was she able to work through them alone?

Sometimes when we are most frightened about something (an event or person), the best way to work through our fears is to share them with someone else. Trying to hold emotions inside can be tiring and stressful—and can make us even more afraid! Instead, talking with someone else can have many positive effects. Perhaps the other person is just as frightened as you are and can offer empathy and closeness (just like Anna did in the cove). Sometimes the other person, particularly if it's an older friend or relative, has experienced a situation like yours and can offer solutions and encouragement. Often, by talking to someone else, we come to realize new aspects of the problem we hadn't thought of before—reasons for us not to be afraid. Children sometimes think that only other children can understand what they are feeling—and sometimes that might be true. However, going to adults and parents can often be your best decision when you are nervous about something. They have experience and maturity which helps them understand what you are going through.

Encourage your student to be open with her fears and allow others to help her with her problems. Sometimes we need to let people know what we're thinking and feeling. Knowing we can go to our friends and family with our concerns is one of our greatest comforts!

Teacher's Note: If your student has enjoyed *Sarah, Plain and Tall* and *Skylark*, she might want to read the rest of the books in the series:

- *Caleb's Story*
- *More Perfect Than the Moon*
- *Grandfather's Dance*

Teacher's Notes

Use this page to jot down relevant info you've found for this *Five in a Row* chapter book, including favorite lessons, go-along resources, field trips, and family memories.

SKYLARK

Dates studied:

Student:

Favorite Lesson Topics:

Social Studies:

Science:

Language Arts:

Fine Arts:

Life Skills:

Relevant Library Resources: Books, DVDs, Audio Books

Websites or Video Links:

Related Field Trip Opportunities:

Favorite Quote or Memory During Study:

Skylark

Skylark - Chapter 1

Name:
Date:
History and Geography: **The Dust Bowl & Great Depression**

After completing the **History and Geography: A Look Back at Drought** lesson, you might want to explore further the timeframe and geographic area of the United States that became known as the Dust Bowl. This period of crisis, primarily in the midwest/southwest U.S., coincided with the Great Depression, which affected the entire United States and many other countries. The Great Depression had many contributing factors and created an economic downturn, which caused industrial production to decline, thus resulting in massive job losses—which increased the economic decline. (*Skylark* takes place two decades before the Dust Bowl and the Great Depression, but this related information is helpful in understanding drought and its consequences.)

As you research this time period, find answers to the questions below.

A go-along book to pair with this activity sheet is:
  Meet Kit: An American Girl Doll 1934 by Valerie Tripp
  Or, you could watch the 2008 movie: Kit Kittredge: An American Girl

What caused the Dust Bowl? _____
_____
_____
_____
_____

What was done to stop the loss of soil and dust storms? _____
_____
_____

Five in Row Volume Seven   109

Skylark - Chapter 2

Name:
Date:
Science: **Canine Gestational Stages**

The **Science: Gestation Periods in Different Animals** lesson gave an overview of different animals' gestation periods. For this activity you will learn more about a dog's (canine) gestation period and the stages of devolopment that occur during that period. The gestation period of a dog is 9 weeks, while a human gestation period is 9 months. Search online to find and fill in information beside each bullet below with what is happening in the weeks durring a puppy's development in the womb.

Optional lesson expansion: Search online or use a resource book from the library to compare human development during gestation with that of the canine, comparing each month of human deveopment to each week of the puppy's deveopment. Do they develop at the same rate if one week of canine developement is equal to one month of human deveopment?

Canine Gestational Stages

- Weeks 1 and 2
  -
  -

- Weeks 3 and 4
  -
  -

- Weeks 5 and 6
  -
  -

- Weeks 7 and 8
  -
  -

- Week 9
  -
  -

Skylark - Chapter 3

Name:

Date:

Science: **Herbivores, Carnivores and Omnivores**

In the **Science: Cows - Herbivores** lesson you learned that cows are **herbivores**: animals that eat plants, not meat. Meat-eating animals are called **carinvores**, while animals that eat both meat and plants are **omnivores**.

Search online for examples of each type of animal: herbivores, carnivores and omnivores. Choose one from each list of animals. Print and paste an image of the animals that you chose into the spaces below, adding details about what they eat or other interesting facts that you find.

Herbivore:

_____

_____

_____

Carnivore:

_____

_____

_____

Omnivore:

_____

_____

_____

Five in Row Volume Seven

Skylark - Chapter 4

Name:
Date:
Language Arts: **Vocabulary Words**

After finishing the fourth chapter, use the crossword puzzle below to review the vocabulary words covered in **chapters 1-3**. The clues and answers are on the following page.

Language Arts: **Vocabulary Words - Crossword Continued**

The crossword clues and answers for the vocabulary words covered in **chapters 1-3** are provided below to be used with the crossword on the previous page.

Across

3. (ch. 2) a baby who is born earlier than the full gestational period

4. (ch. 2) the act or process of the young developing in the uterus

6. (ch. 3) to spit back up after being swallowed

7. (ch. 3) second stomach of an animal which continues the digestive process

11. (ch. 2) colors created by blending primaries

13. (ch. 3) the partially digested food the animal chews again

Down

1. (ch. 3) a fourth stomach where the food meets acids and enzymes to fully digest the proteins

2. (ch. 3) the first stomach of an animal; food lands almost immediately after being swallowed

3. (ch. 2) red, yellow and blue

5. (ch. 2) colors created by blending a primary and secondary

8. (ch. 2) colors which are opposite in origin

9. (ch. 3) third stomach, continues to digest food

10. (ch. 1) a recurring idea, feature or theme

12. (ch. 2) colors which are similar, close on a color wheel

flip for vocab words: reticulum | complementary | omasum | motif | secondary colors | analogous | cud

abomasum | rumen | premature | primary colors | gestation | tertiary colors | regurgitate

Skylark - Chapter 5

Name:

Date:

Art: **The Colors of Drought**

Draw or paint a picture into the frame below that illustrates the prairie in this chapter—"There was no green." You could use only blue tones for the sky and shades of brown for the earth and trees. Or, create an illustration that is entirely shades of brown.

If you completed the art lesson, **Art: Composition in Drawing** of the prairie during your study of *Sarah, Plain, and Tall*, compare the two illustrations upon completion of this lesson. Note the differences in the colors chosen to represent the *same* prairie under very different circumstances.

Skylark - Chapter 6

Name:
Date:
Science: **Ecological Benefits of Fire**

In the **Geography: Areas Where Fire Is a Constant Risk** lesson you learned about the destruction that fires can cause. Are there any benefits to fires (specifically, brush or forest fires—not house fires)?

What is a "controlled burn" and how can it be used as a conservation tool? Search online for "fire benefits" and list some of the things that you learn below.

_____
_____
_____
_____
_____
_____
_____
_____

Skylark - Chapter 7

Name:
Date:
Language Arts: **Poet's Use of Analogy**

Through the use of comparison, poets use analogies to pain vivid word pictures with deep layers of meaning. In the **Language Arts: Analogies** lesson, you learned that an analogy is a comparison of two things; often the two things being compared include a complex concept and a concept that is easier to understand.

Choose either the poem "There Is No Frigate Like a Book," by Emily Dickinson, or "Nothing Gold Can Stay," by Robert Frost. Find and note below the author's use of analogy in the poem of your choice.

If you are unsure what the poem is referring to through its analogies, discuss it with your teacher or search online, "what does the poem (title here) mean?"

Example: no frigate like a book ... to take us lands away (a frigate is a ship—therefore, like a ship, books can help us travel to many far-off lands)

_____
_____
_____
_____
_____
_____
_____

Skylark - Chapter 8

Name:

Date:

Language Arts: **Author's License - Breaking the Rules on Purpose**

After completing the Language Arts: **Author's License - Breaking the Rules on Purpose** lesson, discuss e. e. cummings' use of the capital letter O to represent the moon and how that is somewhat similar to an author's use of analogy that you learned about in chapter 7.

Here are a couple of discussion questions to consider: How is using a capital letter O to represent the moon similar to an author's use of analogy? What other letters or type formatting could an author use to represent an object or idea?

How might you arrange the words if you wanted to represent something growing, to show tears flowing, or to represent things rising up or getting louder/bigger?

This technique is called Photo Poetry. See an example below and then create your own Photo Poetry piece of writing/artwork.

TO REST ON THE GROUND

To see examples of Photo Poetry book cover illustrations, search online for, *Wet Cement: A Mix of Concrete Poems*, or *Lemonade: and Other Poems Squeezed from a Single Word*. Both books are by Bob Raczka.

Skylark - Chapter 9

Name:
Date:
Science: **Watertable Experiment**

Use the instructions from the **Science: Watertable - What It Is and How to Create Your Own** lesson, then note your observations on the spaces provided below. Finally, fill out the summary at the bottom of this page with what you've learned about the purpose of a well and how the watertable relates to it. Feel free to change the day numbers to match what happens in your experiment (heat, humidity, and sunlight may affect how many days you observe).

Day 1: Observations (include measurements and description of water and "earth.")

Day 2 or 3: Observations

Day 5: Observations

Summarize the purpose of a well and how the watertable relates to it.

Skylark - Chapter 10

Name:
Date:
Geography: **Maine - Plan a Vacation**

TRAVEL

The lesson **Geography: Maine** provides several ideas for additional research. Another idea is to plan a vacation to the state of Maine. Many decisions must be made when planning a vacation. Use this activity sheet to plan; older students can also project expenses and create a budget for the vacation.

Vacation planning resources might include: online research, library books and travel guides, state official tourism website: www.visitmaine.com, and online video tours of atrractions in Maine.

1. How many miles away is Maine and how will you get there? (driving? flying?)
_____

2. Where will you stay? (area/city? camping/RVing, hotel? rental?)
_____

3. What time of year and how long will you stay?
_____

4. What/where will you eat? (cook own meals? eat out? campground meals?)
_____
_____

5. What activities will you do? (biking? hiking? in water or in woods?)
_____
_____

6. What sites do you want to visit? (historic? nature?)
_____
_____

Skylark - Chapter 11

Name:
Date:
Language Arts: **Vocabulary Words**

After finishing chapter eleven, use the crossword puzzle below to review the vocabulary words covered in **chapters 5-11**. The clues and answers are on the following page.

Skylark

Language Arts: **Vocabulary Words - Crossword Continued**

The crossword clues and answers for the vocabulary words covered in **chapters 5-11** are provided below to be used with the crossword on the previous page.

Across

3. (ch. 5) a condition caused by excessive exposure to heat and characterized by cold, clammy hands and general symptoms of shock

5. (ch. 10) the ocean waters as a single body of water, worldwide

7. (ch. 9) the level below which the ground is saturated with water

8. (ch. 11) balanced; opposite sides which are equal

11. (ch. 6) the chemical result of oxygen combined with other substances

13. (ch. 7) a story or example which helps simplify a more complex idea

14. (ch. 5) the process of converting lands to make them more suitable for a different use

15. (ch. 9) a place where water is stored and collected for use

16. (ch. 10) the rise and fall of the ocean, approximately every twelve hours, due to the movement of the sun and moon in relation to the earth

Down

1. (ch. 8) freedom of action, speech or thought

2. (ch. 6) the temperature of the air required to create combustion

4. (ch. 9) a hole in the ground from which water (or oil or natural gas) can be withdrawn

6. (ch. 6) a rapid oxidation accompanied by heat and light

9. (ch. 9) water held beneath the earth's surface

10. (ch. 8) a resinous substance (obtained from the lac insect) melted into thin flakes, used for making varnish

12. (ch. 5) collapse or sudden illness with fever and dry skin, caused by overexposure to excessive heat

flip for vocab words:
tides, reservoir, land reclamation, analogy, heatstroke, oxidation, shellac, groundwater, symmetry, license, kindling temperature, heat exhaustion, well, global ocean, combustion, watertable

Skylark - Chapter 12

Name:
Date:
Fine Arts: **Planning a Special Event**

Sarah's aunt serves tea under the moonlight—but you could make up, plan and host any special event. What makes the moonlight tea so extraodinary? Simply the fact that Sarah's aunt planned the tea at a different time than would be expected and in an unusual location.

Plan an event that takes place in an unexpected location and at a time that it wouldn't typically occur. An example could be a **family movie morning** instead of the typical family movie night. What would you serve instead of popcorn, candy and soda at a "movie morning?"

Questions to ask yourself as you plan:

What is the event?

What is the typical time for the event?

What is the normal location for the event?

Are there decorations that are frequently used at this event?

Are any foods/drinks often served at this event?

How can I change the time/location/decorations/food to make it an unexpected and special event?

Write your answers on a separate piece of paper and plan your party. You could simply plan the party out on paper, or, you might choose to actually throw the party for your family or friends. If you choose to have an actual party you can set a budget with a parent and work on purchasing invitations/food/drink/decorations, staying within the given budget.

Skylark - Chapter 13

Name:
Date:
Science: **Genetics**

Reread the second and third paragraphs in the **Genetics** lesson, and then search "genetic traits" and "dominant human genetic traits" online.

1. Make a list of traits:

2. Which human traits are often dominant?

3. Do you or your family members possess any of the dominant traits? What about the recessive traits?

Skylark - Chapter 14

Name:
Date:
Language Arts: **Character Chart - One Year Later**

After completing the **Language Arts: Creative Writing - The Wittings One Year Later** lesson, use the character chart below to note changes that could have occured for each character a year afer the final chapter. Use this list to create your story.

Sarah

Papa

Anna

Caleb

Baby

Skylark - Chapter 15

Name:
Date:
Language Arts: **Vocabulary Words**

After finishing chapter fifteen, use the crossword puzzle below to review the vocabulary words covered in **chapters 12-15**.

Across

3. (ch. 13-15) a gene which expresses itself most often

4. (ch. 13-15) a gene which is expressed less often

6. (ch. 12) the name of the previously used long range navigational device in the United States and Canada (it can also contain a hyphen and capital C after the name)

7. (ch. 13-15) a distinguishing characteristic

Down

1. (ch. 12) an object in water which is anchored and then floats; may have bells, whistles, or lights attached

2. (ch. 13-15) the branch of biology dealing with heredity

5. (ch. 12) a map used on ships

flip for vocab words: recessive, dominant, genetics, trait, LORAN, chart, buoy

The Story of George Washington Carver

Title: The Story of George Washington Carver
Author: Eva Moore
Copyright: 1971

Chapter 1

Teacher Summary

Moses Carver and his wife Susan live in Diamond Grove, Missouri. The year is 1864. One night, robbers come and steal Moses' slave, Mary, and her baby son, George. Mr. Carver is outraged and hires a man named Bentley to go and bring back Mary and the baby. Bentley tries to find the young mother and son, but returns with only the child. The baby is sick and frail. The Carvers decide to keep him, along with his older brother, Jim. The baby will later become known as George Washington Carver.

What we will cover in this chapter:

Social Studies: History - Genealogy: Knowing Who You Are*
Social Studies: Geography - Diamond, Missouri
Social Studies: History and Geography: Civil War
Language Arts: Writing and Discussion Question
Language Arts: Vocabulary

Social Studies: History - Genealogy: Knowing Who You Are*

Draw your student's attention to the photograph of George Washington Carver at the beginning of this chapter. Take a moment to read the caption together. It says no one, not even George himself, knows the year of his birth. What would that be like? Can your student imagine not knowing what day he was born, or even what year?

Knowing about your past and mapping out your ancestry (family tree) is called studying your **genealogy**. Has your student ever considered where he gets his blue eyes? Why does his name sound French? Why does he look so much like his great-grandfather? (Some of these questions can be answered through the study of genealogy, and some through the study of genetics. See the lesson earlier in this volume on Genetics in *Skylark*, chapters 13-15, for a review of this topic.)

To begin learning about your past, it's important to discover all you can about yourself. Encourage your student to make up a personal "portfolio" of his own life. Start with the basics: eye color, hair color, height, weight, physical build, etc. Next, he can begin recording all he knows about his birth: his full name, the date, year, hospital, what the weather was like, etc. Find baby books, birth certificates, diaries, letters and family pictures to provide more information for your student about what his immediate family is like. Your student can begin to ask a lot of questions. His parents, grandparents, aunts and uncles—all his relatives—can provide him with interesting family anecdotes and facts. If your student isn't sure where to begin with his questions, share the following list of question ideas with him. Answers to these questions will help him gain a better understanding of his immediate roots:

Questions for Parents and Grandparents:

1. What is your full name (as it appears on your birth certificate)?
2. When and where were you born?
3. When and where were you married?
4. What are the full names of your parents?
5. When and where were your parents born?
6. When and where did your parents marry?
7. When and where did your parents die? (if applicable)
8. What are the full names of your grandparents?
9. When and where were your grandparents born?
10. When and where did your grandparents marry?
11. When and where did your grandparents die? (if applicable)

When your student has finished gathering his information, or data, encourage him to begin organizing it some way: a journal, a timeline, a three-ring notebook—anything which makes sense to him in which he can easily display the information.

If your student gets interested in his genealogy and wants to know more than he can obtain from personal accounts, here are some places which can provide more information: libraries; public, private and church census records; state and federal agencies; and cemeteries. With parental supervision, he can also find certain information online, or by using a company that does genealogy research for a fee.

George Washington Carver was never sure of his own birthday. Celebrate with your student the joy of knowing as much as possible about his heritage. Help him get started on his own genealogy today!

History and Geography: Diamond, Missouri

Our story tells us George Washington Carver lives in a town called Diamond Grove in Missouri. The town's name has since been shortened to "Diamond," and the George Washington Carver National Monument has been erected there. It is the first unit of the National Park Service dedicated to an African American, and it contains a museum, interactive exhibits about history and science, and a walking trail where you can see George Washington Carver's birth site, the Moses Carver house, and the burial sites of Moses and Susan Carver.

Using a detailed map, help your student find Diamond, Missouri. It is located in southwestern Missouri, a few miles southeast of Joplin. Have your student mark this site on the map. Be sure to notice how *many* states border Missouri and their names (Missouri and Tennessee each have eight bordering states—more than any other state!). Throughout our story, we will continue to hear of the new places that Carver moved to. Following chapter 9, your student can create his own "geographic timeline" of Carver's life—making note of each new town and state.

Social Studies: History and Geography: Civil War

Teacher's Note: Your student may have encountered this complex topic previously in his *Five in a Row* studies, in such units as *Follow the Drinking Gourd* (Vol. 2) or *Thomas Edison* (Vol. 6). Discuss with your student what you both remember from those studies and build on that knowledge with this lesson.

The Story of George Washington Carver begins during the time of the Civil War. This was a time of sadness and division in America's history. Take this

The Story of George Washington Carver

opportunity to share some information on the Civil War, including some facts your student may not have heard before.

The Civil War is sometimes called "The War Between the States." It began on April 12, 1861, when southern troops fired on Fort Sumter at Charleston, South Carolina. The war was a bloody, terrible event, and lasted nearly four years. It officially ended on April 9, 1865.

Two basic causes contributed to the start of the Civil War—the issue of slavery and the economic/agricultural needs of the South. These two causes are in many ways inextricably linked. The country was divided horizontally—north against south. The South (Confederate) wanted to continue using slaves as plantation workers to support its heavily agricultural economy. The North (Union) believed that slavery was morally wrong. General Ulysses S. Grant was the commander of the Union armies. General Robert E. Lee was the head of the Confederate armies. In 1861, the United States had 19 "free" states and 5 "slave" states. President Abraham Lincoln called our country "a house divided."

You may wish to explore other fascinating, and more intimate looks at the war with your student including books on women and their participation in the event, and the history of African American soldiers in the Civil War.

One great resource book entitled *A Separate Battle: Women and the Civil War* by Ina Chang, talks about the women of the day and how they served their communities. Thousands of women served as nurses, both in hospitals and on the battlefield, and even fought (disguised as men). According to Chang, "Dozens of women were discovered posing as male soldiers during the Civil War, and hundreds more may have done so without being discovered. Women enlisted for many reasons. Some couldn't stand to be separated from the men they loved; others felt they could serve their country best on the battlefield."

Another resource title you may wish to obtain is *Between Two Fires* by Joyce Hansen. This book explores the rarely-told story of the brave African American soldiers who fought in segregated regiments through the war. Here is an excerpt: "The black soldiers served even though they would not be afforded the rights of prisoners of war if caught by the enemy, did not receive equal pay, and had little opportunity of becoming officers. They faced the fires of war and hatred hoping that people of African descent in America would finally have the right to 'life, liberty and the pursuit of happiness.'"

Teacher's Note: Although these books may be beyond the reading level of your student, they are both excellent resources for information you can share. You may also want to look for other books on these topics at your local library.

The famous African American abolitionist, orator and writer, Frederick Douglass, said of this event, "Once let the black man get upon his person the brass letters, U.S.; let him get an eagle on his button, and a musket on his shoulder and bullets in his pocket, and there is no power on earth which can deny that he has earned the right to citizenship in the United States."

If your student is interested, help him locate books, maps, biographies, and other materials about the Civil War to assist his exploration. Personalities that might be of interest include: Abraham Lincoln, Robert E. Lee, Ulysses S. Grant, Clara Barton, Sojourner Truth, Harriet Tubman, and Frederick Douglass.

The Civil War was a tragic time in the history of the United States. It is important to study an event of this magnitude so we can better understand the mistakes we've made in the past, and we can resolve to never make them again. Noted historian and author Shelby Foote once said, "The Revolutionary War created the United States, but the Civil War *defined* us." Much that is both right and wrong with America today has its root in our Civil War. It is a subject worth studying in depth. This subject and its related tangents provide a major section of history in this unit study. Begin with several simple Civil War-related topics now and keep a Civil War notebook to add lessons to in the future.

Language Arts: Writing and Discussion Question

According to our story, Moses Carver did not believe in slavery, but he had slaves anyway. Why do you think he kept slaves if he truly thought it was wrong? Why didn't he free Mary and her children before? How might the story of George Washington Carver's life have been different if this had happened?

Language Arts: Vocabulary

genealogy   The study of the descent of a person from his or her ancestors.

Chapter 2

Teacher Summary

George is a sickly baby, and he grows very slowly. Even when he is about seven, he is still small for his age. His brother, Jim, helps Uncle Moses out in the fields, but George stays in the house and helps Aunt Susan. George loves being alone in the woods and looking at plants. There are so many things to see and touch! George begins to learn about different plants, and starts to care for Aunt Susan's roses. A neighbor, Mrs. Baynham, stops in one day and notices Aunt Susan's beautiful roses. She invites George to come and help her with the roses at her home. Soon everyone starts asking little seven-year-old George what he thinks about their plants, and he becomes known as The Plant Doctor.

What we will cover in this chapter:

Science: Photosynthesis - How Plants Are Fed*
Language Arts: Writing and Discussion Question

Language Arts: Vocabulary
Fine Arts: Making Charcoal Bark Rubbings
Life Skills: Stuttering - Understanding More About It
Life Skills: Developing Expertise

Science: Photosynthesis - How Plants Are Fed*

George understands that plants need sun. Does your student know why? Plants need three things to live: water, air, and light. Take this opportunity to share with your student the fascinating process of **photosynthesis**.

First, look at the word in two parts: photo (light) and synthesis (to put together). Photosynthesis is the name for a chemical process by which green plants convert light into energy. Photosynthesis is the main function of a plant's leaves.

Photosynthesis is a highly complex and miraculous process, but it can be understood quite easily if it is broken down into specific steps. To first understand photosynthesis, your student must have an understanding of what is in a leaf.

A leaf is made up, in part, of small cell-like bodies called **chloroplasts**. By themselves, the chloroplasts would be colorless (and so would the leaf), but inside is a green pigment (a colored substance) called **chlorophyll**. How does the plant use these little green-filled cells to make energy?

Every plant needs three things: water, air and light. Air is all around the plant. Remind your student that the chemical makeup of water is two parts hydrogen and one part oxygen (H_2O). When light (energy) is absorbed by chloroplasts, it causes the cells to draw water up from the roots of the plant and into the leaves. As water reaches the chloroplasts, the energy from the light splits the molecules of water and divides the hydrogen from the oxygen.

Next, hydrogen molecules combine with carbon dioxide (the plant gets carbon dioxide from the air around it) and forms a simple sugar-food for the plant. This simple sugar is called **glucose**. Oxygen left over from the water molecules is released by the plant. It provides essential oxygen for the air we (and other animals) breathe every day.

To help your student understand how the water travels up the cells of the plant, take a piece of celery and cut off the base, cleanly. Now place the stalk in a glass filled with water colored with food coloring. Ask your student what he thinks will happen. Leave it for a few hours or overnight and then remove the celery. With your help, have your student slice through the celery stalk several times, starting from the bottom. Can he see the colored liquid that has been absorbed by the plant's cells? How far up the stalk did the water travel?

If your student is having difficulty understanding the process of photosynthesis, take some time and help him make a poster or large drawing of each step. Find good library books or a video online to supplement your teaching on plants and photosynthesis.

Language Arts: Writing and Discussion Question

George is fascinated by plants and flowers. That is the area of nature that interests him. What aspect of science or nature has caught your interest? Explain why.

Language Arts: Vocabulary

chloroplasts   Tiny bodies in the cells of green plants which contain chlorophyll.

chlorophyll   The green pigment which fills the chloroplasts, located in the cells of green plants.

photosynthesis   The process by which plants convert light and water to a food source.

glucose   A simple sugar.

expertise   Knowing a lot about a particular subject.

Fine Arts: Making Charcoal Bark Rubbings

George enjoys spending time in the woods and studying the plants around him. He likes to feel the plant leaves and to look at their interesting patterns.

Has your student ever stopped to look at or feel the bark of a tree trunk? What strange textures and shapes! What kinds of trees does your student have around his house? Help him identify as many as he can and write down the name of each. Next, let him observe and feel the bark of each tree. What does it look like? Can he make a quick sketch? What does it feel like? Have him write down his descriptions and put each with the appropriate tree name.

One way to see the beauty of bark is to make a charcoal rubbing. (You can also use crayons or colored pencils, but charcoal pencils work best.) Lay a piece of white drawing paper against the trunk of a tree and, lightly at first, begin rubbing the charcoal across. Can your student see the design and texture beginning to appear? He may need to go back and forth over the same patch several times until the design is clear. Just make sure you don't move the paper around, only the charcoal. He may repeat these steps on trees that have different types of bark.

After he has completed his bark rubbings, he can assemble his own "Bark Observation" Notebook, by compiling the names of his trees, his own descriptions and the relief charcoal rubbings he created. George would have enjoyed a project like this!

Life Skills: Stuttering - Understanding More About It

Draw your student's attention the beginning of the chapter, where we learn that George was small for his age, sickly and that he stuttered when he spoke. Does your student have a friend who stutters? Perhaps your student, himself, has this speech difficulty.

Stuttering is a speech/language difficulty which usually starts before the age of three. No one knows exactly what causes it. Most people who suffer from stuttering find it difficult to speak clearly on the phone, in public, or in situations where they feel particularly insecure. More males stutter than females, worldwide, and it is more common in Western societies and in more affluent economic groups.

Stuttering has nothing to do with intelligence. You should never make fun of or draw attention to someone who stutters. Being sensitive and patient when you are with someone who stutters will help him gain confidence and relax, which will sometimes ease the stammering.

Stuttering can affect anyone. Some very famous people in the world have stuttered. For example, Winston Churchill, one of the most respected statesmen of all time, stuttered terribly as a child. James Earl Jones, the actor whose voice has now been called a national treasure, stuttered so severely as a child that he was unable at times to speak at all. This difficulty persisted through his adult life, but through speech therapy he has overcome it and has become famous for his acting and voice.

Encourage your student to be kind to any friends who stutter and people he meets with this problem. And remind him that we *all* have things which are different about us—stuttering is just something everyone is able to notice more easily.

Life Skills: Developing Expertise

George is becoming known as the "Plant Doctor." He has studied plants and the world around him, gathered his own information and knowledge, and now he can help others learn how to care for their plants—just like he helps Mrs. Baynham with her roses.

Even though George is only seven, he has gained expertise in the area of plants. When you are an expert about something, it means you know a lot about it and can help others. As George proves, you don't have to be an adult to develop expertise on a topic.

What is your student interested in? How can he learn more about it? Where can he go and serve the community (or a neighbor) to help others with his knowledge? Encourage your student today by reminding him that even kids can become experts on topics and can help make a difference!

Teacher's Note: If your student used FIAR Vol. 4, does he remember *The Tree Lady*? This picture book tells the story of Katherine Sessions, another young person who loved plants and nature, and who overcame great odds to have a career based on this early interest. Sessions was a contemporary of George Washington Carver.

Chapter 3

Teacher Summary

George continues to learn more about plants and animals. He learns to sew and knit from Aunt Susan, and he takes up whittling. Aunt Susan gives him a spelling book and George sits by the fire to study. But there is so much to learn! George wants to go to school, but there are no schools in Diamond Grove for black children. He tries to learn as much as he can on his own.

One day, by accident, George finds himself in Mrs. Baynham's house. She shows him her paintings and George is fascinated. He has never seen a painting before! Quickly George goes home and makes up his own "paint" from pokeberries. Then with his finger, George paints pictures of flowers on a large, flat rock. George decides he loves plants and painting!

What we will cover in this chapter:

Social Studies: History - Segregation*
Language Arts: Book Recommendation - *The Secret Garden*
Language Arts: Writing and Discussion Question
Fine Arts: Juice Paints and Vegetable Dyes

Social Studies: History - Segregation*

George wants to go to school. He knows he's learning a lot through his own studies, but he doesn't have all the resources that school would provide. We learn that George is unable to attend school in Diamond Grove because there aren't any schools for black children—only schools for white children.

Take this opportunity to share with your student some background information on segregation and its role in America's history.

Segregation means to set one racial group apart from a larger group or society. The term desegregation means stopping these divisions. In the United States, racial segregation (as we recognize it today) began very soon after the Civil War ended. These segregation laws required blacks and whites to use separate public facilities—bathrooms, restaurants, schools, drinking fountains, parks, etc.—and became known as the Jim Crow laws. A minstrel song featuring a black character named Jim Crow became popular in the 1830s and people borrowed the name for the legislations.

It is important to impress upon your student the painful aspect of these laws. For no other reason besides the color of their skin, black people were discriminated against and forced to use separate public facilities. Imagine how humiliating and dehumanizing such treatment would make you feel!

By the 1930s, African Americans were gaining in the arena of politics, forming groups and speaking out. In 1954 an historic ruling came down from the Supreme Court in the case of Brown vs. The Board of Education. In this landmark decision, the Supreme Court ruled against racial segregation in public schools. All children, of all races, should be able to attend school classes together. This was what George needed but was unable to find 80 years earlier—schools that anyone could attend.

If your student is interested in learning more about segregation and the ways by which the United States has changed some of its most offensive laws, you might suggest studying one or more of the following topics and people: Rosa Parks, Dr. Martin Luther King, Jr. (winner of the 1964 Nobel Peace Prize), and Plessy vs. Ferguson—1896. (We will also cover Dr. Martin Luther King, Jr., in a later lesson for this book.)

As your student begins to study the history of segregation in America, he will see the phrase "separate but equal" used again and again. For many years, this was the belief and sentiment of many white Americans and of the government. It is important to discuss with your student why "separate but equal" is not possible. Separate facilities (particularly in the realm of education) are not equal. They can only be equal when each child can attend any school, and have the same texts, teachers and opportunities for friendships.

Part of the beauty of the United States is how widely diverse its people are—immigrants from all over the world have made America their home. It is important to learn how to respect diversity, share common ground and remember that we are all Americans. Segregation was an ugly and painful time in our history. We must work together to prevent it from ever happening again.

Language Arts: Book Recommendation - *The Secret Garden*

George enjoys helping sick and dying plants get better. He finds ailing plants and transports them to an area in the woods he calls his "secret garden." If your student is interested in plants and gardens, in particular, or just enjoys a good story, he might want to read *The Secret Garden*, by Frances Hodgson Burnett. The story centers around a young girl named Mary Lennox. Having lost her parents to cholera in India, Mary is sent to live with a distant uncle in the Yorkshire moors. Mary is lonely and willful, but through extraordinary circumstances she finds friends, health and happiness.

Your student will become instantly absorbed in this classic tale. It is ideal for reading aloud even with younger children. The story not only teaches wonderful lessons relating to the human experience, but also shares valuable information on flowers, gardening and the joy of working with nature.

Language Arts: Writing and Discussion Question

George is very smart. Aunt Susan tells George he doesn't need to go to school— that he already knows more than most school children. Do you think it is necessary for a child to go to school to receive a good education? Why or why not?

Fine Arts: Juice Paints and Vegetable Stains

George enjoys painting with the juice of pokeberries. He doesn't have paints so he invents his own! Your student may wish to try this interesting art form by steeping some berries (blueberries, strawberries, raspberries, etc.) in boiling water, straining the juice and painting with it. Or, if he wants to try George's method, he can simply crush the berries and paint with his fingers on rocks or bark. (You may want to suggest disposable gloves if you don't want him to have purple fingers for the next few days!)

A great art activity following this theme involves exploring natural dyes. By taking scraps of white muslin or other cotton fabric, your student can try his hand at vegetable and fruit dyes. Onions, beets, the powdered spice turmeric, and even loose, black tea leaves can create fascinating variations of yellow, orange, and brown dyes. If your student wants to try his hand at fruit dyes, encourage him to experiment with blackberries, blood oranges and strawberries.

To extract the dye from any of these sources, tie the fruit, skins or spices in a piece of cheesecloth and submerge in cold water. Place your fabric in the cold water and then bring it to a gentle simmer. Stir regularly, and have your student watch the fabric and notice the change in color. When it has reached the desired shade, which may take anywhere from 30 minutes to 3 hours, he can lift the fabric out of the pan. (Be careful when handing fabric taken from hot water!) Rinse the fabric in clean, warm water until it runs clear. Allow the fabric to air dry.

Chapter 4

Teacher Summary

George begins to attend church with Mr. and Mrs. Baynham. He particularly loves the singing. George is also excited about being able to attend Sunday school. Instead of learning about things like math and science, George learns about Noah and the ark. He begins to think he needs to move to Neosho. George will miss Aunt Susan and Uncle Moses, but he has to go to a real school! Finally, the day arrives for George to leave home. Aunt Susan gives him a few corn dodgers, and with his small satchel, George sets out alone for Neosho.

What we will cover in this chapter:

Language Arts: Writing and Discussion Question
Language Arts: Vocabulary*
Fine Arts: Choirs and Singing
Fine Arts: Cooking - Corn Dodgers
Life Skills: Acting in Determination

Language Arts: Writing and Discussion Question

Why doesn't George's brother, Jim, wish to accompany him to Neosho? Jim says he doesn't think he needed an education. What do you think an education can give you? Why is school important?

Language Arts: Vocabulary*

vocal cords   Two pairs of tissue membranes in the throat, near the voice box.

larynx   The upper end of the windpipe where the voice box and the vocal cords are located.

contralto   The lowest range in a woman's singing voice.

mezzo-soprano   The mid-range in a woman's singing voice.

soprano   The highest range in a woman's singing voice.

tenor   The highest range in a man's singing voice.

baritone   The mid-range in a man's singing voice.

bass   The lowest range in a man's singing voice.

determination   A great firmness in carrying out a purpose.

Fine Arts: Choirs and Singing

We learn that George enjoys singing along with the church choir. Has your student ever been involved in a singing program? If so, does he enjoy solos or singing with a group? Take this opportunity to share with your student the basic terms and categories for singing and voice.

Every person's voice is slightly different, but all voices can be classified in three categories: high, mid-range and low. These categories are defined by what is called a voice's **pitch**. Pitch means the voice's position on a musical scale—what range of notes the person can accurately and easily sing. For women, the category names are **soprano** (high), **mezzo-soprano** (mid-range), and **contralto** (low). For men, the terms are **tenor** (high), **baritone** (mid-range) and **bass** (low). The average voice belongs in either the mezzo-soprano or baritone categories.

Does your student know what allows him to speak? What makes each person's voice different? Why do men's voices generally drop lower than women's? The human voice is produced by two thin folds of tissue **(vocal cords)** that are stretched across the voice box **(larynx)** in the back of the throat. When air, or breath, moves those folds back and forth they vibrate, producing sound.

The human male's vocal cords tend to be thicker and wider than that of females. For this reason, the male's voice is generally lower.

In our story we read that George has a "soft, high voice." George Washington Carver had a higher voice than usual for a male, but he was said to have spoken with intensity. You can access recordings of Carver speaking and let your student listen to his voice.

Five in Row Volume Seven

If your student is interested in learning more about singing, perhaps a field trip to a music hall or event would be appropriate. Can he pick out which voices are sopranos? Basses? If he enjoys singing himself, then getting involved in a choral group or singing lessons might be appropriate also.

Fine Arts: Cooking - Corn Dodgers

George loved eating corn dodgers. Aunt Susan must have made them especially well, because they were his favorite food. Why not take some time and talk with your student about George Washington Carver over a plate of steaming hot corn dodgers? Here is the recipe:

Corn Dodgers
1/2 cup flour
3 tsp. baking powder
1-2 Tbs. sugar
3/4 tsp. salt
1 1/2 cups yellow cornmeal
3 Tbs. melted butter
3/4 cup milk
1 beaten egg
4 strips bacon, fried crisp
2 green onions, finely chopped

Begin by frying four strips of bacon in a skillet (cast iron preferred). When the bacon is crispy, remove and either leave the drippings in the skillet (if a cast iron skillet is being used) or transfer the drippings to a glass baking dish. Mix together the flour, sugar, baking powder and salt. Add cornmeal. Gently fold in butter, milk and egg. Crumble the bacon and gently stir into the batter, along with the chopped onion. Pour the corn dodger mixture back into your hot skillet or the baking dish, and bake in the skillet or 8"x8" glass pan at 400° F. for approximately 25 minutes—or until a toothpick comes out clean. Cut into wedges and serve in a little napkin. Delicious!

Life Skills: Acting in Determination

George desperately wants to attend school in Neosho. Imagine being so young and setting off all by yourself on such an adventure. George has to leave behind Jim, Aunt Susan, Uncle Moses and all of his friends and activities in

Diamond Grove. But he is determined!

How would your student define the word **determination**? It usually means the ability to carry out plans or thoughts for a specific purpose—without distraction. A determined person is focused on a goal. Determination isn't the same as rebellion. George does not run away from home without discussion or goodbyes. He doesn't tell his family they are wrong. Instead, he purposely continues to discuss his situation and his desires. He is motivated and seeks input. When a person is acting in rebellion, then he is not open to other people's opinions—he is being selfish. Instead, George acts with determination.

Later in his life, George Washington Carver said, "We are the architects of our own fortune and the hewer out of our own destiny." Talk with your student about this quote and what he thinks it means.

Can your student remember a time when he was focused on a goal? When he exhibited determination? Discuss living with purpose and ways by which each can learn to seek out our goals more effectively.

Chapter 5

Teacher Summary

George arrives in Neosho in the evening. He hurries to find a place to sleep for the night. He is also hungry, having eaten all of his corn dodgers earlier. Finding some wild berries for dinner, George finally falls asleep in an empty horse stall. The next day, a woman named Mariah Watkins discovers George and takes him to live with her and her husband, Andy. George is overjoyed! This nice couple is willing to let him live with them and attend the school designated for black children as well. Each day after school, George helps Aunt Mariah clean the house and cook for Uncle Andy. Each Sunday, the Watkins take George with them to services at the African Methodist Church. Now George can go inside and listen to the sermons, because this is a church for black people. George decides he wants to be like the minister when he grows up.

What we will cover in this chapter:

Social Studies: History - Last Names
Social Studies: History - African Methodist Church
Social Studies: History - A Quick Comparison: Edison and Carver*
Life Skills: Learning More About Adoption

Social Studies: History - Last Names

George had been a slave, owned by Uncle Moses. Moses and Susan's last name was Carver, so George was known as "Carver's George." When he made it to Neosho, George became known as George Carver. What is your student's last name? Also called a surname, the last name is like a family title, often shared by immediate family members. What would it be like to never have a last name?

Many slaves, just like George, took their owner's surname as their own after they became free. Others chose their own last names—often taken from famous American leaders (such as Washington or Jefferson) or even as combinations of words (such as Freeman).

As slaves, black people were stripped of all identity. No personal belongings. No equal education. No last name. Talk with your student about what it would be like to not have a surname. How does sharing a name with your family help to bond you with them? How does it help to shape your own identity?

If your student was given the opportunity to choose his own last name, what would it be? And why?

Social Studies: History - African Methodist Church

George attended an African Methodist Church in Neosho with Aunt Mariah and Uncle Andy. This was a place of worship where black people were not only accepted, but were also on staff. Known today as the A.M.E. (African Methodist Episcopal Church), this denomination is one of the largest Methodist denominations in the United States and exists in dozens of countries around the world.

Founded in 1787 by Richard Allen and Absalom Jones, the A.M.E. is still thriving and influential today. In 1787, in the city of Philadelphia, large groups of black Americans began protesting the St. George Methodist Episcopal Church. This church discriminated against blacks and was a segregated group. Allen and Jones were the leaders in the separation from St. George's, and they formed their own group. The church name is intended to remind us that this denomination was founded by people of African descent. Today with nearly 3 million members, the church continues to grow and accepts members of all races to attend services.

If your student is interested, locate an African Methodist Episcopal Church in or near your area. Visit a service and see what George found so delightful. If you attend a denominational church, you might also make a project of investigating the history and origins of your denomination as well.

Social Studies: History - A Quick Comparison: Edison and Carver*

Draw your student's attention to where our author tells us, "George was always asking questions the teacher could not answer." What person does your student think of when he hears this description of George? Who else have we studied that was constantly asking questions? Thomas Alva Edison! Another brilliant scientist we studied in Five in a Row Volume 6.

If your student is interested, go back and review some of the situations in which Edison found himself at school with his instructors. Note for your student that later in his life George Washington Carver became *friends* with Thomas Edison.

The Story of George Washington Carver

Edison even offered him a position to work with him on some research events. Great minds must often think along similar lines!

Life Skills: Learning More About Adoption

Aunt Mariah and Uncle Andy did not have any children of their own—they were glad to have George around. Although they did not legally adopt George, they took care of him and helped him a great deal. Sometimes, however, couples who either don't have any children or want more, adopt a child. Adoption is a legal process by which a person can take as their own a child who is not biologically his or hers.

Does your student have any friends who have been adopted? Siblings? Perhaps your student is adopted himself. Adopted children are just like other children. They are loved, cared for and are legally entitled to all the same treatments—including the right to inherit property.

Adoptions in the U.S. can sometimes be facilitated by an agency, a lawyer or physicians. Without an agency, an adoption is called a private adoption, which is legal in some states and not in others. Agency adoptions take three main steps to be complete: 1) the child must be legally separated from his birth parents, 2) the custody must belong fully to the agency, and finally 3) the parental rights are then given to the adoptive parents along with the child. In agency adoptions, the people in charge of choosing the parents (caseworkers) screen each and every applicant carefully. They understand how important it is to place each baby or child with a family where both the child and the family benefit. Every consideration is taken to ensure a successful adoption. Some people wish to adopt children with special needs and these parents are screened even more carefully.

Note for your student that adoption is not a recent legal creation. In fact, one of the earliest written law codes—the Babylonian Code of Hammurabi (1700s B.C.), included a long section describing the laws of adoption. You might want to learn more about Hammurabi's code. Locate a complete timeline of history and show your student how far back in history the Babylonian civilization existed!

If your student is interested in learning more about adoption and what it involves, contact a local agency and request a tour or information packets. These brochures will answer many of your student's questions. You can also research your state's specific adoption laws online.

Adoption is a loving and caring way for children to be a part of a family. It allows families the blessing of one or more children that they may never have been able to have.

Language Arts: Writing and Discussion Question

Why do you think the name of George's school was Lincoln School? Discuss where they may have come up with the name and why.

Chapter 6

Teacher Summary

George leaves Neosho and his good friends the Watkins, and sets off for Fort Scott, Kansas. He has heard there is a different free school there. George hopes the teacher at the new school will be able to answer more of his science questions. Before he leaves, he and Jim get their picture taken together.

When George reaches Fort Scott he meets a wonderful woman named Mrs. Payne. Mrs. Payne invites George to live with her, in return for cooking meals and helping around the house. George accepts. Soon he is attending school and living happily with the Paynes. But one day, George witnesses a white mob beat a black man to death in town. George is horrified and leaves Fort Scott immediately. He never goes back.

What we will cover in this chapter.

Social Studies: History and Geography - Kansas and Missouri*
Language Arts: Writing and Discussion Question

Social Studies: History and Geography - Kansas and Missouri*

George is certainly moving a lot, isn't he? This chapter takes our budding scientist from Neosho, Missouri to Fort Scott, Kansas. Take some time and share with your student a few interesting facts about each of these states, and locate both states on a map.

Missouri (mih ZOOR ee) entered the Union on August 10, 1821. Jefferson City is Missouri's capital and Kansas City is the largest city in the state. Boasting primarily industry and farming, Missouri continues to expand and grow. The name, Missouri, probably comes from a Native American word meaning "town of the large canoes." Most states have nicknames, and Missouri is no exception. The most common nickname is "The Show-Me State." In 1899, Congressman Willard Vandiver of Missouri was speaking at a convention. He said, "...eloquence neither convinces nor satisfies me. I am from Missouri. You have got to show me." The phrase caught on, and is now used to describe the genuine and somewhat stubborn citizens of Missouri.

Missouri has been the birthplace and home to many famous Americans, including Harry S. Truman, Mark Twain, Walt Disney, Joseph Pulitzer, General John Pershing, Maya Angelou and, of course, George Washington Carver.

George left both Diamond Grove and Neosho in order to attend school in Fort Scott, Kansas. Kansas is often referred to as the "Wheat State" and the "Breadbasket of America" because of its tremendous wheat production. It lies immediately west of Missouri. The Native American Indians who originally inhabited this region were called the Kansa or Kaw, and it is from these names that we get the word Kansas.

Most of Kansas is covered by flat plains. Over 200 different kinds of grasses grow in Kansas and the most prominent flower is the sunflower. Wichita is the largest city in Kansas, but Topeka is the state's capital. President Dwight D. Eisenhower grew up in Abilene, Kansas. You can still visit his birthplace and spend an afternoon in Abilene yourself.

If your student is interested in discovering more facts about Missouri or Kansas, he can obtain books at the library to help him in his search. Making maps, tracing the path of different rivers, showing where the major cities are located—all these activities can further your student's understanding of these two fascinating states.

Language Arts: Writing and Discussion Question

Our book tells us that while George was in Fort Scott, there was "...no one to take care of him. He had to look after himself, earn money to buy his meals and to rent a room to sleep in." How would you feel to be on your own? What could you do to earn money? What do you think you would enjoy most about being independent right now?

Chapter 7

Teacher Summary

George moves around from town to town in Kansas, and finally settles in Olathe. He finds a nice couple, Lucy and Chris Seymour, and they take the young boy in. George helps Aunt Lucy with her laundry business each day, and he attends school. When George finishes the sixth grade, he and the Seymours move to Minneapolis, Kansas.

Instead of attending school, George begins to seek out college information. He is sure he can do university level work, if only he can find a college that would accept him. George waits each day for responses from his applications, but there is someone else in town named George Carver. George is always getting that man's mail. He wants to be sure he is getting his own. To clear up the mistakes in mail service, George takes a middle initial for himself—W. When his friends joke about the letter, George decides it should stand for something. He decides on Washington. Now George Washington Carver has his own full name.

What we will cover in this chapter:

Social Studies: History - Postal Service
Language Arts: Writing and Discussion Question
Fine Arts: The Accordion
Life Skills: Education - Exploring College Applications*

Social Studies: History - Postal Service

George wants to make sure he's getting all of his mail. To ensure the proper delivery, he changes his name so it is unique to him. What do we do in large cities where hundreds of people might have the same name? Discuss with your student how he should address an envelope for the mail. What do we include?

Each letter the United States Post Office delivers requires at least five pieces of information to be present on each envelope or package it delivers. The recipient's name, street address (apartment number), city, state (or province), and a ZIP code. Post Office employees say the most critical piece of information is the ZIP code.

Does your student know what his ZIP code is? What does it stand for? What do the numbers actually represent?

ZIP stands for Zoning Improvement Plan. Introduced in 1963, the Zoning Improvement Plan was begun in order to speed the sorting and delivering of the mail. That same year, the Post Office Department introduced a series of two-letter state abbreviations. For example, Missouri became MO. New York became NY. California became CA. These state abbreviations are always written in capital letters, *without* a period following. In this way, the city, state and ZIP code can all fit on the same line.

But what do these numbers in the ZIP code mean? The Post Office Department has divided the United States into 10 geographic areas. For example, let's examine the ZIP code 22207. The first number, 2, represents Area 2. Area 2 combines the District of Columbia, Maryland, North Carolina, South Carolina, Virginia and West Virginia. Have your student locate this region on a map.

The next two digits, in this case "22", represent the city area or section. In our case, "22" represents the Arlington area in Virginia. Finally, the last two digits, 07, represent the specific village district, neighborhood, or township where the mail is headed.

In 1983, the Post Office Department introduced four-digit codes, in addition to the basic five-digit ZIP Codes. For example, the person in Arlington, VA above might have the ZIP code 22207-4509. The last four digits represent the exact house or apartment for delivery. In this way, there is no possibility for mail delivery error, except for human mistakes.

Does your student know his ZIP code? His ZIP+4 code? Has your student ever addressed an envelope or mailed a letter? Take this opportunity to write a short note to a grandparent or friend. Fill out the envelope completely, including the address of the recipient and your student's return address. Don't forget a first-class stamp. Maybe your student will receive a letter in return!

Language Arts: Writing and Discussion Question

George selected the middle name of Washington. What would you pick for your middle name if you could choose it yourself? Why?

Fine Arts: The Accordion

We read that George plays the accordion in school concerts. Does your student know what an accordion is? Has he ever seen someone play an accordion? Explore this unusual instrument together.

Accordions are perhaps most synonymous with German polka bands. Locate some polka music for your student to listen to, or watch a video online. When your student listens, can he pick out the accordion?

Accordions are unique instruments. Somewhat like a mini-piano, they have a keyboard, which the player plays with his right hand.

The player's left hand is used to pump the bellows. As the air is pushed by the closing of the bellows, it vibrates against metal reeds and produces sound. Playing an accordion can be complicated, but the result when mastered, is beautiful.

Watch for examples of accordion music or instruments to point out to your student. George is a special person in so many ways. Even his musical instrument is uncommon!

Life Skills: Education - Exploring College Applications*

George is interested in going to college. He fills out applications to see if he is accepted. Has your student ever had the opportunity to look over a college application or requirement sheet? Even though it is early for your student to be seriously looking at colleges, it might be fun and informative for him to see exactly what a community college or university application includes.

What kinds of classes will he have needed to complete? What is a G.P.A. (grade point average)? How is it calculated? What does it mean when a class is described as "a three-hour class?" What is an "elective" versus a "requirement?"

If your student is interested, look online for a community college or university course catalog and application. Then sit down with your student and explore it together. In this way, your student will have a better understanding of the serious choices George had before him.

Chapter 8

Teacher Summary

George has finally received an acceptance letter from a university! Highland College wants George to come and be a student on their campus. He can sign up for classes in the fall. George is thrilled. He sells his laundry business equipment and raises enough money for the train trip to Highland.

When George finally arrives at Highland College, he goes to visit the head of the university. George shows the man the letter he received and is stunned by the response he gets. Highland College won't accept George after all. The man tells George they didn't know he was black. Highland College doesn't accept Negroes. George leaves in tears.

Instead of running back to the Seymours, George decides to work and save money. As he works, he meets a man who tells him of a new government plan in the west. If a man works on a piece of land and lives on it for five years, he can own it. It's called homesteading. George thinks this is a fine idea. A farm of his own! At 22 years of age, George moves to Western Kansas. Although he does the best he can, after two years, no crops are growing well. George gives up and moves back east.

What we will cover in this chapter:

Social Studies: History and Geography - Homestead Act of 1862
Language Arts: Writing and Discussion Question
Life Skills: Injustice - Feeling Judged
Life Skills: Ingenuity - Creativity in Your Finances*

Social Studies: History and Geography - Homestead Act of 1862

George hears about a plan whereby he can secure a large farm in return for living on the land and working it for five years. In the end, George's farm isn't successful. The land is too dusty and dry for crops to grow well there. But wasn't the plan a good one? If a person didn't have much money, here was a way by which he could secure a piece of land himself and build a farm for his family.

George was just one of hundreds of thousands of Americans who took advantage of this idea. Like George, people living on farms under this plan were known as "homesteaders." The United States Congress, in May of 1862, passed a law called The Homestead Act.

The Homestead Act stated that anyone over 21 years of age who was the head of a family and a citizen of the United States, could find, live and work on a 160-acre plot of land. (This included women who were single, widowed, divorced, or deserted.) If, after five years, he was still living on the land and improving it (using it for cattle, farming or industry), then he owned it—free and clear! In other words, if a person was willing to work very hard and make something out of an open plot of land, then he should have the right to call it his own.

Hundreds of thousands of people moved west from 1862 to 1900, setting up homesteads and securing farms for their families. Even during the early 1900s, homesteading was still being accomplished in Alaska. In 1976, the Homestead

Act was terminated for all states except Alaska. In 1986, the Homestead Act was abolished altogether.

Language Arts: Writing and Discussion Question

George was extremely excited at the prospect of attending Highland College. When he was told he would not be welcome there, George cried. Have you ever been excited about something and then felt sad when circumstances prevented it from happening? Write about a time when you felt as George did and what you did to overcome the disappointment.

Life Skills: Injustice - Feeling Judged

George was told by the head of Highland College that he was not wanted there—because of the color of his skin. What an injustice! Perhaps your student, like George, has dealt with discrimination. However, even people who haven't felt racial injustice can sympathize with the emotion. Has your student ever felt wrongly judged? People can be cruel and often judge others' entire worth by details such as his clothes, or his job, how much money he makes, or even how much he weighs.

Talk with your student about a time when perhaps you, yourself, have felt your worth brought into question. How did it make you feel? Were you able to ignore the comments or move past them? How?

Perhaps your student has been involved in a similar situation, or maybe he has made the mistake of treating someone else with injustice. Learning to treat others with respect is part of what helps others have respect for you. Encourage your student to think about how he can work on seeing beyond superficial differences in others and focus on the strengths of each person he meets.

Life Skills: Ingenuity - Creativity in Your Finances*

George knew he would need money for a train ticket. How could he secure the funds? George decided to sell some of his belongings (a laundry tub, iron and ironing board). George used common sense and some ingenuity to raise the money. Learning to make money and to save some of it are things even younger children can begin to understand.

Give your student a hypothetical situation. For example, pretend (or don't, if there is a real circumstance which is similar) that he wants a new bicycle for the summer. He decided in January on the bike he wants and it costs $150. He has until May (five months) to pay for the bike. What could he do to make money? Yard work? Help clean the house? Wash cars? Babysit? How much money, on average, would he make at each job? How quickly would those dollars add up?

Another topic of discussion is learning to save money. Being able to budget accurately, stick to a plan and realize your goal is a vital part of becoming mature. Does your student get an allowance? Does he have a budget? What things are included in the savings portion of his budget?

Learning to be creative and think of new ways to make money, and then having the maturity to save and spend wisely are all things your student can be learning and practicing while still young. George had an excellent head on his shoulders when it came to budgeting and money-making. He didn't have many opportunities when he was young, but he made the most of what he had. We can all learn a lesson from George!

Chapter 9

Teacher Summary

George travels for three months, heading east and north. He does odd jobs and laundry and soon finds himself in the town of Winterset, Iowa. In Winterset, George is hired as a cook at the Schultz Hotel. One day, a man at George's church introduces himself as Dr. John Milholland. George and the Milhollands become good friends. They help him open his own laundry business. Now George has work each day, but he is still actively learning new things about plants and flowers. Mrs. Milholland thinks George definitely belongs in college. The doctor tells George about Simpson College. George finds he can be accepted as a student even though he is black. So, on September 9, 1890, George is in college for the first time. He is much older than the other students, but delighted to be there!

What we will cover in this chapter:

Social Studies: Geography - Iowa: A New Place for George*
Social Studies: Career Path - Illustrator
Language Arts: Writing and Discussion Question
Life Skills: Self-Directed Study: Being Your Own Teacher

Social Studies: Geography - Iowa: A New Place for George*

George Washington Carver has been in many cities in Kansas and Missouri. This chapter, however, introduces yet another state—Iowa. Share with your student some interesting facts about this state.

Iowa is a farm state. Producing nearly 1/5 of the corn grown in the United States, Iowa is often referred to as the "land where all the corn grows." However, Iowa's most renowned nickname is the "Hawkeye State" in honor of the famous Native American chief, Black Hawk. The Black Hawk War of 1832 was also named for this chief, who led his group of Sauk and Fox against white settlers in an attempt to reclaim traditional tribal lands that the U.S. had claimed in a treaty of 1804. The Native Americans were defeated, but the battle went down in history because of the fierce fighting and the land which the settlers gained through the victory.

Many famous Americans have been born in Iowa, including President Her-

bert Hoover, Carrie Chapman Catt (leader in the women's suffrage movement), celebrities Johnny Carson and John Wayne, and Norman E. Borlaug (winner of the 1970 Nobel Peace Prize).

Iowa is a rich and fertile state. More than 85% of the state's land is used as farmland. Although the chief crop is corn, Iowa also produces soybeans and processes many pork products.

If your student is interested in learning more about Iowa, he can find books at the library, or search online for websites and videos about this state.

Social Studies: Career Path - Illustrator

In this chapter, we're told again how much George loves to paint. The young man enjoys painting pictures of the flowers he is studying. Is your student interested in art? Does he find himself drawing and painting just for fun? Perhaps a career as an illustrator is something he should explore.

When someone says, "I'm an illustrator," we often think of the person who draws the pictures in books, primarily children's books. However, the area of illustration is much broader in scope than that. What about those pictures of plants and cells in a science textbook? Who draws the designs and beautiful covers on greeting cards? What person draws people, scenery, and objects depicted in jigsaw puzzles, board games or video games? The possibilities for illustration work are endless—including technical books, science/medical books, architectural plans, children's books, advertising, science fiction and many more.

Many illustrators use traditional mediums (i.e., watercolor, chalk, pencil/pens, paints, etc.) to create beautiful artwork. Illustrators may also use digital media to create their artwork. Some digital art programs function in much the same way as traditional drawing or painting, while others are quite different and require different skills and techniques.

Because the employment and career options are so varied in the area of illustration, college degree requirements also differ. Illustrators may obtain a studio art or illustration degree from a 2- or 4-year college, where they will assemble a portfolio of their work. This portfolio is most often the key in obtaining a job in illustration.

For more information, contact an area college or university and ask for information on their art programs. Illustrating, whether books or technical materials, is a rewarding way to earn a living. Would your student like to see one of his pictures in a book someday?

Language Arts: Writing and Discussion Question

What is a topic you would like to pursue in a self-directed study? Do you have an area of interest you are already learning about on your own? Describe it.

Life Skills: Self-Directed Study - Being Your Own Teacher

Draw your student's attention to where Mrs. Milholland says that George is running his own school. She tells people that "he is the teacher, and the pupil too." What does that mean to your student? Can a person be their own teacher? Absolutely! Sometimes, self-directed study can be the most beneficial and inspiring learning method in the world. Can *anyone* be their own teacher? Of course! Any child can find a particular subject that fascinates him and begin to educate himself.

What is a subject your student finds particularly interesting? Is it something he could get a book about at the library? Does he know someone he could talk with who knows more about it? What about documentaries or films on the subject?

Encourage your student to follow George's example. If George, a financially struggling, young black man in the late 1800s, was able to find sources for learning and form a self-directed study, then surely your student could also do this!

Chapters 10 and 11

Teacher Summary

George enjoys attending Simpson College. He makes a lot of friends and begins teaching others about his beloved plants and flowers. George continues to paint, but soon realizes that the life of an artist is too unstable. He also understands that the country isn't yet ready to accept a black artist. Instead, with the help of his teacher Miss Budd, he decides to pursue a degree in science and agriculture. George soon transfers to Iowa State College and begins to learn about farming and how crops grow.

In just a few years, George has learned a great deal about science—he has even written a booklet on plant diseases. People begin to talk about George Washington Carver and how brilliant he is. One particular person who hears about George is Booker T. Washington. Booker was the head of a college for black people in Alabama, called Tuskegee Normal School. Booker invites George to come and teach at Tuskegee. George accepts the offer. Soon he will be the director of the Agriculture Department. George Washington Carver is becoming very well known!

What we will cover in these chapters:

Social Studies: History - Tuskegee Normal School*
Social Studies: History - Booker T. Washington*
Science: Learning More about Birds
Language Arts: Writing and Discussion Question
Language Arts: Vocabulary
Fine Arts: Finger Painting - Being Messy Creatively

Social Studies: History - Tuskegee Normal School*

Teacher's Note: A "normal school" is the traditional name for an institution that trains teachers. They were trained in the "norms" of pedagogy (teaching methods) and curriculum.

George has been invited to teach at Tuskegee Normal School in Alabama. What an honor! Has your student ever heard of Tuskegee University (the current name for the institution)? Take some time to review a quick history of this famous place of learning.

Founded in 1881 by Booker T. Washington, Tuskegee University was a private school specifically set up for the education of black Americans. George Washington Carver is the school's best-known instructor. With a strong emphasis on agriculture and the sciences, Tuskegee is still a successful and active college campus today. The school offers more than 60 degree programs, including courses in agriculture, home economics, business, education, engineering and architecture, nursing and veterinary medicine.

Included on the campus today is the George Washington Carver Museum, which can be toured and visited. This historic site, which includes the museum, was established in 1974 by Congress.

Social Studies: History - Booker T. Washington*

Booker T. Washington invited George to come and teach at Tuskegee Normal School. Washington had heard of George and his amazing work with plants and crops at Iowa State. Does your student know anything about Booker T. Washington?

Beyond being the founder and director of Tuskegee University, Washington was the most influential black leader of his day. Advising two presidents (Theodore Roosevelt and William Howard Taft) on racial issues, writing an autobiography (*Up From Slavery* in 1901), founding the National Negro Business League and supporting a variety of black-owned newspapers helped Booker T. Washington to have a dramatic impact on American culture and history.

However, not everyone appreciated or believed in the work Washington was doing for the black community. Other civil rights leaders began to attack and criticize the way in which Washington was fighting for his beliefs. The chief critic was historian and writer **W. E. B. Du Bois**. Du Bois believed that blacks should be allowed to attend all universities and colleges. He didn't appreciate Tuskegee limiting black students to agriculture and technical degrees. Du Bois wished that blacks would have more opportunities for higher education in all subjects, not just agricultural and industrial.

Washington gave a speech in Atlanta, Georgia in 1895 which set off sparks in many arenas of civil rights. He said, "In all things that are purely social we can be as separate as the fingers, yet as one as the hand in all things essential to mutual progress." Du Bois and others found this statement infuriating and dangerous. They were joined together to fight

Five in Row Volume Seven

for complete equality, and did not wish to settle for segregation at any level. Washington and Du Bois differed significantly in other areas, as well, such as primarily desiring economic advancement (Washington) vs. primarily desiring advances in civil rights (Du Bois).

By 1910, Du Bois and other leaders began new movements and the "reign" of Booker T. Washington's ideas began to diminish.

Despite the differences in opinions about his work and life by others in the community, Washington did a great deal of good for black Americans. He certainly provided a platform for George Washington Carver to share his ideas and do good for others. Take this opportunity to research and report on Booker T. Washington and W. E. B. Du Bois and their surrounding histories.

Science: Learning More about Birds

George teaches his friends about birds and birds' songs. Is your student interested in birds? Does he enjoy watching the nesting process in the spring and the new baby hatchlings? Does he ever wonder which birds have blue eggs and which have brown eggs with spots? Has he ever heard a bird singing in a tree and wondered where it was and what it looked like? All of these questions are different ways that people can learn to identify birds. Bird watching (sometimes called "birding") is a highly popular hobby. Learning about birds is a complex science, known as **ornithology**.

Birds are fascinating creatures. They are beautiful, colorful, smart, and can fly! They build functional nests and homes for their young. A bird may migrate each year if need be, to stay in the weather conditions they require. Birds are graceful and lovely, but some can be fierce hunters as well. Did your student know that birds helped with the development of the first successful airplanes? Scientists and developers weren't able to make aircraft work until they studied the bird's wing and fashioned the airplane wings in a similar manner.

There are nearly 10,000 kinds of birds, ranging from the hummingbird (2 inches in length) to the ostrich (nearly 8 feet tall). There are birds in the tropics, the arctic, the desert and the mountains. Each bird is adapted to live well in its own climate. The bee hummingbird weighs only 1/28th of an ounce, while the ostrich can weigh over 300 lbs.!

Birds help us in a variety of ways. They provide many balancing effects for the environment. For example, hummingbirds feed on the nectar of flowers. As they move from flower to flower, just as bees do, they pollinate the blossoms. Another bird, the bobwhite, feeds on seeds. One bobwhite may help a farmer rid his fields of nearly 15,000 weed seeds daily. Hawks and other birds of prey assist farmers by eating mice and rats—animals that can ruin stored grain. Fruit-eating birds help spread seed by eating berries. The skin, pulp and nutrients are absorbed by the bird, but the viable seeds pass through their system and are dropped. Of course, as a direct source of food for humans, birds can be eaten. Ducks, turkeys, chickens, pigeons, quail, and other birds are often hunted or raised by and consumed by people.

If your student is interested in learning to identify birds, he can use many pieces of bird information to assist him in his research. Each type of bird has a different type of feather, body shape, egg, beak, song and nest. First, he may enjoy identifying all the birds common in his neighborhood. If your student lives in an urban or suburban area, these birds are often wrens, robins, blue jays, titmice, starlings, and sparrows. However, each area of the United States has specific birds which are common to that region. What birds are in your student's backyard? Can he identify them by sight? By song? Has he looked them up in a book and noticed what their nests and eggs look like? Here is a topic that your student can research on his own and have a fun time learning. By drawing pictures or gathering found feathers, your student can compile his own notebooks or art books of all the birds he learns about. Encourage your student to open his eyes and begin learning about the beauty and life of the birds around him!

Language Arts: Writing and Discussion Question

George took better care of his health because he realized he had work he needed to do—people needed him. You're needed by your family and friends, too. What are things you can do to improve your health and take care of yourself?

Language Arts: Vocabulary

ornithology The study of birds.

W. E. B. Du Bois Black American leader, historian and sociologist (1868-1963).

Fine Arts: Finger Painting - Being Messy Creatively

Our author tells us that when George was working on an art project he sometimes put down his brush and painted with his fingers! Did your student think that finger painting was just for little kids? Certainly not. Finger painting is a wonderfully messy and delightful way to create art—and adult artists sometimes use finger painting techniques as well!

If it has been awhile since your student has had the pleasure of creating a work of art with paints and his fingers, why not take this opportunity to let him try it again? If he holds two or three of his fingers together, or his whole fist squeezed together he can create different textures and designs in the paint. If he is feeling really daring, have him close his eyes and set a timer. When the timer goes off, have him open his eyes and see what he created by just feeling the paper and the paint.

Have a great time with this method of painting! If the

teacher wants to join in the fun, by all means do so!

Chapter 12

Teacher Summary

George, settling into his new role at Tuskegee, begins by observing the local farmers and their fields. Astonished by the poor soil quality and the sagging crops, George decides to begin working on ways to increase the productivity of the farms. First, he must increase the richness of the soil by adding nitrogen back into the land. But before all of this, George decides he and his students need a building of their own on campus. By making their own bricks from clay, the students build an agriculture building. They set up a laboratory from things they find and scrap material that they collect. Soon they have their own "Experiment Station" set up as well. On this piece of land, they can set up "mock" farms and research what helps the soil and crops.

What we will cover in this chapter:

Science: Soil - What Role Nitrogen Plays
Science: Composting
Science: Legumes - What Are They?*
Language Arts: Writing and Discussion Question
Language Arts: Vocabulary
Fine Arts: Making Bricks Out of Clay

Science: Soil - What Role Nitrogen Plays

Dr. Carver and his students did experiments with nitrogen and soil in the Experiment Station. Nitrogen is essential for all living organisms, both plants and animals. Nitrogen is a part of all amino acids—the base of all proteins. Plants can produce all the amino acids they need (thereby receiving their nitrogen), but animals (including people) must get the rest of these amino acids by eating other plants and/or animals.

In a cycle of chemical reactions called the nitrogen cycle, nitrogen is removed from the air, deposited into the earth and then returned to the air. Some plants, like legumes (cowpeas, beans, sweet peas and peanuts) grow in pods and give out nitrogen through their roots. When different plants are then grown in that same plot, the nitrogen remains in the soil and helps them grow. Later, the legume crops can be planted in that same plot again. This way of farming and gardening is called **crop rotation**.

Use this opportunity to learn more about nitrogen. Encourage and help your student to find library books appropriate for his age level on the nitrogen cycle, nitrates, nitrites and the greenhouse effect. You can also help your student search for this element on the periodic table of elements.

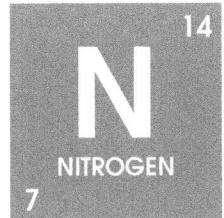

Science: Composting

Dr. Carver encourages his students to gather up garbage, grass clippings, manure and leaves and place them in a fenced-in pen. Then he tells them to add some soil from the woods and swamps and wait for it to rot. Is Dr. Carver crazy? Why would this help the farmland? What was he trying to accomplish?

Dr. Carver was teaching his students about **composting**. Has your student ever heard this term? Maybe your student has seen composting done in his own yard, or that of a neighbor's.

A compost pile is a collection of plant material, food waste products (vegetable skins, coffee grounds, etc.) and soil which is left to rot. As the materials break down and decay, nutrients become concentrated and provide rich nutrition for the soil.

Anyone can work on his own compost pile. If your student would like to try his hand at one, encourage him to set up a pen, similar to Dr. Carver's, somewhere outside. Even chicken wire can be formed into a small cylinder and stuck in the ground to make a great compost center. Now, have him begin collecting leaves, dirt and food scraps from the family. Remember—no meat products, but lots of vegetable matter. Old coffee grounds make a great addition! Encourage your student not to have a lot of any one addition, but instead to create a nice, even mixture of many things. He can sprinkle his compost pile with a little water to help speed up the decay process.

This experiment is best done in early spring and summer, since the heat of the sun helps break down the plant materials. When several weeks have gone by and your student's pile has rotted, he can try out his compost by planting some seeds in one pot, using only plain soil. Some more seeds can be planted in another pot using some soil *and* some compost. Which plants grow more quickly? Which are stronger?

If your student continues to compost, he'll soon have enough rich material to add to the soil all around his own yard, to nourish plants, flowers and gardens. Composting is an excellent way to grow bigger, better crops and recycle at the same time!

Science: Legumes - What Are They?*

Dr. Carver encouraged his students to plant cowpeas, instead of cotton. He told them cowpeas are legumes and that they are good for the soil. Has your student ever heard the term **legume** before? Take this opportunity to share a few essential legume facts with your student.

Legumes (LEG yooms or leg YOOMS) are all the

plants that belong to the pea family—the second largest family of all flowering plants. Botanists have identified over 16,000 species of legumes! Legume species vary a great deal—from low shrubs to herbs and even trees! Delicious peanuts are legumes.

Legumes are good for the soil because they take in nitrogen from the air through their roots. Little nodules, or knot-like growths, form along the roots of the legumes. These nodules house bacteria, and this bacteria is what changes the nitrogen from the air to a valuable source of growth for the plant.

Because of the legumes and their way of infiltrating soil with nitrogen, many farmers plant legumes as cover crops (crops that area grown primarily to benefit the soil rather than for eating) and in crop rotation. If your student is interested in learning more about legumes, encourage him to find a book about peanuts, peas or the nitrogen cycle.

Language Arts: Writing and Discussion Question

Dr. Carver told his students they didn't have any excuses. He said, "There's no need to whine, 'Oh, if I only had so-and-so!' Do it anyhow. Use what you find around you." Has there been a time you were forced to be inventive and use what you had around you? What did you do? How did it turn out? Have fun recalling and writing an explanation of your creativeness.

Language Arts: Vocabulary

legume   Any plant belonging to the pea family.

refractory brick   A brick used in high-temperature areas, such as furnaces and fireplaces.

building brick   A brick made to be uniform and attractive and used for building outdoor exterior walls and homes.

composting   A process by which plant material is broken down and decayed to produce high-nutrient material for gardening and farming.

Fine Arts: Making Bricks Out of Clay

Dr. Carver's students worked hard to build their own agriculture building. By using the clay found in their area, they made bricks and built a functional two-story building for their classes.

Bricks are the oldest known man-made building material. In ancient times (by 6000 B.C.), sun-dried bricks were prevalent in the Middle East. By 3500 B.C., kiln-fired bricks were also being produced. Even today, in the American Southwest and in Mexico, sun-dried brick homes are still common. They are called adobe homes. Adobe (uh DOH bee) is the Spanish word for sun-dried brick. To make traditional adobe bricks, the workers mix sandy clay, a small amount of water and some straw or grass together. Then the mixture is placed in some sort of form (wooden or metal) and dried into bricks. When the clay is dry, the bricks are removed and laid in the sun for 10 days to 2 weeks. Then they can be used for building. Adobe homes are not practical for cold or rainy areas, because the sudden change in temperature or the wetness can compromise the integrity of the bricks and cause them to crumble.

Today, there are two main types of bricks commonly manufactured—building bricks and refractory bricks. **Building bricks** are extremely uniform in size and shape and are used to build walls, chimneys, houses, buildings, etc. **Refractory bricks** are made to handle very hot temperatures (2,000°-4,000° F.) and are used in factories, furnaces, and fireplaces. To make these bricks so heat resistant, they are often composed in part by materials such as alumina, carbon, and zircon.

If your student is finding this discussion of bricks interesting, why not let him try his own hand at building a few bricks? Even a mini-building? He can decide on the size of his bricks, how he will shape them and how many he will make. By using dirt, straw and water, he can make some very simple sun-dried bricks at home. If he wants to make a model or small structure that will hold up for a longer period of time, it might be wise to go to an art store and purchase some sculpting clay to mix with the dirt.

Then, get dirty and have fun! And remember how much work it must have taken for the students to build their agriculture classroom building!

Chapter 13

Teacher Summary

Dr. Carver was happy in his role as professor and was much loved by his students. Everyone liked his gentle manner, intelligent teaching style and silly humor. Beyond teaching his students, Dr. Carver began to hold monthly meetings for the farmers in his area. By teaching them about their land and plants, Dr. Carver was teaching them how to be more successful farmers! Sometimes, Dr. Carver also led the group of farmers in prayer and song. He taught them how to sew and cook as well. Dr. Carver was busy helping everyone build stronger lives, better families and more prosperous farms.

What we will cover in this chapter:

Social Studies: Career Path - Teacher
Science: Insects - Identify Three New Insects Today*
Language Arts: Humbug - A Literary Reference
Language Arts: Writing and Discussion Question
Life Skills: Dealing with Practical Jokes - Learning to Laugh at Yourself

Social Studies: Career Path - Teacher

Dr. Carver was an outstanding teacher. He made his subject interesting, encouraged his students to strive for excellence and never quit learning himself. Has your student ever thought about becoming a teacher? Teachers are a respected and vital segment of our workforce today. Educating and training the children of our country is a large responsibility.

If your student is interested in looking into education as a career choice, remind him there are several basic requirements. First, does he enjoy learning? The best educators are people who love to learn themselves. Second, does your student enjoy passing information on to others patiently? These are two essential ingredients to being a successful teacher.

Teachers can be found in nursery care, preschools, grade schools, high schools, colleges and universities, technical and trade schools, specialized learning centers, boarding schools, after school programs for children, and many more places! To become a teacher, a four-year college degree and either graduate work or certification are almost always required. Teachers can be certified for specific grades, specific subjects, children with special needs, or all of the above. Hundreds of universities include a school of education and teaching certification programs.

If your student enjoys learning and sharing his knowledge with others, becoming a teacher might be a good career path to explore. For more information, contact your local university or library for brochures, books, and resource materials. If your student knows a teacher, perhaps a visit to his or her classroom for observation might be helpful. Your student can take notes on what he sees and then write a paper on his discoveries. Did he enjoy a "day in the life of a teacher?"

Science: Insects - Identify Three New Insects Today*

Dr. Carver wanted his students to learn the names of every plant and insect they saw. What a wonderful goal Dr. Carver had for students. He wanted everyone to know as much about nature as they could. By following his example, encourage your student to take a moment and look online or in a reference book and learn about three new insects today. What insect looks humorous? Which insect looks frightening? Is there a butterfly or type of ant that has always interested your student?

By drawing or coloring a picture of each of the three choices, writing down a few facts and telling you about his discoveries, your student can broaden his knowledge of the outside world today—just as Dr. Carver's students did each and every day. This might be a good opportunity to visit the library and find an age appropriate book on the insect world for your student.

If your student wants a few suggestions for insects to research, here are a few ideas: cicada killer, katydid, bagworms, silverfish and the spittlebug.

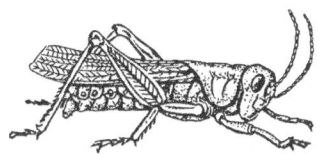

Language Arts: Humbug - A Literary Reference

Dr. Carver's students play a trick on him by combining parts of several insects to make a "rare" bug. Dr. Carver calls it a "humbug." Does your student understand his joke? What does humbug mean? A humbug is someone who pretends to be something he is not—a fake. Perhaps the most famous association with this term is found in Charles Dickens' masterpiece *A Christmas Carol*.

Ebenezer Scrooge, the main character in this classic drama, doesn't believe in the Christmas spirit or in charity at all. Often in response to those who are much more cheery than he, he will respond, "Bah, humbug." If your student or family has not shared this story before, do so now! It's a great book to read at anytime—not just at Christmas. As the changed Scrooge says in the end, "I will honor Christmas in my heart and try to keep it all the year."

Language Arts: Writing and Discussion Question

Dr. Carver helped teach farmers how to grow better gardens. He encouraged his students and friends to plant legumes. If you could select the flowers and vegetables for your own garden, what would they be and why?

Life Skills: Dealing with Practical Jokes - Learning to Laugh at Yourself

Dr. Carver's students played a joke on him by pretending to find a very unusual bug. Instead of getting embarrassed or upset with the teasing, Dr. Carver laughed it off and made his own joke. Has your student ever had a trick played on him? Has he ever been the brunt of a practical joke? Sometimes in life, people will tease us and instead of becoming frustrated or angry, it is best to learn to laugh at ourselves, and shrug off the teasing.

Learning to deal with other people and new situations is what growing up is all about. Encourage your student to laugh and join in the next time he is tricked or teased. It is the most fun and mature way to deal with those situations.

Chapter 14

Teacher Summary

Dr. Carver and his students continue to research better ways to grow crops. They begin to plant sweet potatoes and soon discover what a simple and delicious crop they are! Dr. Carver wants to share his knowledge with even more farmers, so he begins to write pamphlets on his discoveries. For the farmers who can't read, Dr. Carver begins to travel and shows them what he has learned. Beyond growing sweet potatoes, Dr. Carver shows his friends and the farmers how to make beautiful yellow house paint from the Alabama clay. He also teaches the women how to make rugs and mats for their homes from dried okra stalks. In 1906, Tuskegee helps build a little school on wheels to take all the information around to area farmers. Dr. Carver is happy he is now able to help even more people.

What we will cover in this chapter:

Social Studies: History - Dr. Carver's Pamphlets
Science: Sweet Potatoes
Language Arts: Folios and Pamphlets - Creating Your Own
Language Arts: Writing and Discussion Question
Fine Arts: Cooking with Sweet Potatoes
Life Skills: Waste Not, Want Not
Activity Sheet: Vocabulary*

Social Studies: History - Dr. Carver's Pamphlets

Dr. Carver began writing pamphlets about his experiences with sweet potatoes. The Tuskegee Institute began to print them and distribute them to farmers in the area. In this way, many more people could benefit from his findings.

In one such pamphlet, entitled *How The Farmer Can Save His Sweet Potatoes—And Ways of Preparing Them For The Table*, Dr. Carver covered such topics as the history of the sweet potato, its origins, the varieties available, how to grow them most effectively and how to cook them most deliciously. The recipes he discovered ranged from baking, frying, pies, glazes, cobblers, doughnuts, croquettes and even breads.

Teacher's Note: Look at the following Fine Arts lesson for a few of the recipes taken from Dr. Carver's pamphlets. Your student can whip up a delicious concoction and know he is making a dish Dr. Carver himself tried.

Today, your student can view these pamphlets (or "bulletins") online. You can also get facsimile copies from the George Washington Carver Birthplace District Association located in Diamond, Missouri.

Science: Sweet Potatoes

Sweet potatoes became a passion for Dr. Carver. Share with your student some more scientific information about sweet potatoes to help enrich his understanding of our story.

Sweet potatoes are actually the edible roots of a plant which belongs to the morning glory family, *Convolvulaceae*. The roots of this plant are bulbous and fleshy, and are the section of the plant we harvest and consume. Originally believed to have been grown in South America, China now produces more sweet potatoes than any other country; in the U.S. North Carolina is the biggest producer. Although the most common color of sweet potato flesh is yellow or orange, there are varieties that offer flesh from purple to white.

Remind your student that although many people confuse sweet potatoes with yams, they are two very different plants. Yams are mostly grown in the tropics, are a vine-type plant, and belong to the *Dioscoreaceae* family. Some yams can grow as large as 100 pounds!

Sweet potatoes are high in carbohydrates and in vitamins A and C. They are good for you, as well as delicious! Dr. Carver was right!

Language Arts: Folios and Pamphlets - Creating Your Own

Dr. Carver was able to spread his ideas and discoveries about sweet potatoes, farming, peanuts and more to a lot of people through the publication of pamphlets. Has your student ever done a research project or learned something exciting and wanted to share it? Take this learning opportunity to teach your student a bit more about the way books and pamphlets are constructed and then help him make one of his own.

Begin by examining a book together with your student. Try to locate a hardback, spined book, so your student can observe the sewn sections (called folios) which make up the book's pages. More expensive books are sewn onto canvas, and less expensive books are often made up of folios which have simply been glued. Find an old book (perhaps you can pick one up from a garage sale or used book sale) in which you are no longer interested or which is already extremely worn. As an interesting and helpful exercise, let your student take it apart and examine each section. Even-numbered pages, your student will notice, are always on the left, and odd-numbered pages are always located on the right.

Take several pieces of paper and fold them in half. Show your student how a stapled pamphlet or booklet would be made, by putting one inside of the other. Label the cover, each of the pages, and the back cover, then take it apart. Your student can see how the pamphlet is assembled (with the first piece being both the front and back cover, etc.).

Once your student understands the basic concept of constructing a pamphlet, encourage him to create his own on whatever topic interests him. Remind him that he'll need to plan each page carefully so when it is folded the pages appear in the proper order. It might be helpful to compile the number of papers he wishes his pamphlet to contain first, and fold them like a book, as described in the above paragraph. Now he can see what pages will show in what order.

When his copy (the written portion) and his illustrations are completed, he can either staple or sew his "binding" together. Be sure to let your student show off his completed booklet to friends and family!

Language Arts: Writing and Discussion Question

Some of the farmers Dr. Carver spoke with about farming could not read. Do you think adult illiteracy is still a problem in the United States? Do some research and discuss your findings. What are some ways you think would be helpful in fighting adult illiteracy?

Fine Arts: Cooking with Sweet Potatoes

Teacher's Note: Does your student's family have favorite sweet potato recipes, either eaten at "everyday" meals or for special occasions? Be sure to share those recipes with your student, as well as Dr. Carver's recipes below.

Just like Dr. Carver, your student can experiment in the kitchen using the same recipes he developed and found to be delicious. The following recipes are from Dr. Carver's booklet *How The Farmer Can Save His Sweet Potatoes* (Copyright 1937, Tuskegee Institute Press, Fourth Edition). Of course, you can always just bake a sweet potato and serve with butter, salt, and pepper—but for a bit more variety, spend some time exploring Dr. Carver's own recipes with your student today!

Recipe No. 25, Baked With Apples (delicious)

Take four medium sized sweet potatoes and the same number of apples. Wash, peel and cut the potatoes in slices about 1/4" thick; pare and slice the apples in the same way; put in baking dish in alternate layers; sprinkle 1 1/2 cups of sugar over the top, scatter 1/2 cup of butter over the top; add 3/4 pint of hot water; bake slowly for one hour; serve steaming hot.

Recipe No. 18, Croquettes

Take two cups of mashed, boiled, steamed or baked sweet potatoes; add the beaten yolks of two eggs and season with salt and pepper to taste; stir over the fire until the mass parts from the sides of the pan. When cold, form into small croquettes, roll in egg and breadcrumbs, and fry in hot oil to amber color. Serve on napkins.

Sweet Potato Biscuits

Take:
1/2 cup mashed sweet potatoes
1/2 tsp. salt
1 cup flour
4 tsp. baking powder
2 Tbs. butter or lard
milk sufficient to make soft dough

Mix dry ingredients together and then begin adding the potatoes in small batches, mixing with knife. Work the butter into the mixture with knife. Now begin adding milk, until soft dough is formed. Turn out onto floured board, pat and roll out, until 1/2" thick. Cut into biscuits; place on greased pans and bake 12 to 15 minutes at 400° F.

Life Skills: Waste Not, Want Not

George Washington Carver believed in using what he saw around him. Wasting was simply not an option. Becoming more aware of what we waste and throw away is helpful in becoming better consumers. Does your student think his family throws away too many things? Food scraps? Paper scraps? Old clothes? Plastic shampoo and soap bottles? Aluminum cans?

Encourage your student to think of at least five ways his family can recycle or reuse items on a routine basis to help cut down on wasteful living. For example, unwanted clothing can always be given to homeless shelters or charity organizations. If a sock has a hole in it, it could be mended and worn again instead of thrown away. Jeans with ripped out knees can be patched and worn as work pants or cut off to wear as shorts. Old newspapers can be rolled and formed into useful fire starter sticks. Many food scraps can be used in composting piles to create rich mulch for garden areas. Plastic products, aluminum cans, and bottles can all be collected and recycled. Partially used printer paper, the back of old school assignments and even junk mail can be cut into uniform squares on a paper cutter, and stapled into scratch note pads for use around the house.

How many more ways can your student come up with to help recycle and reuse items around his house? Learning to use what we have most effectively allows us to get more out of what we have. Using good stewardship can also benefit others and save our natural resources for future generations.

Chapter 15

Teacher Summary

Dr. Carver has now been teaching at Tuskegee for over ten years. In 1909 a new agriculture building was built, and Dr. Carver and his students had a brand-new laboratory to work in. Dr. Carver finally had so many speaking engagements, he was forced to give up teaching, but he still maintained relationships with his students. Sometimes he held special nature classes for very young children. His students and friends found him to be a sweet man who didn't care about his clothes or personal possessions. He just wanted to help people and teach them more about the world around them.

What we will cover in this chapter:

Science: Parts of a Flower*
Science: Gardening
Language Arts: Writing and Discussion Question
Life Skills: Owning A Pet

Science: Parts of a Flower*

George Washington Carver loved flowers and plants for his entire life. He devoted many years to studying them, painting them, and teaching others about them. As we near the end of our study of this famous **botanist** (an expert in the scientific study of plants), here's an opportunity for your student to study flowers in the same way a budding scientist would: by dissecting a flower, identifying its parts, and making a labeled drawing of the findings.

Flowering plants (phylum Anthophyta) contain the reproductive organs that the plant needs to reproduce. Flowers may look very different on the outside, but they share some characteristics that are illustrated below:

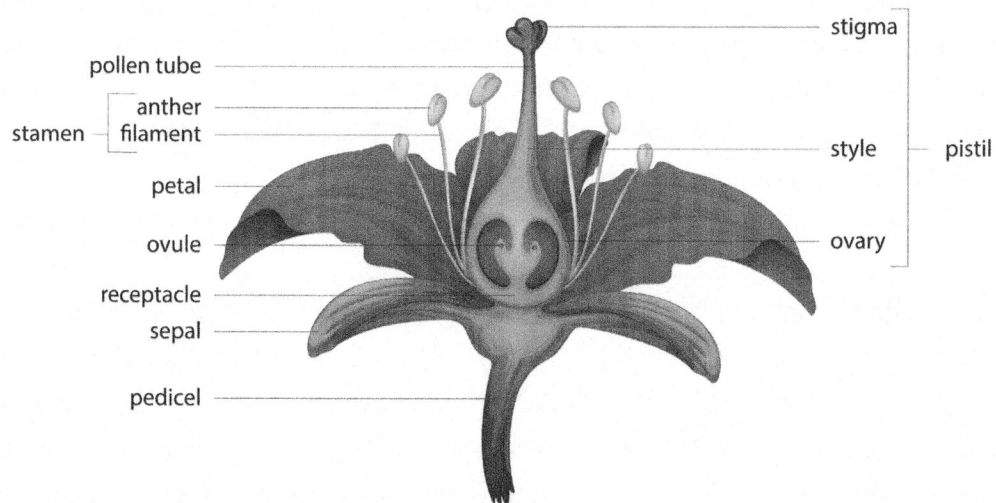

The activity sheet for this chapter will require you to obtain a large flower whose parts can easily be seen, identified, and drawn by your student (you might want to get two or three flowers and do this activity with your student!). Certain types of flowers work best for this activity—you will want ones that have structures that are clearly visible and easy to identify. Stargazer or rubrum lilies work best and can easily be found at most florists; tulips can also work. To begin your dissection, cut the flower in half, making a cross-section as in the illustration above.

After labeling the parts of his flower, your student may want to use colored pencils to make his work of science also into a work of art!

Science: Gardens and Flowers

Dr. Carver thought each child should have a little garden of his own. Why does your student think he said this? Gardening can provide children with several key learning opportunities. First, it helps teach responsibility. It can stimulate interest in educational topics like horticulture, botany, the water cycle, heredity, nutrition, art, etc. Does your student have a little garden of his own? Would he like to make one? Even in a window box or pot, a child can create a flower garden, an herb garden, or even have a tomato or pepper plant.

Gardening is a satisfying hobby. It provides exercise, keeps you in contact with the outdoors and can be very relaxing. It can also be rewarding if you are able to eat your crop!

If your student is interested, encourage him to locate some books on gardening from his local library to learn more about what is involved—watering, fertilizer, soil erosion, growing regions, plant varieties, pesticides, insects, weeding, harvesting, flower cutting, etc. If he is able, perhaps he would like to plant a garden of his own and give it a try. No matter how successful it is, Dr. Carver would have been proud!

Language Arts: Writing and Discussion Question

Dr. Carver tells his young friend, "Now take it back and turn it loose, my boy. Take it back to its mother. It is terrible when a young bird is taken from its mother." Why do you think Dr. Carver said this? Why was he upset by the baby bird being taken from its mother? What personal attachments might he have to this scenario?

Teacher's Note: This question requires your student to recall biographical information about Carver's early life and how it related to the baby bird incident. Recalling and synthesizing information to form conclusions is an important academic and life skill.

Life Skills: Owning A Pet

George Washington Carver believed that all children should be able to care for small animals. Does your student have a pet? Does he want one? Perhaps if there is an animal your student is highly interested in (or one he has always wanted to have for a pet) he can do research on all the things required for that pet. For example, lizards need heat lamps, sometimes live food, rocks, glass tanks and fearless masters. Parakeets require seed, cage, toys, grit, beak bones, papers changed each day, and an attentive owner.

Owning a pet is a great deal of fun, but it also demands a high level of commitment. Being responsible for an animal is perhaps the first way many people learn certain aspects of parenthood. If a puppy is that much work, imagine how much work a human baby would be!

When your student has done his research on a particular pet, encourage him to either write a paper or give an oral report. He can create posters and visual aids on his topic and present it to siblings, parents or friends.

Chapters 16 and 17

Teacher Summary

Dr. Carver continues to work on his experiments with the sweet potato, and then begins working with peanuts as well. He develops scores of uses for each plant and is soon being called "The Wizard of Tuskegee." Famous people like Thomas Alva Edison begin to approach Dr. Carver. They want him to come work with them, but he chooses to stay at Tuskegee. Dr. Carver wants to help support his black friends and give back to them his knowledge and training.

What we will cover in these chapters:

Social Studies: History - Royal Society
Social Studies: History - Dr. Martin Luther King, Jr.: "I Have A Dream" *
Science: Sweet Potatoes and Peanuts - The Uses and Products of Dr. Carver
Language Arts: Writing and Discussion Questions

Social Studies: History - Royal Society

Dr. Carver's experiments were so profound and exciting he was invited to join an elite group of scientists through an organization called The Royal Society of Arts. Is this prestigious group still in existence? Yes. In fact, it has been around for a very long time.

The Royal Society for the Encouragement of Arts, Manufactures and Commerce (but often called The Royal Society of Arts or RSA), this group is the world's oldest known existing scientific organization. Founded in 1754, the Royal Society is devoted to development and recognition of scientists in areas such as biology, chemistry and mathematics. The Royal Society has over 30,000 members worldwide.

Social Studies: History - Dr. Martin Luther King, Jr.: "I Have A Dream" *

Teacher's Note: Before beginning this lesson, take a few moments to review the topic of racial segregation as presented in Chapter 3 of this unit. Consider doing the activity sheet for that chapter if your student hasn't already done so. This chapter provides an excellent opportunity to introduce or expand your student's knowledge of Dr. Martin Luther King, Jr., and his famous speech on August 28,

Dr. Martin Luther King, Jr.

1963, during the March On Washington.

Why does the guard ask Dr. Carver to leave the city park? In response to the guard's request, Dr. Carver says quietly to himself, "They don't understand." Another man, famous in our history, said similar words to himself on many occasions. Dr. Martin Luther King, Jr., was a black social rights activist and Baptist minister who worked tirelessly for the end to segregation and an overall improvement in race relations in the United States.

Born in Atlanta, Georgia, in January of 1929, young Martin Luther King excelled in school and graduated from high school at fifteen. Entering Morehouse College at that same age, Martin decided to become a minister just like his father and grandfather. In 1953 King married Coretta Scott. By 1955 at the age of 26, King had obtained a bachelor's degree, a Divinity degree, and a Ph.D. in Theology.

King began his interest in civil rights in 1955 during and after the Montgomery bus system protest and Rosa Parks' stand for justice. Urged by fellow activists, King began giving speeches on his beliefs regarding civil rights and the problems America faced. Unlike some of his colleagues, however, King insisted on non-violent protests.

Although he had many successful boycotts, sit-ins and speeches, perhaps no moment more clearly defines the Civil Rights movement or King's life than his speech given on August 28, 1963, at a massive march in Washington, D.C. On that day, over 200,000 Americans (including many white people) crowded around the Lincoln Memorial. In his speech, entitled "I Have A Dream," Martin Luther King, Jr., spoke of his hope for our nation. You might want to watch and listen to the most famous parts of this speech online, but you can begin by discussing this quote from the speech:

"I have a dream that one day this nation will rise up and live out the true meaning of its creed: 'We hold these truths to be self-evident: that all men are created equal.' I have a dream that one day on the red hills of Georgia the sons of former slaves and the sons of former slaveowners will be able to sit down together at a table of brotherhood."

On April 4, 1968, while in Memphis, Tennessee, Dr. Martin Luther King, Jr., was shot and killed by a white escaped convict, James Earl Ray. On King's tombstone are the words, "Free at last, free at last, thank God Almighty, I'm free at last."

If your student is interested and you live near these areas, you may want to visit the National Civil Rights Museum located in Memphis at the site of King's assassination, or the Martin Luther King, Jr. Memorial located next to the National Mall in Washington, D.C.. Also, draw your student's attention to the third Monday in January each year—Martin Luther King, Jr., Day. It is a federal holiday honoring King, his life and his work for each of us.

Science: Sweet Potatoes and Peanuts - The Uses and Products of Dr. Carver

Dr. Carver developed over 300 uses for the peanut and over 100 uses for the sweet potato. Have your student try to guess what types of products these were and then show him the following lists and see if he is surprised by the diversity. Remind your student of Dr. Carver's favorite adage, "Waste not, want not."

Peanuts	**Sweet Potatoes**
margarine	synthetic rubber
massage oil	molasses
glycerine	starch
explosives	tapioca

Peanuts (cont.)	**Sweet Potatoes (cont.)**
paper board	dyes
plastic filler	flour
salad oil	postage stamp glue
soap	coffee
cosmetics	
insulation	
fertilizer	
illuminating oil	
medicines	
bedding for livestock	
sweeping compounds	
artificial wool	

Language Arts: Writing and Discussion Questions

1. Why do you think Dr. Carver "holed" himself away in his laboratory by the hour? What purpose could that serve? If you were conducting experiments, would you act the same way? Why or why not?

2. Dr. Carver made an entire meal out of peanuts, each different dish being made from the versatile legume. Describe what you think each dish might have been and how they would taste. Would you like to try a meal like that? Why or why not?

Chapters 18 and 19

Teacher Summary

Dr. Carver spends more and more time giving speeches all around the world. Wherever he goes, all the seats are filled. He never gets married, but instead lives alone, doing his experiments and research projects. At age 72, in 1936, Dr. Carver still lives at Tuskegee in his two-room dorm and has been at the college for 40 years. The college hires an artist to make a statue of Dr. Carver for the anniversary celebration. (Later, in 1948, the United States Post Office honored Dr. Carver with a commemorative stamp with his picture on it.)

For the next few years Dr. Carver works as much as he can on plans for the George Washington Carver Museum located at Tuskegee. He meets President Franklin D. Roosevelt while working on this project and receives a special medal for his service.

In 1941 the museum opens and Dr. Carver is there for the ceremony. Early in the morning on January 5, 1943, George Washington Carver dies at age 79. He lived a life of service.

What we will cover in these chapters:

Science: Synthetics - What They Are and How They Help Us*
Language Arts: Writing and Discussion Question
Fine Arts: Crayons and Carver
Life Skills: Living a Life of Service - Developing a Servant's Heart

Science: Synthetics - What They Are and How They Help Us*

Your student may have noticed a word he is unfamiliar with in this chpater: synthetics. Dr. Carver worked on what is now known as synthetic chemistry. Synthetic chemists work on developing new substances or compounds from two or more elements. Synthetics are things like all plastics, Styrofoam, nylon, vinyl, plastic wrap, spandex, acetate, polyester and many more.

Take a look through your kitchen—plastic bowls, plastic spoons, plastic cups, plastic plates, soap bottles, etc., are all synthetic products. Can you imagine our world without plastics? And what about your student's pajamas? Or bicycle? Or sports equipment? Or shoes? So many pieces of our daily life reflect the development and use of synthetics.

Chemists and manufacturers produce synthetics by combining elements such as carbon, nitrogen and oxygen in various quantities and under different conditions. As these compounds are formed, the chemical processes create different synthetics. The most common chemical process by which scientists can create synthetics is called polymerization. Polymerization involves converting small molecules into larger ones.

George Washington Carver was one of the first scientists in history to experiment with synthetics and realize their importance.

To help your student grasp how important synthetics have become in our daily lives, sit in a specific room and have him guess (without trying to count) how many synthetic items he thinks are around him. Then, with your help, start at one side of the room and begin listing each item he sees which is made using synthetics. You will both be amazed! Dr. Carver was truly a scientist ahead of his time. Your student may want to learn more about synthetics in general or specific plastics from library books or articles or videos online.

Language Arts: Writing and Discussion Question

Do you find it interesting that Dr. Carver refused the fame and fortune that so many offered him? Would you refuse such offers? Why? Why not?

Fine Arts: Crayons and Carver

Although our book does not include this aspect of Carver's discoveries, your student may be interested in knowing that he developed the early synthetic pigments and waxes used to make the first crayons—long before Crayola® jumped into the picture! How many young children, every day, eat a sandwich made with peanut butter (also invented by Carver) and color with crayons? Millions! Those two contributions alone have provided many children (and adults) with a great deal of enjoyment!

Why not take a break and enjoy a peanut butter sandwich in honor of Dr. Carver? And while you're at it, draw a picture with some crayons. Perhaps a portrait of the kind inventor himself, or whatever your student wishes. And while you're munching and drawing, be thankful for the inspiring spirit of creativity and servanthood Carver demonstrated through his life.

Life Skills: Living a Life of Service - Developing a Servant's Heart

When the young George Carver was first setting out on his own to Neosho to attend school, little did he know the path his life would take. Fame and fortune were certainly not his goals, but instead, to serve others and provide his fellow black brothers and sisters with tools which would enable them to help themselves. He was offered many working positions around the world from people as famous as Thomas Edison, Henry Ford and Josef Stalin. These men offered great sums of money and unlimited resources to Carver in exchange for his technical expertise and commitment. But Carver insisted on staying near his roots and serving at Tuskegee. Carver never married, and in 1940 he gave his life savings of $33,000 to the Tuskegee Institute. He asked that the funds be used to establish the George Washington Carver Research Foundation—dedicated to furthering agriculture research.

What does your student think of Carver's approach to life? Certainly not everyone is as devoted to a life of service as Carver, but we can all learn to develop more of a giving heart by looking to him as an example. What can your student do, even at his age, to help others and exhibit a servant's heart? By offering to help around the house, reading to an elderly person or grandparent, spending time with his siblings, purchasing a toy for an underprivileged child, helping out at a soup kitchen or shelter house, etc., each of us can find a few moments in our daily lives to help someone who is less fortunate. Encourage your student to think of Carver as an example of what we should each strive for in our lives.

Teacher's Notes

Use this page to jot down relevant info you've found for this
Five in a Row chapter book, including favorite lessons, go-along
resources, field trips, and family memories.

THE STORY OF GEORGE WASHINGTON CARVER

Dates studied:

Student:

Favorite Lesson Topics:

Social Studies:

Science:

Language Arts:

Fine Arts:

Life Skills:

**Relevant Library Resources:
Books, DVDs, Audio Books**

Websites or Video Links:

Related Field Trip Opportunities:

Favorite Quote or Memory During Study:

Five in Row Volume Seven

The Story of George Washington Carver - Chapter 1

Name:
Date:
History: **Genealogy - Personal Profile**

After finishing the **Genealogy - Knowing Who You Are** lesssion, you can use the questions below to begin collecting information on your personal identity and the history surrounding your birth.

All About Me

Eye color: _____

Hair color: _____

Height: _____

Weight: _____

Physical build: _____

Full name: _____

Born at (hospital, home, etc.): _____

Born on (date and time): _____

Weather on day of birth: _____

Age of parents when I was born: _____

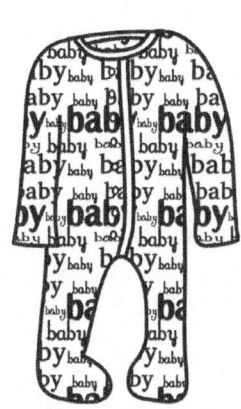

The Story of George Washington Carver - Chapter 2

Name:
Date:
Science: **Photosynthesis**

Using what you learned in the lesson **Photosynthesis - How Plants Are Fed**, color the image and fill in the blanks on this activity sheet.

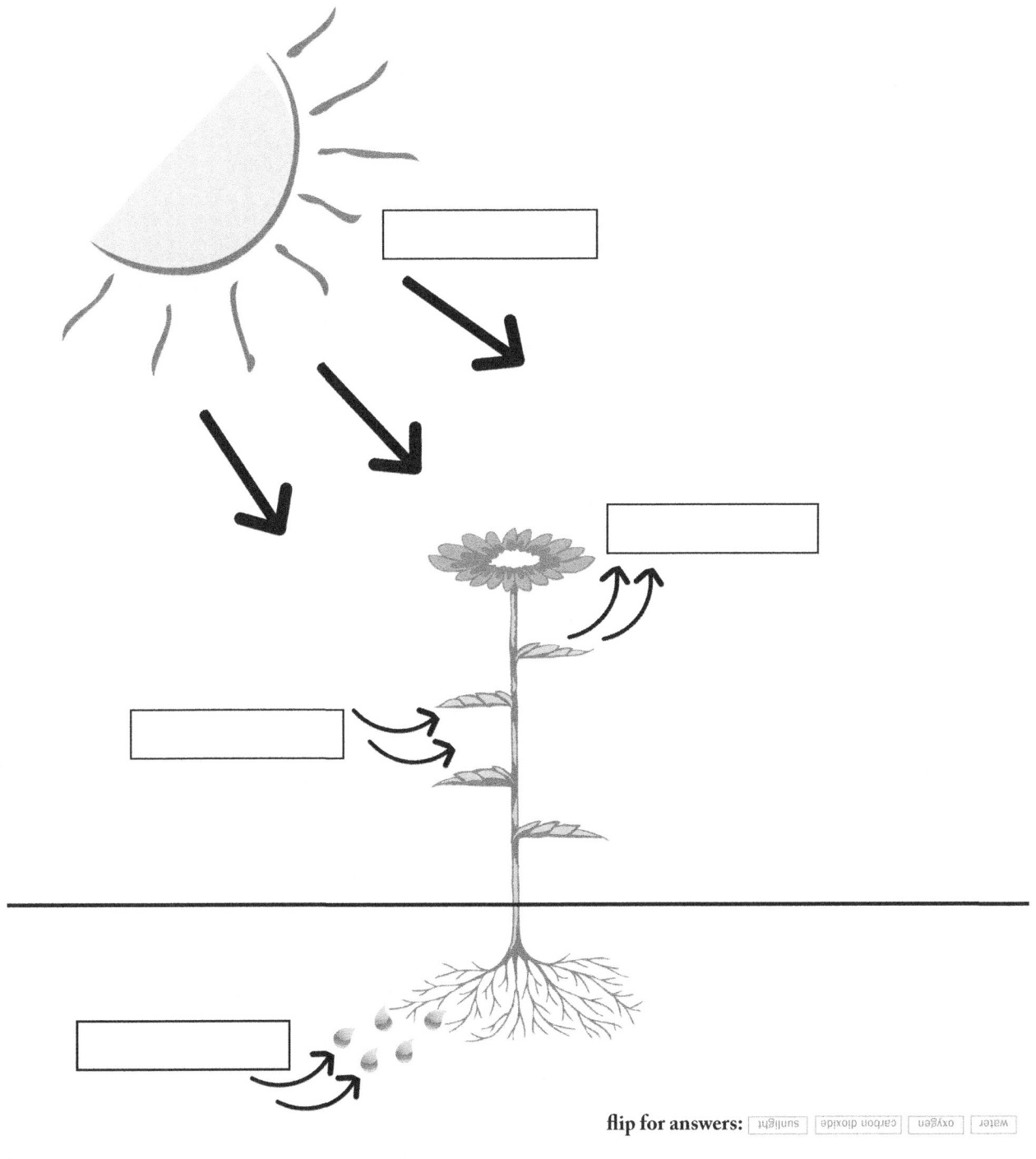

flip for answers: sunlight | carbon dioxide | oxygen | water

The Story of George Washington Carver - Chapter 3

Name:
Date:
History: **Biography - Who Am I?**

Rosa Louise McCauley Parks was an activist during the Civil Rights movement. After refusing to give up her seat on a bus, which inspired the Montgomery Bus Boycott, she became known as the "Mother of the Civil Rights Movement." Once you've completed the **History: Segregation** lesson, research Rosa Parks. You can serach online or use books from the library.

A go-along book that you could use for research is: *Who Was Rosa Parks?* by Yona Zeldis McDonough

Print and paste an image of Rosa Parks into the frame.
Write information gathered through your research into the spaces below.

Name: _____

Lived: _____

Known for: _____

_____

_____

Connections to story: _____

_____

_____

The Story of George Washington Carver

The Story of George Washington Carver - Chapter 4

Name:
Date:
Language Arts: **Vocabulary Words**

After finishing chapter four, use the crossword puzzle below to review the vocabulary words covered in **chapters 1-4**. The clues and answers are on the following page.

Language Arts: **Vocabulary Words - Crossword Continued**

The crossword clues and answers for the vocabulary words covered in **chapters 1-4** are provided below to be used with the crossword on the previous page.

Across

1. (ch. 2) a simple sugar

3. (ch. 4) the mid-range in a man's singing voice

5. (ch. 1) the study of the decent of a person from his/her ancestors

9. (ch. 2) the process by which plants convert light and water to a food source

10. (ch. 2) tiny bodies in the cells of green plants which contain chlorophyll

11. (ch. 2) knowing a lot about a particular subject

12. (ch. 2) the green pigment which fills the chloroplasts, located in the cells of green plants

14. (ch. 4) the highest range in a man's singing voice

15. (ch. 4) the highest range in a woman's singing voice

Down

2. (ch. 4) the lowest range in a woman's singing voice

4. (ch. 4) the mid-range in a woman's singing voice

6. (ch. 4) the lowest range in a man's singing voice

7. (ch. 4) a great firmness in carrying out a purpose

8. (ch. 4) two pairs of tissue membranes in the throat, near the voice box

13. (ch. 4) the upper end of the windpipe where the voice box and the vocal cords are located

flip for vocab words: soprano | tenor | larynx | chlorophyll | expertise | chloroplasts | photosynthesis | vocal cords | glucose | contralto | baritone | mezzo-soprano | Genealogy | bass | determination

The Story of George Washington Carver

The Story of George Washington Carver - Chapter 5

Name:
Date:
History: **Biography - Who Am I?**

George's questioning nature was compared to Thoma Alva Edison's in the **History - A Quick Comparison: Edison and Carver** lesson. The lesson ended with, "Great minds must often think along similar lines!"

Another brilliant scientist who encouraged questioning was Albert Einstein, who once said, "The important thing is not to stop questioning. Curiosity has its own reason for existing. ... Never lose a holy curiosity." Research Albert Einstein. You can search online or use books from the library.

A go-along book that you could use for research is:
Who Was Albert Einstein? by Jess Brallier

Print and paste an image of Albert Einstein into the frame.
Write information gathered through your research into the spaces below.

Name: _____

Lived: _____

Known for: _____

_____

_____

Connections to story: _____

_____

_____

The Story of George Washington Carver - Chapter 6

Name:
Date:
Geography: **Kansas and Missouri**

After completing the **History and Geography: Kansas and Missouri** lesson, research each of these states online or using resource books from the library and fill in answers to the questions below. Add any additional information that you learn and want to note in the final section.

Kansas

State Flower: _____

State Tree: _____

State Bird: _____

Motto: _____

Capital City: _____

Population: _____

Admission to Statehood: _____

State Nickname: _____

Origin of State Name: _____

Region: _____

Missouri

State Flower: _____

State Tree: _____

State Bird: _____

Motto: _____

Capital City: _____

Population: _____

Admission to Statehood: _____

State Nickname: _____

Origin of State Name: _____

Region: _____

Notes: _____

_____

The Story of George Washington Carver - Chapter 7

Name:

Date:

Life Skills: **Exploring Trade School Options**

After completing the **Life Skills: Education - Exploring College Applications** lesson and researching what a college application looks like, you can also look into what degrees or certificates a trade school has to offer. If there's interest, compare the application process. Trade schools offer many specialty training degrees in **health and beauty**; **technology, engeneering and media**; **manufacturing, construction and technical jobs** (electrician, pipefitter, refrigeration, heating and air conditioning, auto repair, veterinary technician); **criminal justice** and **business**. Choose three of the degree titles above and reserach what degrees a trade school offers in that category. Write a degree title into each box and then fill in the blank space below with information about that degree or about specific jobs available within that category. It's very beneficial to learn about different education options beyond high school.

Trade School Degree: _____

Trade School Degree: _____

Trade School Degree: _____

The Story of George Washington Carver - Chapter 8

Name:

Date:

Life Skills: **Ways to Earn Money and Save Money**

The lesson **Life Skills: Ingenuity - Creativity in Your Finances** discusses ways to make money and the importance of saving money. Below are a few questions about specific ways you might be able to earn and save money. Read through and consider the questions, then write your answers in next to each question and see if you discover any ways you could work, or things you could create/make, to earn money.

What skills or interests do you have? _____
_____
_____
_____

What work needs to be done? _____
_____
_____
_____

What do people around you want or need? _____
_____
_____
_____

The Story of George Washington Carver - Chapter 9

Name:
Date:
Geography: **United States - Midwest Region Map**

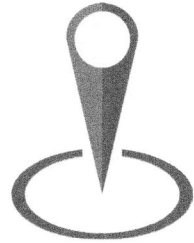

Chapter 9 sees George move to Iowa as discussed in the lesson **Geography - Iowa: A New Place for George**. George has now lived in several states in the midwest region of the United States. Use the map included in chapter 10 of our book to mark the important locations of George's life onto the map below.

The Story of George Washington Carver - Chapters 10 and 11

Name:
Date:
History and Geography: **Tuskegee University**

Virtual FIELD TRIP

Chapter 11 introduces a new location (Alabama) and a new job for George, at Tuskegee Normal School (known as Tuskegee University today). Head to www.tuskegee.edu/tours and scroll down to *virtual tour*. Take notes below of any information you learn about Tuskegee University, any famous alumni, or the degrees that the college offers. Print and paste an image of the university or an image from the George Washington Carver Museum into the frame above.

_____
_____
_____
_____
_____
_____
_____

The Story of George Washington Carver - Chapters 10 and 11

Name:
Date:
History: **Biography - Who Am I?**

In the **History: Booker T. Washington** lesson, you were introduced to a man who taught himself how to read, built a schoolhouse so that everyone could come to school, worked multiple professions before becoming the founder and director of Tuskegee Univerity, and was the most influential black leader of his time.

Booker T. Washington is a fascinating man who fought for what he believed in and is worth studying further. Research him online or use resource books from the library.

A couple of go-along books that you could use for research are:

Who Was Booker T. Washington? by James Buckley, Jr.
With Books and Bricks: How Booker T. Washington Built a School by Suzanne Slade

Print and paste an image of Booker T. Washington into the frame.
Write information gathered through your research into the spaces below.

Name: _____

Lived: _____

Known for: _____

_____

_____

Connections to story: _____

_____

Five in Row Volume Seven 183

The Story of George Washington Carver - Chapter 12

Name:
Date:
Science: **Learning About Legumes**

The **Science: Legumes - What Are They?** lesson discusses why Dr. Carver encouraged his students to plant legumes: there are many benefits that legumes offer the soil.

Serach online for "types of legumes" to see the variety of foods that are part of the legume, and therefore, the pea family. From fava beans to green peas; peanuts to pinto beans; garbanzo beans to great northern beans, alfalfa to lentils; the list goes on and on and contains so many delicious legume options.

Did you know you can make "cookie dough" from garbanzo beans (which are also known as chickpeas)? Legumes are power-packed morsels, full of fiber and protien ... so the "cookie dough" recipe below is really good for you!

COOKIE DOUGH BITES WITH LEGUMES
(or double legumes—with peanut butter)

Ingredients:
- 1 can garbanzo beans or chickpeas (drained)
- 1/3 cup peanut butter (or alternate nut/seed butter)
- 1/4 cup oat or almond flour
- 1/4 cup maple syrup (or 2 TBS brown sugar)
- 1 tsp vanilla (or almond) extract
- a pinch of salt
- 1/2 cup mini or regular chocolate chips

In a food processor, add all the ingredients except the chocolate chips and pulse until combined and fairly smooth. (If you do not have a food processor you could try to mash the chickpeas with a fork or potato masher and then add the other ingredients and stir to combine—but the result will not be smooth and the dough will be lumpy and may not taste the same.) Stir in the chocolate chips. Form dough into small balls (1 TBS or the size of a quarter is good). Chill in the refrigerator for 30 minutes. Enjoy!

The Story of George Washington Carver - Chapter 13

Name:

Date:

Science: **Insect Identification**

After completing the **Science: Insects - Identify Three New Insects Today** lesson, use the page below to document the three insects you chose to study. Draw or print and paste an image of each insect into the frames below. List the insect name and 3 facts about each insect in the blanks provided.

Insect Name: _____

Fact #1: _____

Fact #2: _____

Fact #3: _____

Insect Name: _____

Fact #1: _____

Fact #2: _____

Fact #3: _____

Insect Name: _____

Fact #1: _____

Fact #2: _____

Fact #3: _____

Five in Row Volume Seven

The Story of George Washington Carver - Chapter 14

Name:
Date:
Language Arts: **Vocabulary Words**

Use the crossword puzzle below to review the vocabulary words covered in **chapters 10-12**. It's been a few chapters since you covered these words. Review the vocabulary words in lessons 10-12 if needed before completing the crossword below.

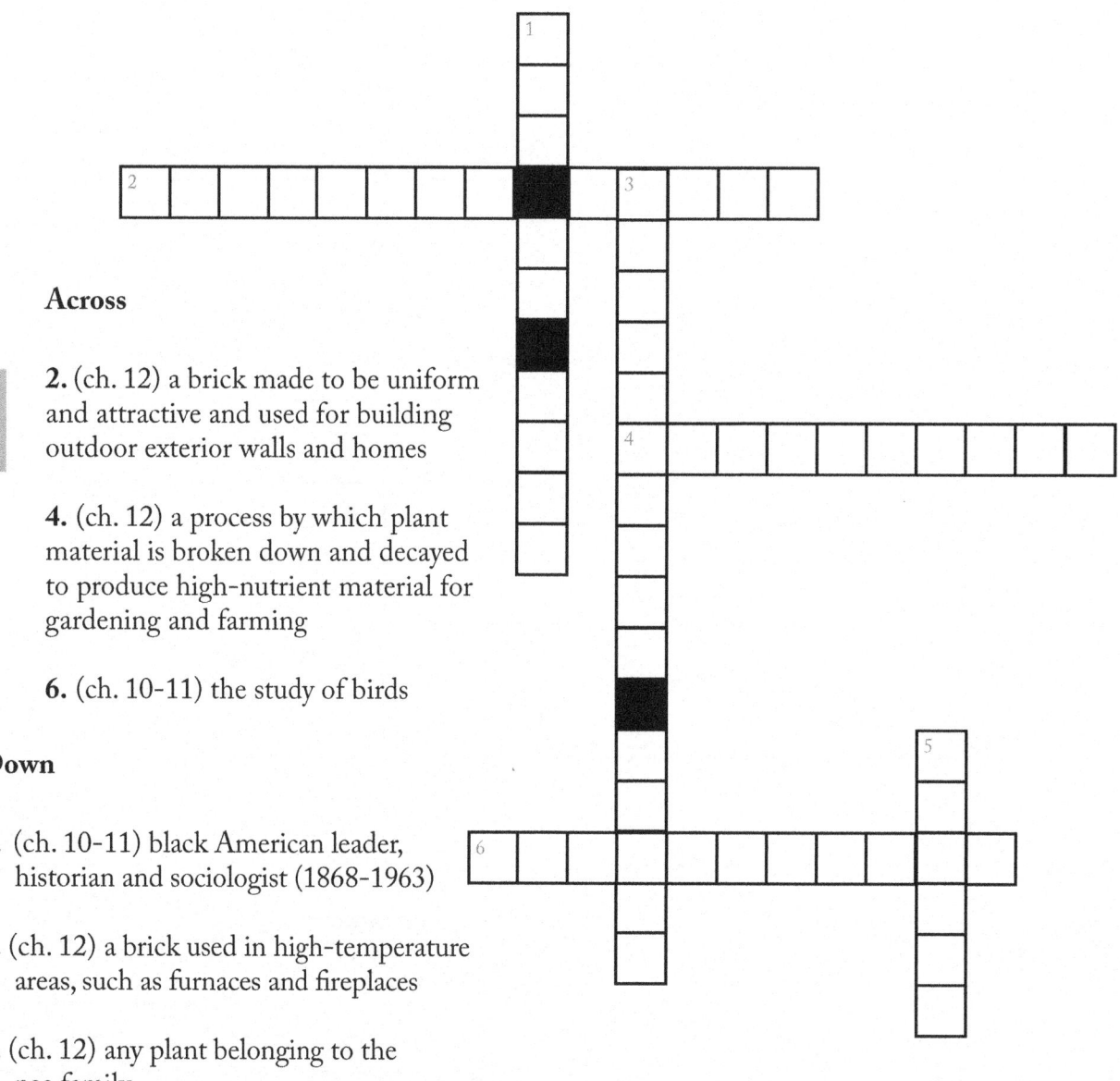

Across

2. (ch. 12) a brick made to be uniform and attractive and used for building outdoor exterior walls and homes

4. (ch. 12) a process by which plant material is broken down and decayed to produce high-nutrient material for gardening and farming

6. (ch. 10-11) the study of birds

Down

1. (ch. 10-11) black American leader, historian and sociologist (1868-1963)

3. (ch. 12) a brick used in high-temperature areas, such as furnaces and fireplaces

5. (ch. 12) any plant belonging to the pea family

flip for vocab words: composting | building brick | refractory brick | legume | W.E.B Du Bois | ornithology

The Story of George Washington Carver - Chapter 15

Name:

Date:

Science: **Flower Dissection Lab**

After completing the **Science: Parts of a Flower** lesson, use the page below to draw a cross-section of a lily (stargazer, rubrum, or another variety of large lily work best) and label the parts. Reread the lesson and use the illustration provided to guide you as you dissect, draw, and label. The parts to label are listed below.

stamen	stigma	petal
anther	style	receptacle
filament	ovary	sepal
carpel (or pistil)	ovule	pedicel

The Story of George Washington Carver - Chapters 16 and 17

Name:

Date:

History: **Biography - Who Am I?**

You learned about Dr. Martin Luther King, Jr. in the **History - Dr. Martin Luther King, Jr.: "I Have A Dream"** lesson. Research online or use resource books from the library to dig deeper and learn more about this activist and civil rights leader and his famous and often-quoted speech.

Go-along books that you could use for research are:
Martin's Big Words: The Life of Dr. Martin Luther King, Jr. by Doreen Rappaport
Who Was Martin Luther King, Jr.? by Bonnie Bader

Print and paste an image of Dr. Martin Luther King, Jr. into the frame. Write information gathered through your research into the spaces below.

Name: _____

Lived: _____

Known for: _____
_____
_____

Connections to story: _____
_____
_____

The Story of George Washington Carver

The Story of George Washington Carver - Chapters 18 and 19

Name:
Date:
Science: **Common Synthetics**

After completing the **Science - Synthetics: What They Are and How They Help Us** lesson, search online for "synthetic products made from oil and gas," to learn more about these everyday items (there are more than 6,000!).

List five items below that utilize synthetics and that you would not want to go without in your daily/weekly life. Print and paste images next to each item.

Item: _____

Item: _____

Item: _____

Item: _____

Item: _____

Five in Row Volume Seven

The Cricket in Times Square

Title: The Cricket in Times Square
Author: George Selden
Illustrator: Garth Williams
Copyright: 1960

Chapter 1—Tucker

Teacher Summary

Our story begins with an introduction to our new friend, Tucker. Tucker is a mouse who lives in an abandoned drainpipe in the subway station at Times Square in New York City. This particular evening, Tucker is finishing up a snack and watching a young boy tend his father's newsstand. The boy is named Mario Bellini.

Tucker feels sorry for Mario because no one is buying any papers or magazines. It's Saturday night, but everyone is rushing from the subway and heading home for dinner, or rushing from home to the subway and heading into the city. Tucker knows Mario works hard for his family in the newsstand. The Bellinis aren't rich and a bad selling night like this is a depressing one for Mario.

Finally, a friend of Mario's, Paul, stops by the newsstand. Paul is a conductor on the subway. Feeling sorry for Mario's poor sales, he picks up a Sunday *Times* on his way back to the shuttle. He even gives Mario an extra 25 cents as a tip. Tucker likes Paul, because Paul is kind to Mario.

Suddenly, Tucker hears a strange noise. He has never heard anything like it before.

What we will cover in this chapter:

Social Studies: History and Geography - New York State
Social Studies: History and Geography - New York City*
Social Studies: History and Geography - Mass Transit
Science: Mice
Language Arts: Organization of a Book
Language Arts: A Fantasy Story - Animals Talk
Language Arts: A Wonderful Opening Line
Language Arts: Writing and Discussion Question
Life Skills: What Is Your World?

Language Arts: History and Geography - New York State

This chapter is your student's introduction to Mario Bellini and Tucker, the mouse. It can also serve as an introduction to New York State, since that is where Mario and Tucker reside.

Begin your discussion by locating New York State on a good United States map or globe. Point out to your student that the state is bordered on its northwestern side by Lake Ontario, and on the west by Lake Erie. On the eastern side of the state your student can find the Hudson River and the Atlantic Ocean.

In a more detailed atlas or online, your student can find the state capital, Albany, and the other major cities: Buffalo, Rochester, Syracuse and, of course, New York City.

Your student may want to record a few main facts about New York. The capital is Albany. New York gained its statehood on July 26, 1788, as the 11th state. The state motto is "Excelsior" which means "ever upward." The state bird is the bluebird, and the state flower is the rose.

New York is nicknamed "The Empire State." Indeed, it has served as the leading state in the United States in banking, communications and finance. It is like a little empire. New York was also one of the original 13 colonies.

Teacher's Note: Here is a list of the 13 colonies and the dates of their first permanent settlements: Virginia (1607), Massachusetts (1620), New Hampshire (1623), New York (1624), Connecticut (1633), Maryland (1634), Rhode Island (1636), Delaware (1638), Pennsylvania (1643), North Carolina (1653), New Jersey (1660), South Carolina (1670) and Georgia (1733).

Henry Hudson, an English explorer, claimed the entire New York region for the Netherlands in 1609. The Dutch named their new land, New Netherland. The English took control of the region in 1664 and renamed it New York, in honor of the Duke of York.

Your student may find it interesting that Manhattan, one of the most expensive areas in which to live and one of the most crowded islands in the world, was bought for less than $24. According to the *Usborne Book of Countries*, after the Dutch had claimed New Netherland, they sent representatives over to explore and settle their new region. One of these Dutchmen, Peter Minuit (the governor of New Netherland) bought an adjacent island from the local Native Americans for some cloth and beads. He thought they were probably worth around $24. He

had purchased what is now known as Manhattan, but he called it New Amsterdam and claimed it as the capital of New Netherland.

Besides its current status in America's history as a leading city of finance and trade, New York City was also considered the capital of the United States from 1785 to 1790. George Washington took his oath of office as the first President of the United States in New York City. New York was the most populous state in America from 1810 until the 1960s when California stepped in as the U.S. state population leader. Share with your student that over one-third of all the battles of the Revolutionary War in America (1775- 1783) were fought in New York.

New York State is a major vacation destination in the United States. The state has such a variety of things to offer, including forests, mountains, gorgeous lakes, beaches and waterfalls. New York City itself draws more than 66 million visitors every year.

New York State, including New York City, has been referred to for many years as a "melting pot." Ask your student what she thinks that might mean. About 40 out of every 100 New Yorkers were born in other countries. New York City is a refuge and home to people from all over the world. Because of this great diversity, New York offers a wide variety of ethnic shopping, dining and trade.

If your student is interested in learning more about New York, here are some related topics she may want to explore: Erie Canal, Hudson River, Niagara Falls, the New York Yankees or Mets, etc.

Language Arts: History and Geography - New York City*

Draw your student's attention to the title of our book: *The Cricket in Times Square*. Does your student know what or where Times Square is? Explain to her that it is a specific location in New York City which is the home of the New York Theater District. More specifically, it is located at the intersection of Broadway and Seventh Avenue, between 42nd and 47th Streets. All throughout Times Square, you can find theaters showing plays, musicals and more. Locate and print or copy a simple, concise New York City map. Point out to your student where Times Square is located, and keep the map for your student's use throughout this unit study.

Because of our story's location and title, much attention will be paid to New York City in the following lessons. Your student may want to begin a small notebook or scrapbook dedicated just to her study of New York City. If your student lives near New York City, then by all means, take a field trip (or two) there so she can see firsthand the amazing sites we will be discussing.

Teacher's Note: Trying to teach a quick, summarized lesson on New York City is like trying to teach a quick lesson on the human body. It is nearly impossible! Instead of giving your student all the information at once, try to find one or two specific things that might interest her and focus on those. A discussion on Times Square is necessary, because that is the locale of our story. Other than that, select from this lesson what you think your student will appreciate or needs to know and leave the rest for later. There will be plenty of opportunities to discuss New York City throughout this unit.

New York City is the largest city in the United States, and one of the largest in the world. With a population of more than eight million, it has more than twice as many people as any other city in the United States.

New York City is considered one of the greatest cultural centers in the world due to its tremendous number of museums, art galleries, publishing houses, theaters, orchestras, dance companies, operas, and more. The Metropolitan Museum of Art (often referred to as The Met), located on the corner of Fifth Avenue and 82nd Street, is the largest art museum in the United States. It is the home to more than two million pieces of art! The museum covers more than four city blocks, but it can still only display a fraction of its pieces at any given time.

New York City is also home to many wonderful parks. In fact, New York City has more park playgrounds than any other city in the United States! Perhaps Central Park is the most famous park in New York City. Located in the middle of Manhattan, it is almost 2 1/2 miles long and 1/2 mile wide. It has beautiful rolling hills with walking paths, trees, fountains and outdoor concert areas.

Explain to your student that New York City is divided into five sections, called boroughs. They are called Manhattan, the Bronx, Queens, Brooklyn, and Staten Island. Locate each of these sections on a map with your student. Within each of these sections, there are nearly 100 different neighborhoods. Some of the neighborhoods have specific names, like Greenwich (GREN ich) Village, Chinatown or Harlem. Many of these neighborhoods are formed by the ethnic groups who live there. People tend to want to live around people like themselves. In the different boroughs, you can find Puerto Rican neighborhoods, Polish neighborhoods and others.

Five in Row Volume Seven

There are so many related lessons and explorations you can do with your student when you discuss New York City. Many of these will come up throughout our unit study, but for now, here are some ideas: the Statue of Liberty; the *New York Times*; the Empire State Building; Wall and Broad Streets (the financial district); Rockefeller Center; Radio City Music Hall (the world's largest indoor theater—5,900 seats); One World Trade Center (the rebuilt World Trade Center after 9/11/2001, now the tallest building in the U.S.); the 9/11 Memorial & Museum; United Nations Headquarters; Saint Patrick's Cathedral (one of the best examples of Gothic architecture in the United States) and so much more.

Social Studies: History and Geography - Mass Transit

Our friend, Tucker, lives in an abandoned drainpipe in the subway station at Times Square. Has your student ever seen or ridden in a subway? If your student doesn't live in a major metropolitan area, then she probably has not. Take this opportunity to share a little information with your student about mass transit.

Living in New York City is so expensive and crowded that most people don't own cars. Instead, many take taxicabs or the subway for transportation. A subway is an electric train which generally has between one and ten cars. These trains can travel at ground level, on elevated tracks or below the ground. Subways are helpful in crowded cities where heavy traffic can make the roadways slow. These electric trains are able to move many people through the city quickly, dropping them off at different destinations.

Share with your student that the first city in the world to have a subway was London. In London, people call the subway the "tube." In the beginning, London's subway trains were pulled by steam locomotives. Today, London's subways are all electric and include ten different lines which take people all over the city.

Other forms of mass transit your student might want to research include monorail systems and maglev systems. Monorail trains straddle a single rail, and are smooth and quiet. Maglev trains are moved by magnetic levitation. Has your student ever noticed how two magnets repel one another? Researchers use this

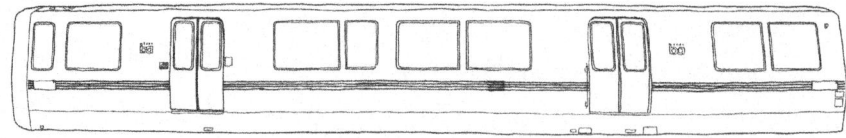

principle to float entire trains using huge magnets. A train that floats isn't slowed by the friction of wheels or rails, and speeds of over 300 miles per hour can be achieved. Maglev lines are in one or two areas of the world, but they are expensive to build and maintain.

As you continue your study of *The Cricket in Times Square*, your student can be thinking about what she has learned about subways. What would it be like for Tucker to live in a subway station?

Science: Mice

Tucker is a mouse—and a talking mouse, at that! Your student knows that mice can't really talk, but what does she know about mice, in general? Take some time to learn about these interesting and diverse animals, so that your student will understand our main character better.

There are 38 species in the genus Mus, which is the Latin word for mouse. Mice are small mammals called rodents. A rodent is an animal with special teeth formed for gnawing. Gerbils, hamsters, lemmings, voles, rats, beavers, squirrels, and capybaras are all rodents, as well as house mice, grasshopper mice, harvest mice and deer mice. Smaller rodents, like mice, often steal food from people's homes and other areas. The word mouse comes from an ancient Sanskrit (which is an ancient language of Asia) word for thief.

Tucker is probably a house mouse. House mice live wherever people live. They can live in buildings, garages, homes or anywhere else. They eat whatever people eat (breadcrumbs, cookies, meat or vegetables) and even some things people don't eat, like leather, tree trunks and glue!

A house mouse's body is usually 2 1/2 to 3 1/2 inches long, with a tail almost the same length. It has soft grayish-brown fur and a bare pink-ish tail. Its two long front teeth, which are shaped for gnawing, never stop growing. They are worn down by chewing on food and housing materials.

Man is one enemy of house mice. He sets traps and spreads poison to kill the mice. Other enemies include owls, cats, dogs, snakes and foxes, which capture and devour mice.

Other types of mice your student may want to explore include American harvest mice, grasshopper mice, deer mice and dormice.

Mice are often the subject of children's stories and poetry. One example would be the nursery rhyme "Hickory, Dickory, Dock." Here is another example:

The House Mouse

Little brown house mouse, laugh and leap,
Chitter and cheep while the cat's asleep,
Chatter and call and slip through the wall,
Trip through the kitchen, skip through the hall.

Little brown house mouse, don't be meek,
Dance and squeak and prance and tweak.
There's cheese to take and plenty of cake
So long as you're gone when the cat's awake.

Jack Prelutsky

Language Arts: A Fantasy Story - Animals Talk

Our story, *The Cricket in Times Square*, is what is known as a fantasy story. Unlike real life, the animals in the story talk with each other and humans. They have lives, feelings, conversations, homes and preferences, similar to humans.

Fantasy stories are a specific genre of children's literature. What are some other stories your student has read which fit in to this category? Perhaps she remembers *Five in a Row* books such as *Make Way for Ducklings*, *Papa Piccolo*, *Babar: To Duet or Not To Duet* and *Peter Rabbit* (and many other Beatrix Potter tales), as well as *The Lion the Witch and the Wardrobe*, *Charlotte's Web*, and *The Jungle Book*. Many children's books include talking animals.

What does your student think makes these kinds of stories so fun and interesting? Why do children like stories about talking animals? Perhaps we all wish animals could talk, so we could know what they are thinking. Sometimes animals have extremely expressive faces. We are just sure they want to tell us something.

Does your student have a pet or a favorite kind of animal? Have your student write a short (or long) story with her pet or favorite animal as the main character. This animal could speak (like Tucker), express its feelings, converse with other animal neighbors or friends, maintain a home, have specific food preferences and fashion preferences, etc.

This writing exercise will stretch and amuse your student in a variety of ways. It will also give her a greater appreciation for our author's skill at giving animals such personality and specific mannerisms. As you read further in *Cricket*, your student will see what a well-rounded character Tucker is.

Language Arts: A Wonderful Opening Line

Draw your student's attention to line 1 of our story: "A mouse was looking at Mario." Without reading further, what does your student think would most probably follow that opening line? Most people would think that the following lines would be from Mario's perspective. For example:

A mouse was looking at Mario. Mario noticed him out of the corner of his eye and stared back. He wondered what the mouse was thinking...

Instead, our author, George Selden, immediately takes us into the fantasy world of our story. His next line says, "The mouse's name was Tucker..."

Suddenly, we realize that this story will be a fantasy tale where the animals have names and personalities. Selden has introduced us to two characters and the genre of his story in just two short sentences. What a masterful writer!

Language Arts: Writing and Discussion Question

When Paul buys a newspaper from Mario, he gives him a half-dollar, instead of a quarter. Why? Write about a recent time you were generous. (**Teacher's Note:** If your student has never seen a half-dollar, get one at the bank if possible, so she can compare it with other coins. Make sure she also understands how much it is worth—twice what a quarter is worth!)

Life Skills: What Is Your World?

This chapter offers you an opportunity to discuss perspective with your student. What does your student consider her world? Here we do not mean the actual planet she lives on, but her world of friends, places she goes and things she does every day. For a person who doesn't leave home much, her world might just be her neighborhood. A business person who travels extensively, however, might feel more at home in a variety of places.

For Tucker the mouse, his main world is his little home and the surrounding area at the Times Square subway station. For Mario, his world probably includes the subway station where he works, his neighborhood, school and home.

One's perspective is the way you look at or perceive something. Depending upon where you live, what you do and where you go, your perspective of your world will change dramatically. Think about how your student's perspective of the world is different from your own.

Learning about how we are different helps us understand one another and ourselves better.

Chapter 2—Mario

Teacher Summary

Mario and Tucker both hear an unusual sound in the subway station of Times Square—the chirp of a cricket. Mario finds the cricket under some trash and is immediately delighted. Tucker watches as Mario carefully shares some of his chocolate bar with the cricket and makes him a bed out of a matchbox.

Soon, Mama and Papa Bellini come to fetch Mario and he shows them his new pet. Mama Bellini isn't happy about the new insect, but Mario's father says he can keep the cricket as long as it stays at the newsstand. Mario is thrilled and tucks his new winged friend into bed for the night.

What we will cover in this chapter:

Social Studies: Geography - Long Island
Science: Crickets*
Science: Insects Spreading Disease
Science: Matches - An Accidental Invention
Language Arts: Organization of a Book
Language Arts: Writing and Discussion Question
Language Arts: Vocabulary
Fine Arts: Garth Williams - Getting to Know Our Illustrator

Social Studies: Geography - Long Island

Mario thinks the odd sound he hears in the subway station is a cricket. He remembers hearing a similar sound when he visited his cousin on Long Island.

Here is an opportunity for your student to add to her research on New York. Find Long Island on your New York map and point out to your student how close it is to New York City. Here are some Long Island facts that you can share with your student. She may wish to include them, if she is keeping a New York notebook.

Long Island is an island that forms the southeastern part of New York. Even though it is very small, there are so many people in Long Island that its population is greater than that of 41 of the 50 states in the U.S.!

Along most of its southern shore, the island is lined with beaches including Long Beach, Westhampton Beach and Fire Island National Seashore.

One of the most important battles in the Revolutionary War—the Battle of Long Island—took place in what is now Brooklyn. There, on August 27, 1776, the British forces defeated the American troops.

Today, Long Island is covered with mostly residential areas.

Science: Crickets*

What was making that funny singing sound that Mario heard? A cricket! What does your student know about crickets? Take this learning moment to share with your student about crickets.

Perhaps your student has seen a cricket. More likely, however, she has *heard* a cricket. Like Mario, she may have heard the long, sad chirp crickets so readily make.

Crickets are jumping insects. They are related to grasshoppers, but they are slightly different. Crickets deposit their eggs from long, tube-like openings called ovipositors. The wings of most crickets lie flat on top of each other on their backs. Most crickets are black or brown, while most grasshoppers are green. And they have long, slender antennae—often longer than their entire bodies.

With your student, listen to cricket sounds online. How do crickets make that unusual song? It is mainly the male crickets that make the chirping songs; they do this by rubbing their two front wings together. Crickets hear with organs in their front legs. The chirping songs help the males and females find each other.

Crickets are found everywhere, and they generally eat plants and other insects.

The most common crickets are the house cricket and the field cricket. Both are about an inch long. If your student is interested in classifications, she may want to know that crickets are in the order of Orthoptera, and the cricket family, Gryllidae.

After viewing several crickets online or in reference or library books, try to find a live cricket, if you can!

Science: Insects Spreading Disease

Discuss with your student Mama Bellini's statement, "Bugs carry germs." Do crickets carry germs? Do other insects carry germs? If so, what kind of germs and how do they spread these germs to humans? Here is a great opportunity to introduce your student to some new discussions in science.

Teacher's Note: Mama Bellini makes the common assumption that insects are bugs, and vice versa. But is that true? Your student may want to research this interesting question. She will find that all bugs are insects, but *not* all insects are bugs! (And crickets are not bugs.)

Mama Bellini was right about bugs carrying germs. But she was wrong, as well. Not all insects carry dangerous germs (even though many can be found living

under piles of trash, or **refuse**, like Mario's cricket was). Crickets, for example, do not. In fact, the only insects that generally spread disease are insects which feed on blood—mainly fleas, ticks and mosquitoes.

These insects, which are blood-sucking creatures, spread infection and disease in a very complex manner. First, some insects obtain dangerous germs in their system by biting a person or animal already carrying that disease. As the mosquito, for example, sucks some blood into its system, the germs it obtains grow and replicate inside its body. Then, as it bites the next person, some of the tainted blood goes into that body, thus spreading the disease.

If your student is older, you may want to introduce a new science vocabulary word: **pathogen**. The germ-ridden blood of an infected insect is filled with what scientists call pathogens. (The word "pathogen" comes from the Greek prefix *pathos*, which means suffering, and the Greek suffix *gen*, which means something that is produced.)

These small micro-organisms are what carry disease into the body. Once in the body, pathogens conquer cells and tissue and use them to help the disease or illness replicate, breeding more of the disease. Scientists group different diseases by the pathogens that cause them. For example, certain sicknesses are caused by bacteria pathogens, others, by virus pathogens, and still others, by worm pathogens.

Mosquitoes can transmit dangerous diseases like malaria and yellow fever. Fleas can spread similar illnesses. Lice can carry typhus. Ticks often carry tick typhus, Lyme disease and Rocky Mountain spotted fever. Each of these diseases is transmitted by way of pathogens.

If you live in an area where Lyme disease is particularly prevalent, (i.e., Northeastern United States, Minnesota or California) then you may want to spend some time talking with your student about ways to prevent the disease. Even if you are not located in one of these high-risk areas, it is still an important and relevant topic for discussion.

Teacher's Note: Flies spread disease by picking up germs on their feet and wings. Flies are drawn to food and thus deposit germs on the foods people eat. Crickets are not generally drawn to food.

Science: Matches - An Accidental Invention

Mario lovingly makes a bed out of a matchbox for his new friend, the cricket. How the match was invented is an interesting true story to discuss with your student.

According to the book *Accidents May Happen* by Charlotte Foltz Jones, an English chemist named John Walker was working in his laboratory one afternoon. It was the year 1826 and he was trying to create a new explosive. He was working with potash (wood or furnace ashes mainly containing impure potassium, which is traditionally used in making soap) and with antimony (a brittle metallic chemical element). As he stirred the potash and antimony, a big glob of the mixture stuck to the end of his stirring stick. Walker couldn't slide the glob off, so he tried to scrape it off on the floor. As he scraped the stick across the floor's surface, his stick burst into flame! Walker had accidentally invented the first friction match! Walker named his new invention "congreves," and he demonstrated the matches in London. Unfortunately, Walker didn't patent his invention, and just ten years later Alonzo Philips, an American in Springfield, Massachusetts, obtained a patent for friction matches and began to mass-produce them.

Average estimates now say that Americans strike over 550 billion matches every year!

Your student also may be interested in learning that there is a name for people who collect matchboxes and matchbooks—phillumenists. Phillumeny can be a fun way to begin collecting things. Matchbooks are inexpensive but have become harder to find. In the past, they were often free in hotels, restaurants and stores.

Teacher's Note: Please caution your student about the dangers of playing with matches.

Remind your student that some of the best inventions in the world have come about because of accidents. When we work on scientific ideas and theories, never discount the importance of experimenting. Sometimes we may discover something we weren't even expecting!

The author of the above book, *Accidents May Happen*, has also written a more recent book called *Mistakes That Worked: 40 Familiar Inventions & How They Came to Be*. This is a high-interest, fun book for readers of all ages to enjoy!

Language Arts: Organization of a Book

One of the basic subjects every middle grader should understand is how a book is organized. Although you may have already discussed this with your student in previous *Five in a Row* studies, why not use *The Cricket in Times Square* as another example?

Explain to your student that all books share certain sections in common. Depending on the type, a specific book, however, may have extra sections. Here is a list of the basic parts of a book. Look over it with your student (or have her copy the list) and discuss which sections are included in *The Cricket in Times Square*.

1. The title page: This is usually the first printed page in a book. It gives you very important information: (1) the full title of the book, (2) the author's name, (3) the publisher's name and (4) the place of the publication.

2. The copyright page: This is the page directly following the title page. On the copyright page, you will find the publication or copyright date, as well as the publisher's name and address, the author's name(s), the ISBN (a unique number given to each book published), and any notes from the publisher on this particular printing.

3. The preface: This section could include a foreword, introduction or acknowledgment, as well. This part of the book might tell you what the book is about, why it was written, who helped or to whom it is dedicated.

4. The table of contents: This section tells you how the book is divided (chapters, topics, units, etc.) and where to find each section.

5. The body: This is the main section of the book.

6. The appendix: This follows the body of the book and may include maps, charts, diagrams, or other extra information.

7. The glossary: This is the "dictionary" portion of a book. It will include an alphabetical listing of words with which you may not be familiar and will include definitions, pronunciations, etc.

8. The bibliography: This is a list of books or articles the author used as sources when preparing to write her manuscript.

9. The index: This is an alphabetical listing of all important topics appearing in the book along with pages where they will be found. It is a little like the table of contents, but much more detailed.

Our story, *The Cricket in Times Square*, is a fiction book. Fiction books usually include a title page, copyright page, table of contents and body. Sometimes, depending upon the author's wishes, you will see an acknowledgment, a preface, a dedication and/or a bibliography included.

Your student will probably notice that *The Cricket In Times Square* doesn't have many of the sections listed above. This is because nonfiction books tend to have more of the other sections, including an introduction or preface, glossary or index. If you have a nonfiction book handy with some of these sections in it (for instance, the *Five in a Row* manual that you're reading now!), show it to your student or have her find them on her own. Or encourage your student to go through her own bookshelves (or yours!) to see what is included in each. She may also want to employ some of these sections in stories of her own. For example, she might wish to write a preface to a story she has written, or to design a title page.

Language Arts: Writing and Discussion Question

Papa Bellini doesn't want to argue with his wife. He is very good at avoiding confrontations. Is avoiding confrontations always a good thing to do? Why or why not?

Language Arts: Vocabulary

monochromatic palette   A palette using only one color.

refuse   Garbage or trash.

Fine Arts: Garth Williams - Getting to Know Our Illustrator

Look with your student at the beautiful, soft illustrations in the first two chapters of our book. Can your student guess who the illustrator is from these pictures? Your student may have read other books illustrated by this same person—Garth Williams. Mr. Williams is best known for his illustrations in E. B. White's *Stuart Little* and *Charlotte's Web*, Laura Ingalls Wilder's *Little House on the Prairie* series, and our story, *The Cricket in Times Square*. He also illustrated for authors such as Margaret Wise Brown, Russell Hoban and Randall Jarrell.

Before you discuss his illustrations and art techniques, share with your student a brief introduction to the man, Garth Williams, and his life.

Garth was born in New York City in 1912. His family was supportive of his talents and also very involved in the art community. His father was a cartoonist and his mother was a landscape painter. As he said, "Everyone in my [childhood] home was always either painting or drawing." Not all artists have had the benefit of such family support.

When he was a young man, his family moved to England and Garth studied painting and sculpture at the Royal Academy of Arts. He moved to Italy and immersed himself in art, but was soon called to serve during World War II. He worked as a Red Cross ambulance dispatcher.

After the war, Mr. Williams returned to the United States. His work was rejected many times, but he was able to publish a few small drawings in *The New Yorker*. Author E.B. White had seen these drawings and liked them. When he sent his final manuscript of *Stuart Little* to Harper and Row Publishing, he attached a small note to the front. It said, "Try Garth Williams." This was the break Mr. Williams had been waiting for.

From then on, Garth Williams worked steadily as an illustrator. During the 1950s, Garth and his wife, Leticia, built a hacienda (a country house on a large estate) in Guanajuato, Mexico. He lived there off and on for the next 40 years and died on May 8, 1996, at the age of 84. Garth and his wife had five children.

What medium does your student think Mr. Williams used for *The Cricket in Times Square*? His illustrations appear to be pen and ink. Draw your student's attention to Mr. Williams' attention to facial expressions. In the first illustration, we see Mario yelling to passing customers. In the second, we see a different Mario—quiet, happy and reflective as he looks at his new friend. Garth Williams is also a master at cross-hatching and shading. Even with a **monochromatic (one-color) palette**, he creates depth, shadow and fullness by using many lines in certain places and just a few in others.

Let your student try her hand at pen-and-ink-type drawings. Ballpoint pens do not work as well as very fine-point markers for this type of exercise. Your student can try to draw like Mr. Williams—using many lines to shade and create shadows, and to draw expressive faces.

Garth Williams loved his work and enjoyed expressing himself through art. He also loved children's literature. He believed that books, "given, or read, to children can have a profound influence." He always worked to "awaken something of importance ... humor, responsibility, respect for others, interest in the world at large."

Chapter 3—Chester

Teacher Summary

Tucker explores the newsstand and finds the cricket's matchbox bed. He introduces himself to the cricket and finds out that his name is Chester Cricket. The two share some liverwurst, and Chester tells Tucker the tale of how he arrived at Times Square.

Chester is from Connecticut. He is a country cricket. One day he was stealing a few nibbles from a family's picnic basket and didn't realize that they were getting ready to leave. Suddenly, he found himself stuck in the picnic basket and on his way to a place he didn't know. When the family stopped to switch trains, he managed to jump out of the picnic basket and found himself in the subway station at Times Square.

Tucker thinks the story is very exciting, and assures Chester that he will love New York City. Chester is suddenly frightened by a large looming cat standing over Tucker. He tries to warn Tucker, but he fears it's too late!

What we will cover in this chapter:

Social Studies: Geography - Connecticut
Science: Bird Migration*
Language Arts: Creative Writing Exercise
Language Arts: Post-Writing Skills - Editing and Proofreading
Language Arts: Writing and Discussion Question
Language Arts: Vocabulary
Life Skills: Making New Friends

Social Studies: Geography - Connecticut

As Chester Cricket begins his amazing tale, we learn he is from Connecticut. Take this opportunity to discuss Connecticut with your student. She can add this information to her notes on New York, since it is a neighboring state. She may even wish to expand her notebook to include other nearby states.

Chester Cricket considers himself a "country cricket." Compared to New York City, much of Connecticut does seem rural. Connecticut is, however, a state brimming with people and alive with many bustling towns.

Known as the Constitution State, Connecticut became the fifth state in the U.S. in 1788. It is located just northeast of New York City, above Long Island Sound. Its capital is Hartford. Locate Connecticut on a map with your student and point out how close Chester Cricket really is to his home. For a cricket, however, it would be a very long distance.

Connecticut is the only state in the country which has more than just a state bird, song and tree. Connecticut has a state hero—Nathan Hale. Your student may have heard the famous quote, "I only regret I have but one life to lose for my country." That was spoken by Nathan Hale before he was hanged in 1776. He was a spy for General George Washington and was caught by British soldiers. Hale was born in Coventry, Connecticut.

Connecticut is the third smallest state in the country. Only Rhode Island (the smallest state) and Delaware are smaller. If your student needs help finding a

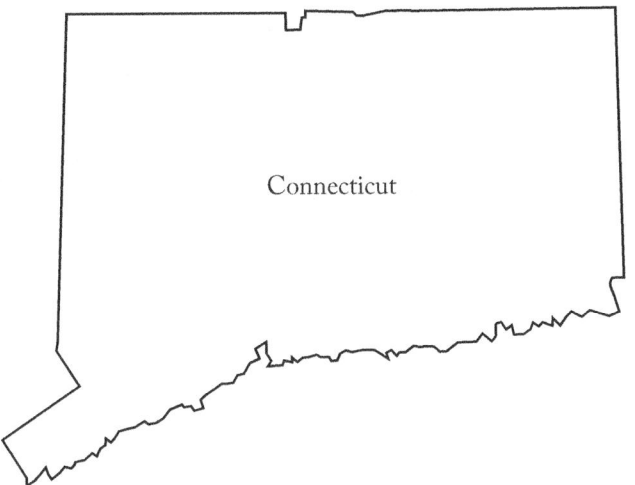

perspective for Connecticut's size, compare it to the largest state, Alaska. Connecticut is so small it would fit into Alaska almost 120 times!

Many famous people besides Nathan Hale were born in or lived in this small state. They include: Ralph Nader, Katharine Hepburn, Paul Newman, Charles Henry Dow, P. T. Barnum, Eli Whitney, Benedict Arnold, Noah Webster, George W. Bush and Samuel Clemens (Mark Twain). Any one of these individuals would make an excellent subject for your student to research for a book or oral report.

Your student may do more research on Connecticut to learn about its natural resources, agricultural products and manufactured goods.

Teacher's Note: Point out to your student that while Connecticut is pronounced kuh-NEH-tuh-kuht, it is spelled in an unusual way (the second "c" is silent). Show her that if she first spells "connect," and then adds "i-cut," she will spell it correctly! The state name comes from an Algonquian (Native American) word, quinetucket, meaning "beside the long tidal river" (the Connecticut River).

Science: Bird Migration*

Chester has never been to New York City, but he has heard of it. Reread the following excerpt with your student:

"You were never here before?" Tucker asked.

"Goodness no!" said Chester. "But I've heard about it. There was a swallow I used to know who told about flying over New York every spring and fall on her way to the North and back."

What an excellent opportunity to introduce animal migration to your student! Your student may have noticed that certain birds seem to be around for one season and gone the next. But does she know why? Does she know where they go?

Many animals leave their home for a season (migration) and then return later. Your student may ask, "But why do animals leave in the first place?" Talk with your student a little about what an animal needs. All animals need food, water and shelter where they can be safe and raise their young.

Seasonal animal migration usually is caused by temperature fluctuations. If a bird such as an oriole, hummingbird, or swallow (there are many others) needs warmth, in order to find food and lay and hatch eggs, then it will have to leave the northern states in the winter and fly south. When temperatures drop, many animals are forced to find warmer climates or they will die.

Some birds, like Chester's friend the swallow, have very lengthy migration routes—often over 1,500 miles! It is easier to understand why birds (and other animals) leave their homes and migrate for a season

than to determine how they know when to leave, and how they find their way back home!

Change in temperatures and hunger seem to be the main clues for a bird's initial departure. But how do birds know which way to go? Scientists, using homing devices and artificial satellites, have been studying the migration of birds for many years now. They now know a little bit about how birds find their way.

The bird has a poor sense of smell, but excellent sight! Birds seem to see and memorize landmarks much as we do. When you leave your house to go to the store, you quickly recognize certain streets and shops that lead you there. Birds do the same thing. This excellent memory and vision seems to account for many birds' abilities to find their way. But it doesn't tell the whole story. By means of experiments with light and shadows, scientists have found that birds seem to direct themselves by using the position of the sun. When migrating swallows are placed in an atrium of glass, they face the direction they should be flying, according to the sun coming through the windows. However, on cloudy days, the birds seem restless and a bit confused. Scientists experimented by shining an artificial sun from a different position. The birds immediately shifted to adjust to this new position. Birds seem to have almost an "internal compass" which allows them to read the sun and know where to fly.

Many other animals besides birds migrate. Your student may want to research the migration patterns and lives of seals, fish, penguins, bats, butterflies or even bees.

The next time your student notices a new bird in her area, remind her of your study of migration. It is truly an amazing aspect of nature.

Language Arts: Creative Writing Exercise

Mr. Selden describes a delicious picnic lunch: "They had hard boiled eggs, and cold roast chicken, and roast beef, and a whole lot of other things besides the liverwurst sandwiches..."

Encourage your student to practice her creative writing skills by assigning her the following project. Have her describe, in detail, her idea of the perfect picnic lunch. Urge your student to fill in every detail she can think of—the basket, linens, food (appearance and taste), beverages, etc. She can either set her lunch description in a new story, write it on its own, or set the description into our story, *The Cricket in Times Square*, as though it were the lunch Chester smelled.

Perhaps when this exercise is completed, your student can fix one or more of the items for lunch and actually partake of her imaginary meal.

Language Arts: Post-Writing Skills - Editing and Proofreading

One important aspect of your student's language arts education should be the study and practice of post-writing skills. Post-writing skills include editing and proofreading her work.

As her teacher, take into account what you know of your student's abilities in this area. Does she seem to understand the concept of (1) drafts, (2) revising, (3) editing and (4) proofreading? If you think these are unfamiliar concepts, or your student needs a review in these areas, take some time to discuss them with her.

Teacher's Note: Be sensitive to your student's age and abilities, and tailor this lesson accordingly. For certain students, erasing words and adjusting spelling is all the post-writing they can handle. For other students, however, the skills discussed in this lesson are appropriate and important to practice.

1. Drafts

As your student is writing anything (reports, creative pieces, research papers, etc.), it is important for her to remember that her first draft of the project is just that—a draft. She may change a little, most of, or all of what she has written. An easy way of working through a draft is to write it on every other line (or double-space on a computer). This way, when she looks back over her work, she can make notes (preferably in a different color pencil or pen) between the lines. Some writers end up writing two, three or even ten different drafts of a project before they are happy with the results.

2. Revising

After your student has written her first draft (or subsequent drafts) remind her to revise. Revising a piece of work means you look over your writing, searching for certain things. Perhaps you think of an example, description or line of dialogue that you feel will help enrich and clarify the text. It is also important during revising to review your sentences and paragraphs. Are they clear? Are they concise? Are they correct? Always think of your readers—will they understand?

It is helpful, during the revision process, to let someone else look over your work. Perhaps something that you thought was clear will not make sense to your reader. You can then work to clarify that part of your writing.

3. Editing

After you have completed your writing and revising, it is time to begin the editing process. Sit down with your text and look it over carefully for any mistakes. Check spelling, punctuation, definitions, capitalization, grammar and so on. Ask a teacher or friend for help if you need to. Fix all errors you find. When you're finished editing, you can either type or neatly write out a final copy of your writing.

Remind your student that when she is writing something, she is in the process of creating. When you are creating, it's difficult to also be correcting. No matter how good your vocabulary is or how accomplished you are with grammar, you will make some mistakes when you write. This is normal. However, to be a good writer, it is important to go back and review what you've written. After you've created, it's time to clarify.

4. Proofreading

When your student has her final copy finished, it is important to do a final check. This is called proofreading. Check for any accidental misspellings or forgotten punctuation. After all this work, words can begin to all look the same. When you're proofreading, it's helpful to also have someone else check your work. They can be more objective and notice problems more quickly because they are less familiar with it than you are.

To help your student practice editing and proofreading, rewrite and print a portion of our chapter, making errors, leaving out punctuation, taking out capital letters, etc. Here is an example—the corrections your student should make are located in parentheses:

Inside the drain pipe, Tuckers ('s) nest was a jumble of papers, scraps of cloth, buttons, lost jewelry, small change, and everything else that can be picked up in a subway station. Tucker tossed thinkgs (things) left and right in a wild search. Neatness was not one of the things he aimed at in life (.)At last he discovered what he was looking for: a big piece of liverwurst he had found earlyer (earlier) that evening. It was meant to be for breakfast tomorow (tomorrow), but he decided that meeting his first cricket was aspecial (a special) occasion. Holding the liverwurst between his teeth, he whisked back to the newsstand.

"Look!" he said proudly, dropping the meat in front of Chester cricket (Chester Cricket). "Liverwurst! You continue the story—well (we'll) enjoy a snack too."

Create the "mistakes" according to your student's level and abilities. Proofreading is a learned skill and practice sessions like the one above can help your student hone this skill.

Language Arts: Writing and Discussion Question

If you were Chester and suddenly found yourself in a completely foreign town or city, what would you do?

Language Arts: Vocabulary

(These words are all found in Chapter 3.)

scrounging Searching about for what you can find.

eavesdropping Listening secretly to a private conversation.

haunches The hindquarters of an animal; back legs.

liverwurst A sausage made from liver.

tuffet A small bunch of weeds or grass; a little mound.

forlorn Alone and sad.

Life Skills: Making New Friends

Talk with your student about Tucker and Chester and their new friendship. Tucker is a very kind and friendly mouse, isn't he? He knows Chester Cricket is new to the neighborhood. As soon as he is able, he introduces himself. He also finds out what Chester likes (liverwurst) and shares some with him.

Introducing yourself to someone new can be a little scary. It may help to think of a time when you were in a new situation and wanted to meet a friend. Encourage your student to follow Tucker's example the next time she meets a new person. Introduce yourself, and talk with her about something she's interested in. If you have something to share verbally, go ahead. People will appreciate your student's forthright and friendly attitude—and she'll make new friends!

Chapter 4—Harry Cat

Teacher Summary

Chester's fears of the cat are short-lived. The cat turns out to be Tucker's best friend, Harry Cat. Chester has never seen a cat and mouse be friends before. He soon learns to like Harry.

Chester, at Tucker's request, shows Harry his amazing talent of chirping. Harry is appropriately impressed. The animals talk a little more, and Tucker decides it's time for Chester to see Times Square. They go up through many pipes and are soon standing on the street. Chester is overwhelmed by the city scene. Being a country cricket, he has never seen anything like Times Square. He is glad when they go back down into the station and he is able to snuggle into his matchbox.

What we will cover in this chapter:

Science: Germs - Bacteria and Viruses
Science: Chemical Element - Neon*
Language Arts: Oral Reading

Five in Row Volume Seven 209

Language Arts: Nonverbal Communication
Language Arts: Writing and Discussion Question
Language Arts: Vocabulary
Fine Arts: Perspective - Near and Far
Life Skills: Silver Linings

Science: Germs - Bacteria and Viruses

Harry, Chester and Tucker discuss Mama Bellini's fear of germs. Share with your student the information about bacteria and viruses listed below.

Your student knows when she feels sick. Her head and body may ache. She may feel very hot or very cold. Her throat might feel scratchy. Why? Germs are often the cause, but how they work against us is a bit more complicated.

To begin, explain to your student there are two main kinds of germs which make us ill—**bacteria** and **viruses**. Bacteria are very tiny and microscopic. Once classified as plants, they are now classified with other single-celled organisms in Kingdom Monera. Using a microscope, scientists can see what bacteria look like. They are shaped in many ways, but sometimes they are spherical balls or rod-like sticks or even spirals. Viruses are even smaller than bacteria.

Bacteria and viruses are all over our world. They are in the water, air and on everything you see. But they don't always make you sick. Some aren't harmful (some bacteria are even beneficial to us), and most of the time your body successfully keeps the harmful bacteria out. The skin works like armor and helps keep germs out. The hairs in our noses catch germs and push them back out. But sometimes, harmful germs do make it in and we get sick.

Discuss with your student that bacteria and viruses attack our bodies in different ways. Bacteria multiply in and on the body. Just a few bacteria can quickly become thousands, even millions. As they increase, they also give off waste products. These waste products are harmful and poisonous to our bodies. As the poisons float through our bodies, they can injure and kill off cells. If they get to enough cells, you begin to feel sick.

When you have a bacterial infection, a doctor can prescribe medicine for you that will kill the bacteria or stop it from multiplying. In a few days, you'll begin to feel better!

Viruses are different from bacteria. Even though they are smaller than bacteria, they are even fiercer. A virus pushes its way into a cell. Inside the cell, it multiplies. Soon, there are so many viruses inside, the cell eventually explodes, releasing all those dangerous viruses into your body. Each virus then invades another cell and the chain begins again. Sicknesses caused by viruses include the common cold, flu, measles and chicken pox, among others. Unfortunately, scientists do not have medicines developed yet that can cure illnesses caused by viruses. Instead, we treat the symptoms. However, some diseases can be prevented by shots called **immunizations**. In this way, you won't get sick in the first place.

There are several things we can do to help ourselves stay healthy. Can your student think of a few? Here is a basic list:

1. Wash your hands often with soap and warm water. (Handwashing kills germs!)

2. Eat healthy meals.

3. Get plenty of sleep at night.

4. Exercise each day.

5. Visit your doctor and dentist regularly for checkups.

6. Get your immunizations.

Your student may want to make a poster or pamphlet with these—and any additional—"rules for health." She may wish to draw illustrations for each rule, design the layout, experiment with lettering (using either stencils, handwriting or computer fonts) and much more. She can also come up with a clever title for her list. For example: "Getting Healthy, Staying Healthy" or "The War Against Germs." When she is finished, perhaps she can show her work to a grandparent, friend or younger sibling.

Science: Chemical Element - Neon*

As Chester looks around him in Times Square, he sees the bright neon lights. Neon is a chemical element with which your student may or may not be familiar. Can she find it with the gases on a periodic table of elements?

Neon was discovered by two British chemists in 1898—Sir William Ramsay and Morris W. Travers. Neon is the Greek word for "new."

Neon is normally a gas and makes up about 1/65,000 of the earth's atmosphere. It is colorless, odorless and doesn't react with other substances. Neon can be liquefied if it is pressurized enough, and it is this liquid which is most often used for lamps and signs. By itself, neon is a reddish-orange. When a small amount of mercury is added to it, neon turns a brilliant blue.

Search online for pictures or videos of Times Square in order to show your student the neon lights. Point out to your student neon signs in shop windows or restaurants.

Language Arts: Oral Reading

An important language arts skill your student should be practicing is oral reading. Many children begin to read by sounding out words and reading out loud to themselves. In time, most children begin to read silently. Both silent and oral reading are important, however, and neither should be overlooked. In this lesson, we will use portions of chapter 4 as practice pieces for your student.

For some children, oral reading is no struggle. For others, it may be more difficult. Consider several criteria when listening to your student read aloud.

1. Does she speak clearly?
2. Does she show punctuation through voice inflection and pauses?
3. Can she follow the writing and maintain a good pace?
4. Does she read with expression or in a monotone?

Use a portion of chapter 4 as practice for your student. A nice section for this purpose begins near the end of the chapter with, "They were standing at one corner of the Times building," and continues to the end of the chapter. This section contains a lot of description and details, some dialogue and several transitions.

Throughout this unit, you may wish to select different sections of text for your student to use for oral reading practice. Most oral reading difficulties are smoothed out by practice alone. If you sense your student has problems reading which are not getting better, however, you may wish to step up your own oral reading to her. This is a great way to spend a special time together enjoying great books, building vocabulary and oral reading skills in your student and making memories to last a lifetime. It will also help your student to read aloud clearly and effectively.

Language Arts: Nonverbal Communication

When Chester Cricket sees the cat looming behind Tucker, he tries to warn him. Our author writes, "The cricket began to make frantic signs that the mouse should look up and see what was looming over him."

Chester Cricket was trying to warn Tucker by using nonverbal communication. Discuss with your student different types of nonverbal communication.

Facial expressions are ways we communicate nonverbally. For example, we can tell if someone is scared, happy, sad, angry or giddy simply by the way her facial muscles and eyes express these emotions. Body movements can also be used to communicate emotions. If a person has a stooped back and lowered head it might tell us she is tired, depressed or lonely.

Another way we communicate without words is through gestures. A hand motioning toward the body can tell someone far away to come over closer. A wave of the hand means goodbye. Holding up your index and third fingers means the number two.

Every person and culture in the world uses nonverbal communication constantly. If two people speak different languages, they can often still communicate with gesture and expression. Even people who are blind from birth use hand gestures and facial expressions as they are speaking.

There are two categories of nonverbal communication—**kinesics** (kin EE sicks) and **proxemics** (prox EE micks). Kinesics is the study of facial expressions and body movements, in conjunction with language. A scientist who studies kinesics might watch a person telling a joke and observe the eye movement (anticipating telling the punchline), the mouth (trying to stay deadpan), etc. Proxemics is the study of personal space and how much separation people maintain between each other in social situations. A scientist studying proxemics will look at two people talking and realize that one of the individuals doesn't feel comfortable. The scientist can see this by the person stepping back a bit, holding his arms crossed and so on.

Nonverbal communication is second nature to all human beings. Discuss with your student things she notices about nonverbal communication. For example, when she meets someone new, does it make her feel more comfortable if they are smiling? How does she feel if someone stands a little too close (or a little too far away) when speaking to her? Learning more about nonverbal communication can help us communicate our own feelings better to others, and help us read others more clearly as well.

Language Arts: Writing and Discussion Question

Chester Cricket feels a little intimidated by the big city. Do you ever feel intimidated by people or situations? Write about one time that you did and what you did to overcome your intimidation.

Language Arts: Vocabulary

kinesics   The study of body and facial movements, in conjunction with language.

proxemics   The study of personal space and how much separation people maintain between each other in social situations.

bacteria   A type of microscopic, single-celled organism that can be either helpful or harmful in our bodies.

virus   A type of germ which invades a cell and multiplies within the cell; viruses cause certain infectious diseases such as rabies, polio, chicken pox and the common cold.

immunizations   Shots which help prevent certain illnesses.

Fine Arts: Perspective - Near and Far

Look, with your student, at Mr. Williams' illustration near the end of the chapter of the people standing in Times Square. This illustration is an excellent example of perspective.

Draw your student's attention to the large buildings in the foreground of the picture and the smaller buildings in the background. Point out the larger people in the foreground, as well as the smaller people in the background. The people in the bottom left-hand corner are incredibly tiny! Ask your student what these different sizes show? The larger the object, the closer it appears, right? (Your student may remember a similar lesson from *All Those Secrets of the World*, FIAR Vol. 2.)

The picture makes us feel very close to the buildings and people, and it also shows us how long the street is. All the buildings and people, growing smaller and smaller toward the back, make Times Square look large and deep.

Garth Williams also effectively illustrates how small Chester, Tucker and Harry are. Notice how the buildings disappear into the top of the illustration. Not being able to see the top makes buildings seem even taller, doesn't it?

Here is what your student can learn about perspective in drawing by studying this one picture:

1. Drawing certain objects larger makes them appear to be closer; drawing them smaller makes them appear to be far away.
2. Drawing many objects, one behind the next, smaller and smaller, gives the picture depth.
3. Failing to draw the absolute top of objects gives them the appearance of being larger.

Encourage your student to try to draw a picture using these techniques. She can try one or all of them.

Life Skills: Silver Linings

Has your student ever heard the expression, "Every cloud has a silver lining?" What does it mean? People use this expression to say that even during difficult experiences, we can find something good.

Talk with your student about Chester Cricket being carried from Connecticut to New York City. The ride was certainly not pleasant, and Chester seemed genuinely frightened. However, Tucker Mouse seems to think the ride could be a good thing, too, when he says to Chester, "...Why don't you give the city a try? Meet new people—see new things. Mario likes you very much."

New experiences and new friends are Chester's "silver lining." Share with your student a time when you didn't think a silver lining was possible, and then how you found one. Learning to look for the positive in our relationships and experiences helps to keep us happy and healthy. Encourage your student to try to avoid focusing on negative experiences she has, and instead to look for a "silver lining" just as Tucker did.

Chapter 5—Sunday Morning

Teacher Summary

The next day is Sunday, and Mario returns to the newsstand with his father. Mario is very excited to see how his cricket is doing, and he brings him breakfast—a crust of bread, a lump of sugar and a cold Brussels sprout.

After breakfast, Mario takes his new pet over to visit his friend Mickey at the lunch counter. Mickey likes the cricket and fixes Chester a special cricket-size strawberry soda. Mario gets some, too!

Back at the newsstand, one of Papa Bellini's best customers, Mr. Smedley, stops by to buy his monthly copy of *Musical America*. Mr. Smedley is impressed by the cricket as well, and he loves to hear him chirp.

Mario soon leaves for Chinatown. He wants to find a little house for his cricket.

What we will cover in this chapter:

Social Studies: History and Geography - Italy
Social Studies: History - Mythology: Orpheus
Language Arts: Meet Our Author - George Selden
Language Arts: Writing and Discussion Question
Fine Arts: Opera - It's Not Boring
Activity Sheet: Vocabulary Words*

Social Studies: History and Geography - Italy

Teacher's Note: Your student may have previously studied Italy with other FIAR books such as *Papa Piccolo* and *The Clown of God* in Volume 1 or *Angelo* in Volume 5. Use this lesson to review and build on previous knowledge, or as an introduction to the country, if needed.

Papa, Mama and Mario Bellini are from Italy. Help your student locate Italy on the map. Notice how it's shaped like a boot. Point out to your student that Italy is surrounded on three sides by the Mediterranean Sea. The country of Italy also includes two large islands—Sicily and Sardinia.

The capital of Italy is Rome. Other large Italian cities include Naples, Florence, Venice, Bologna and Palermo. Rome is known for its many architectural masterpieces such as the Basilica of St. Peter's, the Colosseum, Trevi Fountain and the Pantheon. Rome is also known for its beautiful public parks and elegant shopping streets.

Italians generally have large, close-knit families. Mealtimes, especially, are events where the whole family comes together. Cooking is a large part of Italy's culture. Large supermarkets are not common in

Italy, so people generally do their food shopping at small stores and local outdoor markets. Small shops in Italy generally sell one specific type of food. For example, you'll find bakeries, fish markets, fruit stores, dairy shops and highly specialized butcher shops that may specialize in just veal or just beef.

Pasta is perhaps the best-known Italian food product. Take your student to the grocery store and look at all the various shapes of pasta that are available. The names are fun to pronounce, such as fusili, ravioli, macaroni, canneloni and more. Buy a pasta that is new to your student and try it at home. Topped with butter and Parmesan cheese or with tomato sauce, this is sure to be a fun meal! Italy is the largest producer of olive oil in the world. If your student isn't familiar with olive oil, buy a small bottle and let her try some. Dip a piece of toasted Italian bread in the oil and taste the flavor. In Italy, olive oil is used on bread instead of butter.

Italians love skiing, cycling and most of all, soccer. Other pastimes include sailing, walking and swimming at the shore.

Italy is known for its fine arts and culture. The country is the birthplace of some of the world's greatest artists, including Leonardo da Vinci and Michelangelo. Italian fashions are often at the forefront of fashion design. Sculptures, fountains, paintings and beautiful architecture are everywhere.

Like the Bellinis, many Italian families love opera. Two famous opera composers are Gioacchino Rossini (1792-1868) and Giuseppe Verdi (1813-1901). Verdi wrote and composed a famous opera called *Falstaff*, which was first performed in Milan in 1893. This opera is still widely performed around the world.

Encourage your student to find one aspect of Italian life that she wishes to explore further. Perhaps she wants to research Italian cooking, famous painters, famous opera singers, Sicily, Sardinia or the Italian automobile industry. She can research online or find books at the library on whatever subject she chooses, and then she can create an oral presentation on that topic. If she chose food, she may wish to fix and serve a few classic Italian dishes. If she chose Italian music, she can include some audio selections as part of her presentation.

Your student will gain a greater appreciation of a new country and cultures, as well as a greater understanding of our friends, the Bellinis.

Social Studies: History - Mythology: Orpheus

Mr. Smedley likens Chester Cricket to Orpheus (OR fee us). Your student may or may not be familiar with Greek mythology. If you would like, take a few moments and explain briefly what myths and mythology are and how Orpheus fits into the bigger picture.

For all of human history, people have tried to understand and explain why certain things occur. For example, people have always wanted to understand why the sun rises and sets, and where people came from. Today, we have scientific explanations for many of these questions. But in very early times, people didn't have the technology to provide truthful answers. Instead, people often explained these natural phenomena through stories they made up. These stories usually had gods, goddesses and heroes.

Has your student ever heard the phrase "Pandora's box"? This is a saying that comes from a Greek myth. Greeks wanted to explain where evil came from, so they created a story. In the tale, all the world's evils and problems were trapped in a single box. When the first woman, Pandora, couldn't resist opening the box, the troubles escaped and have remained in the world ever since.

Orpheus was a mythological figure who was said to be a great musician. His harp playing was so beautiful that it charmed and tamed all the animals around him. Orpheus was said to exist in a land called the upperworld, but even his ability to charm all creation with his music did not make him happy. Long before, his wife Eurydice (yoo RID i see), had stepped on a snake on their wedding day and died. When she died, she went to the underworld (another mythological region). Orpheus, longing to find his true love, ventured to the underworld and played for the king. The king was so thrilled by the music, just as the animals had been, that he promised Orpheus he would release Eurydice from her eternal slumber and allow her to accompany him back to the upperworld. Orpheus was thrilled and then he heard the king say something else. The king made Orpheus promise he would not look at his wife until they reached the upperworld. Orpheus agreed and was soon on his way, with his wife behind him. At some point during the walk, however, Orpheus couldn't hear Eurydice's footsteps. This made him nervous, so he turned to look. Unfortunately, once he had stolen a look at her, the king pulled Eurydice back into the underworld forever.

Your student may wish to explore the great tales of Greek and Roman myths further. If she is interested, you may want to locate *d'Aulaire's Book of Greek Myths* by Ingri and Edgar d'Aulaire. This classic children's book is a great place for children to learn the fascinating tales of ancient mythology.

Language Arts: Meet Our Author - George Selden

Now that your student has read several chapters of *The Cricket in Times Square*, she may wish to learn more about our author, George Selden.

George Selden's full name was George Selden Thompson (1929-1989). His stories were most often animal fantasy (like our story). Selden wrote light, entertaining tales of pure imagination. His stories always delight children, but they also enlighten them by showing them subtle glimpses into human behavior.

Thompson was born in Hartford, Connecticut and attended the Loomis School in Windsor. In 1951, he received a Bachelor of Arts degree from Yale University and was editor of their literary magazine.

Teacher's Note: If you studied the lesson on Connecticut in chapter 3 with your student, then you may wish to note this Connecticut detail, in particular. Your student might want to include George Selden in her notebook or map of Connecticut.

Selden's first book, *The Dog that Could Swim Under Water* (1956), was the story of a dog named Flossy. It told about the animal's experiences and inventiveness. Selden wrote nearly 20 books, but he is best known for *The Cricket in Times Square* (1960). Adults and children alike fell in love with this book, and it was this story which made Selden famous.

Selden, a New Yorker himself, said in an interview, "One night I was coming home on the subway, and I did hear a cricket chirp in the Times Square subway station. The story formed in my mind within minutes." George Selden, a lover of and expert on opera, wove the idea of a musical cricket into his tale and it has since become a classic.

Your student may be interested in knowing that *The Cricket in Times Square* is the first of seven books with the same characters. Some of the titles in the series include *Tucker's Countryside* (1969), *Chester Cricket's New Home* (1983) and *Harry Kitten and Tucker Mouse* (1986). Garth Williams illustrated all of these books as well.

Language Arts: Writing and Discussion Question

Mario was so excited to see Chester, he couldn't even sleep in on a Sunday morning. Write about a time in your life when you couldn't wait to go somewhere or to see someone.

Fine Arts: Opera - It's Not Boring

Both Mr. Smedley and the Bellinis love opera. An opera is a dramatic performance where the characters sing all, or most, of their lines. Opera is a very complex and beautiful art form because it includes acting, singing, orchestral music, costumes, scenery, dance and technical aspects (lights, amplification, etc.). Opera uses music and the power of the human voice to communicate feelings of anger, jealousy, love, joy and sadness to the audience.

Operas are normally performed in special buildings called opera houses. Opera houses are generally larger than most traditional theaters and are built with special spaces and equipment so that large sets and orchestra pits have plenty of room. The orchestra pit is where the musicians and the conductor are placed. Most opera houses were built during the 1700s or 1800s, but a few are modern. The best-known opera houses in Europe include The Royal Opera House in London, the Opera House in Rome and the State Opera in Vienna. The most famous opera house in the United States is the Metropolitan Opera in New York City. The Sydney Opera House in Australia is another venue recognized worldwide for its unique architecture.

Teacher's Note: Locate the Metropolitan Opera on the New York City map with your student.

Even someone who is completely unfamiliar with opera can begin to understand this art form with a few simple definitions. First, an opera has two basic elements: 1) the libretto and (2) the music. The libretto (which means "little book" in Italian), consists of the words of an opera—what the actors are singing. The music, usually called the score, includes both the instrumental and vocal music.

It is important for your student to understand that for anyone to fully appreciate and enjoy opera, she should read the libretto (or a complete summary) of the opera before she attends it. It is especially vital if the opera is in a foreign language. Many people attend their first opera and leave confused because they couldn't follow the story. This problem can be solved easily by simply learning the story line of the opera before you go. You can look up a summary online, or libraries have books that contain summaries of the action in individual operas.

Your student should have at least a fundamental understanding of opera. It is one of the oldest and most beloved forms of art in the world. Beyond this lesson, your student can learn a lot by simply listening to a portion of an opera (or an opera in its entirety). An excellent opera for your student to begin with is called *The Marriage of Figaro*, by Mozart. This opera, the Bellinis' favorite, is in Italian and contains both dramatic sections and beautiful arias, or solos.

Chapter 6—Sai Fong

Teacher Summary

Mario rides the subway to Chinatown and finds a little shop that is open. The store is owned by an elderly Chinese gentleman named Sai Fong. His shop is filled with hundreds of gifts, clothes and curios from China.

Sai Fong tells Mario the legend of the first cricket, and shows Mario an authentic cricket house that he has for sale. It is shaped like a pagoda, and Mario finds it very beautiful. He buys it for 15 cents and takes it home for Chester.

What we will cover in this chapter:

Social Studies: History and Geography - China*
Social Studies: Geography - Yangtze River
Language Arts: Writing Accents
Language Arts: Writing and Discussion Question
Fine Arts: Create Your Own Wind Chimes

Social Studies: History and Geography - China

Teacher's Note: Your student may have previously studied China with *The Story About Ping* (FIAR Vol. 1) or *Paper Lanterns* (FIAR Vol. 5). Use this lesson to build on previous knowledge or to introduce the subject if you haven't covered it before.

Mario visits the shop of Sai Fong. Sai Fong is from China and his shop is filled with beautiful and intriguing Chinese objects. Here is a great opportunity to introduce your student to Asian culture and the fascinating land of China.

With your student, locate China on a world map. Look at how big it is! China is the world's largest country in population and the third largest in area. Nearly one-fifth of all the people in the world live in China. The country covers more than one-fifth of Asia. Only Russia and Canada are larger.

Almost all of the people in China live in the eastern third of the country—where most of the major cities and farmland are located. More than 75% of Chinese people live in rural villages, since agriculture is the chief economic activity in China. Although fewer Chinese people live in cities, these cities are very populated. The two largest cities in China are Shanghai and Beijing (the nation's capital).

China is one of the world's oldest civilizations. The written language of China is nearly 4,000 years old. The Chinese people are a proud and noble group. They were the people to first develop the compass, paper, porcelain and many types of cloth like silk and tapestry.

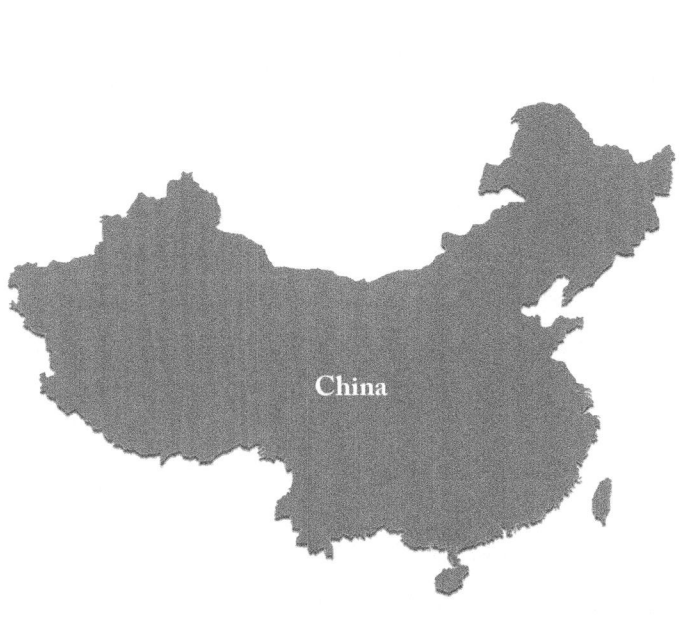

Here are simple Mandarin phrases your student can learn:

Hello	Hao (how)
How are you?	Ni chiguo fan mei? (nee CHUR gwaw FAHN may)
I'm fine.	Chiguo le (CHUR gwaw leh)
Yes	Shide (SURE duh)
No	Bu shi (BOO sure)
Goodbye	Zaijian (zay GEE en)

Chinese people normally place their family name (or last name) first. For example, Sai Fong's first name was probably Fong. However, during conversations with strangers or in business, Chinese people generally go by their family name. What would your student's name be if it were reversed?

Teacher's Note: A heartwarming go-along book that discusses difficult-to-pronounce names is *The Name Jar* by Yangsook Choi. Note with your student that the girl in this story is Korean, not Chinese (find both countries on the map!). But the story, about learning to be proud of your name and background, is one that can apply to anyone.

The Chinese language is spoken by over one billion individuals. Western countries refer to the Chinese language as Mandarin. Mandarin is the national language of China and is spoken by over 90% of the people. Other languages spoken by smaller communities include Cantonese, Tibetan, Mongolian and Dai. Many of these languages have no written form.

Ask your student how many characters are in the English alphabet (26). In order to easily read a Chinese newspaper, a Chinese person needs to learn almost 2,500 characters! In the 1950s, the Chinese government wanted to make it easier for its people to learn to read. The written form of Mandarin was developed, but learning to read in Chinese still requires many years of memorization. Also, Chinese characters cannot be written easily with a Western-style keyboard. This makes it very difficult for China to enter the modern world even today.

Since 1949, China has been a communist country. Communism is a strict, non-democratic way of governing. It is an economic and political system in which private ownership is abolished, and all industry is controlled by the state. It is also a way of life. Because of communism and its concern about overpopulation, Chinese families, for many years, were only allowed to have one child. This law has since been changed, but the number of children allowed is still determined by the government. Also, men must be age 22 to marry, and women must be age 20. Religion is not encouraged in China. People who disagree with communism in China are often sent to remote areas and put into labor camps. For this reason, many people in China (and other communist countries such as North Korea) are unhappy but never voice their concerns.

If your student is interested in learning more about China, help her find information or videos online, or check out books from the library. Related topics your student may wish to explore include Chinese inventions, cooking, watercraft (like junks), silk, tea, rice, religions, kites, fireworks, traditional clothing, communism and the Mandarin language.

Social Studies: Geography - Yangtze River

Sai Fong shows Mario the little silver bell in the cricket house. Sai Fong tells Mario, "Sound like littlest bell in Silver Temple, far off up Yangtze River." If your student has read *The Story About Ping* (FIAR Vol. 1), she is probably already familiar with the Yangtze River. Take some time to share with your student a few facts about this very important waterway.

The Yangtze River is the world's third longest river. Only the Nile and the Amazon are longer. It is China's longest and most important river. It is almost 4,000 (3,915) miles long and follows a wavy course from the Tanggula Mountains to the East China Sea. Almost half of all China's ocean trade is carried over the Yangtze and its many branches. Millions of people (1/15 of all the people in the world!) live along the banks of the Yangtze. Yearly floods often force many people from their homes temporarily.

Find a simple book or video on the Yangtze River at your library. Then locate the Yangtze River on a map with your student. Let her trace her finger down the entire length of this massive waterway. It is truly amazing!

Language Arts: Writing Accents

Draw your student's attention to the way our author, George Selden, writes Sai Fong's dialogue. Ask your student why words like cricket are spelled "clicket." Is our author suddenly misspelling things or does he have a reason for the change?

This chapter gives your student an excellent example of an author writing a character who speaks with an accent. George Selden isn't writing the words the way Sai Fong would *write* them; he's writing the words the way Sai Fong would *speak* them.

George Selden, like many authors, has made *The Cricket in Times Square* more authentic and believable by having a character speak with an accent or dialect (other examples authors might use would be a Southern accent from the southeastern U.S., a Scottish brogue, a cockney accent from working-class London or Yorkshire accent from northern England). Notice with your student the ways that George Selden conveys Sai Fong's Chinese accent, and discuss the information below.

Sai Fong is likely a first-generation immigrant to the United States. Like many immigrants, he has overcome a tremendous hurdle in learning a very challenging language—English! Native Chinese (Mandarin) speakers, like many other immigrants, not only have to learn the language itself, but also sometimes face big differences in the types of sounds that the two languages make. For native Mandarin speakers, some of the biggest differences are: learning to speak the r, v, l, and n sounds, learning to use "the" in sentences, and leaving off consonants at the ends of words. Of course, in the native language of a Chinese speaker, these issues are not problems at all! But when learning a new language, the sounds you are used to making in your first language will affect your ability to pronounce things correctly in a foreign language.

Writing accents effectively is difficult. To do so, the writer must have a good ear for language, pronunciation, and accents, and know how to translate those successfully to the written word. If your student is interested, spend some time looking carefully at how Selden achieves this in Sai Fong's dialogue in this chapter.

Language Arts: Writing and Discussion Question

At the begining of our chapter, Mario and Chester are riding the subway to Chinatown. Chester isn't used to the bumps on the subway and he nearly falls out of his matchbox. If Chester hadn't been found by Mario, where do you think he would have ended up next? Write about what you think his next set of adventures would have been.

Language Arts: Vocabulary

(These words are all found in Chapter 6.)

jig   A fast, joyful solo dance, usually done in a folk style.

spire   The top part of a steeple or tower which narrows to a point.

pagoda   A temple or other sacred building with many stories forming a tower.

incense   A substance which gives off a sweet smell when burned.

kimono   A silk robe held together by a wide sash.

chopsticks   A pair of long, slender sticks used by many Asian people to raise food to their mouths.

novelties   Small, unusual items such as toys and cheap jewelry.

Fine Arts: Create Your Own Wind Chimes

In some of Chinatown's store windows, Mario sees "...the glass wind harps that tinkle when they're hung in the window where the breeze can reach them." What a lovely description of wind chimes! Your student can have great fun creating her own wind chimes. They won't be made of glass, but they will make beautiful tinkling music, just the same.

To make an easy, homemade wind chime, your student will need:
• one coat hanger
• string or heavy fishing line
• something noisy/metal to hang as the chimes (e.g., soda cans, metal food jar lids, old pieces of silverware, etc.)

To make a wind chime, your student can begin by tying pieces of string to the hanger. They should vary in length, alternating in size down the length of the hanger. Tie the string tightly so the chimes won't slide. Next, tie the chimes to the bottom of the strings. One item should be tied to only one piece of string. Now, your student can hang her wind chime outside and wait for the wind to blow.

This project can be simple and rustic, or your student can make something quite ornate. For a round frame to hang her chimes on, your student can use a plastic or wooden embroidery hoop. Craft stores sell inexpensive bells or metal trinkets your student can use for chimes. Have fun listening to the tinkle of music, just as Mario did!

Chapter 7—The Cricket Cage

Teacher Summary

Harry and Tucker think Chester's new house is splendid. Tucker, in particular, is quite taken with the gilded pagoda with the tiny silver bell. Chester likes the new house as well, but he prefers his little matchbox for sleeping. Chester offers his new house to Tucker for the first night, and Tucker is thrilled.

The animals decide that Tucker needs a little bedding in the pagoda, so they take two $1 bills from the Bellinis' cash box. Tucker uses one bill for a bed and the other for a blanket. He is soon comfortable. Chester beds down in his matchbox, and everyone goes to sleep.

What we will cover in this chapter:

Social Studies: History - United States Currency
Science: Sleep

Language Arts: Dictionary Skills*
Language Arts: Writing and Discussion Question
Language Arts: Vocabulary
Fine Arts: Design and Create Your Own Currency

Social Studies: History - United States Currency

Tucker decides to use dollar bills for bedding in the pagoda. Share with your student some information about money and United States **currency**.

Discuss the three main functions of money with your student. First, it allows people to exchange money for things they need. It is a medium of exchange. If you want to buy a pizza, the restaurant will take your money and hand you the pizza. Second, money is a way to keep track of costs. A storeowner will tell you the price of his apples by how many cents per pound they cost. A car salesman will tell you what your car is worth, in terms of dollars. Finally, money allows people to store their wealth. Money can be kept in a safe, drawer or bank and later be used to buy things.

For this lesson, have on hand one of each of the following: penny, nickel, dime, quarter, half-dollar, $1 coin, $1 bill, $5 bill, $10 bill and $20 bill. (Obviously, you can also include a $2, $50 and a $100, if you would like.) Spread the money out and look at it with your student. What does your student notice about each coin?

Dimes, quarters, half-dollars and coin dollars have ridges around the edges called reeding or milling. Reeding was begun in the late 1700s to deter people from shaving off small amounts of precious metals from the coins. Have your student feel the reeding on a dime and then feel the edges of a penny. The penny is smooth, isn't it?

Federal law also requires that coins be dated with the year they were made. All U.S. coins must also bear the word Liberty and the Latin motto, "E Pluribus Unum", which means "out of many, one." This motto reminds us of becoming one nation from 13 colonies. Most U.S. coins are minted in Denver and Philadelphia.

Draw your student's attention to the paper money you've displayed. Paper bills are officially called Federal Reserve Notes. They are made of a very special kind of paper that is 25% linen and 75% cotton. The paper is nearly cloth-like and wears well.

Each U.S. bill includes several key items on its face. Using the $1 bill, try to locate each of the features with your student:

(1) Federal Reserve Seal—Located to the left of the center portrait, this seal features a bold letter (from A through L). This letter identifies which Federal Reserve Bank issued that particular bill.

(2) Federal Reserve Number—Located four times on the bill (to the left of the Federal Reserve Seal and in the other three corners), this one- or two-digit number also helps identify where the bill came from.

(3) Note Position and Plate Serial Number—This letter-number combination appears in very small type. It identifies the engraving plate and position on the plate when the bill was printed.

(4) Serial Number—This large alphanumeric code appears twice on each bill (in the lower left and upper right corners). The first letter refers to what bank the bill came from and the last letter refers to the specific print run.

Occasionally, our currency is redesigned by the Federal Reserve banks to update the look, help prevent

counterfeiting and bring new bills into circulation. Your student might enjoy the United States currency designs throughout our history. What did the first $10 bills look like? What do they look like today? How have they changed?

For more information on what each thing on our bills mean, check your local library for books on money or currency, or look online for explanations of other symbols on the $1 bill or other currency.

Science: Sleep

Tucker, Chester and Harry bed down for the night. Tucker is happy to be sleeping in the pagoda, and Chester is enjoying sleeping in his comfortable matchbox.

Why do we need sleep? What does our body do with sleep? Does the body completely stop during sleep? Even scientists who study sleep every day don't know everything there is to know about sleep. No one really knows all the reasons people need sleep. But to stay healthy, scientists know it's important to get a good night's sleep every night.

Every person's brain has a tiny bit of electric activity. Electric currents flow along our brain cells and this is how scientists study our sleep patterns. Scientists study sleep by putting little metal disks against a person's head. These little disks are called **electrodes** and they are connected to a machine called an **EEG** (electroencephalograph).

As a person sleeps, electrodes detect the electricity in the brain, and the EEG records these waves on paper. Even when a person is completely asleep, the EEG shows that the brain continues to give out little electrical impulses.

Even though understanding EEGs and electricity in our brains is complex, it does make sense that our brains don't completely stop working while we're asleep. After all, we don't stop breathing. The body continues to function (pump blood through the heart, digest food, etc.). If we're cold, our bodies tell us and we pull up blankets. If we hear someone talking, we may even answer her without knowing it.

Scientists have conducted many sleep deprivation experiments. They want to know if humans really need sleep to function. Sometimes they have people stay up all night for one night, and they have even had people try to stay awake for a whole week! Scientists have found that after just one night with no sleep, people are irritable and have trouble thinking clearly. After two or more days, people begin to get sick very easily and may even begin hallucinating (seeing things that aren't really there). We need sleep. It restores our bodies and helps keep us sharp.

What can you do if you don't get enough sleep in one night? Take a nap the next day. Scientists have found that our bodies are a little like a bank. We can put sleep in our "sleep account" when we've gotten too low. Naps are a great way to refresh your mind and body. You'll feel better, stronger and more energetic after a good nap.

If your student is interested in learning more about sleep, then she may wish to research REM sleep, alpha and delta waves, the reticular activating system, nightmares and dreams, sleepwalking, sleep apnea and snoring.

Tonight, as your student goes to sleep, encourage her to remember how much her body is looking forward to the rest and how much work her brain still has to do!

Language Arts: Dictionary Skills*

Our author, George Selden, uses several difficult and possibly new words in this chapter. Here is an opportunity to review dictionary skills. Even in an era of quick answers online, learning to use a dictionary is a skill your student should sharpen. Review with your student what a dictionary can help her do (define, spell, pronounce and discover the origin of words).

For every word entry, a dictionary gives us several key clues about that word. For example, find with your student where her dictionary shows the part of speech label. A dictionary can tell us if a word is a noun (n.), an adjective (adj.), an adverb (adv.) or another part of speech.

A dictionary also shows us how to pronounce the word and the word's origin. And finally, a dictionary defines what words mean and how meanings change in different contexts.

Locate a print dictionary and look it over with your student. Three words your student may wish to look up from this chapter include:

soufflé
admiration
rumble

Assign or assist your student in looking up each of these words in her dictionary. She can write down what the word means, where it comes from and what kind of word it is. Help her understand how to read the pronunciation guide as well.

Review dictionary skills with your student often, and encourage her to use her dictionary (whether online or in print) when she writes and during the editing/proofreading process. A dictionary is a vital tool for students who wish to become excellent writers, readers and speakers!

Language Arts: Writing and Discussion Question

Tucker seems to think that Chester's new pagoda is the perfect place to sleep. Where do you think the perfect place to sleep is? Write about your dream sleeping quarters.

Language Arts: Vocabulary

soufflé   A frothy, baked dish made light by including beaten egg whites and baked in a hot oven.

rumble   A deep, heavy, continuous sound.

admiration   A feeling of pleasure and approval of something fine or well done.

currency   A country's money.

EEG (electroencephalograph)   A machine used to monitor brain waves.

electrode   A disk which detects electric activity.

Fine Arts: Design and Create Your Own Currency

Your student knows about United States currency. Why not let her design her own? This Fine Arts project can be as simple or elaborate as your student wishes.

She doesn't have to use paper (although she most certainly can), but wood, cloth or plastic instead. She can name her denominations whatever she wishes. For example, perhaps her currency could include a small paper disk called a bawk, a larger paper disk called a jilk and a heavy clay bead she calls a lipto.

This art project works well if your student imagines and creates her own little country. She can name it, place it anywhere on the globe (or in space) and then begin to design the currency. She can draw, paint or sculpt the currency. If she uses paper currency, like our bills, then she can include different designs (the center portraits might be of friends or family members), her own system of serial numbers, etc.

This project allows your student's imagination to go as far as she wants. It also relates to the three main functions of money (discussed in the first lesson of this chapter). No matter what her currency is made of or looks like, it still must (1) be a form of exchange, (2) be a unit of account, and (3) be a way to store wealth. In your student's country, the money can be whatever she wants it to be!

Have fun with this lesson, and perhaps when her currency is complete, she can set up a little "store" where it is taken. Your student can trade her currency for a drink of lemonade or a cookie.

Chapter 8—Tucker's Life Savings

Teacher Summary

During the night, little Chester walks in his sleep over to the Bellinis' cash register. Thinking it is a leaf, he picks up a $2 bill and begins to munch. He awakes later to realize that he has eaten half of the bill!

Tucker and Harry try to convince Chester of several schemes to cover up the missing money, but Chester insists on being honest. That morning, the Bellinis arrive and Mama notices the missing money. She is furious and she knows that Chester chewed it. She tells Mario that Chester has to stay in his cage all the time, until Mario can pay the money back.

Chester feels terrible that Mario is paying for his mistake. Finally, Tucker admits that he has almost $3 in savings. Tucker, admirably, offers Chester $2 to use to repay the Bellinis. Chester takes the money thankfully and the next day the Bellinis discover the replaced money. No one can explain how it got there, but Mama Bellini keeps her promise and lets Chester out of his cage.

What we will cover in this chapter:

Social Studies: History and Geography - Coney Island
Social Studies: History - Learning More about the U.S. Legal System
Language Arts: Writing and Discussion Question
Life Skills: Honesty
Life Skills: Dealing with Stress and Anxiety
Activity Sheet: Vocabulary Words*

Social Studies: History and Geography: Coney Island

As your student is compiling information on New York throughout this unit, she can continue to add more details to her notes and map. Here in chapter 8, we find another piece of New York information your student can include.

Mario wants to go to Coney Island for a swim. Has your student ever heard of Coney Island? Locate Coney Island on your student's map of New York City. Coney Island is found at the southernmost tip of the borough of Brooklyn.

Coney Island was really once an island, but land has been filled in to make it a peninsula. In the summertime, just like Mario, many New Yorkers ride subways to Coney Island's beaches and to its famous Boardwalk. The Boardwalk, by the water, is lined with trinket shops and souvenir stores, sideshows (like magic acts) and other attractions. Many years ago (during the '30s, '40s and '50s), Coney Island had many large amusement park rides, but today many of these park areas have been replaced by housing developments or other recreational features.

The food most associated with Coney Island is a hot dog—chili dogs, in particular. Many restaurants serve chili dogs and call them "Coneys."

Social Studies: History - Learning More about the U.S. Legal System

Chester has committed a terrible act—eating some of the Bellinis' money! Even though it was on accident, Mama Bellini treats Chester like a criminal. This chapter can serve as an introduction to the U.S. legal system. Throughout the chapter, we see words such as jail, sentence and punishment. Take some time to talk with your student about what these words mean.

In our society, certain evil acts are considered illegal. We call them crimes. People the police think may have committed a crime are called suspects. People who did commit a crime are called criminals. The study of criminal behavior is called criminology, and experts in this field are called criminologists. Criminologists study crimes and the people who commit them to see if they can detect where, when and why certain crimes occur. They hope to find effective ways to prevent crime. Sometimes people commit crimes (like stealing, for example) and are not caught. But if they are caught, several things usually happen.

Police officer(s) question the suspects, the victims and any witnesses. The police gather as much information as they can from the people involved. They also try to gather information from the area—this is called evidence. Evidence such as fingerprints, weapons and stolen property can all be used later in court.

Police officers must follow many specific procedures when they question a suspect and gather information. Every person in America is considered innocent until proven guilty. After the police are finished asking questions and gathering evidence, they usually take the suspect into the police station or jail. More procedures are followed there, such as fingerprinting, pictures and more discussion.

As the teacher, you know your student's interest and learning levels. This lesson can be expanded greatly for those interested. Additional topics to explore include, but aren't limited to, judges, trials, juries, correctional facilities, rehabilitation, bail and bond, federal prisons, lawyers and the U.S. and specific states' Constitutions.

Understanding how our laws work, learning what police officers do to serve the public and how we as a society are expected to behave are important parts of your student's education.

Language Arts: Writing and Discussion Question

Do you think it was wise for Chester to be honest about his mistake? Write or discuss what might have happened if he had chosen to be dishonest. (You might want to combine this lesson with the Life Skills lesson below on honesty.)

Life Skills: Honesty

Chester knows he ate the $2 bill. Tucker and Harry know it, too. Talk with your student about the animals' conversation. Tucker encourages Chester to run away. He also suggests that he try to tape the bill and pass it off as a $1 bill. Tucker even says that maybe Chester should eat the rest and then the Bellinis wouldn't know what happened to it.

None of these solutions are honest, are they? Chester is an honorable cricket. He knows he'll have to let the Bellinis know what happened, but he's worried about how it will work out. Later, Tucker admits he has enough money of his own to replace the eaten bill.

Being honest is an important part of being a person of integrity and a good citizen. Even when we're not sure how a problem will be solved, it is important to be honest about the situation. Being honest isn't always easy. Punishment and consequences almost always follow if we've done something wrong. But when we're dishonest, we make the situation worse—the problem is still there, no one knows how to fix it and we feel terrible!

Encourage your student to be brave and honest, like Chester.

Life Skills: Dealing with Stress and Anxiety

Chester is scared and upset. He can't believe he accidentally ate that $2 bill! Even with the support of Tucker and Harry, Chester is still very worried.

Children, just like adults, can be stressed and anxious. Problems which may seem small and easily solved to adults can weigh on children's minds. Learning to deal with stress and anxiety is a part of growing up. Part of the solution is learning to talk to your parents and others when you're upset. Discuss this principle with your student. Does she find a parent or friend to talk to when she's stressed? Even if a solution isn't found right away, simply talking our worries over with someone helps alleviate our stress.

Sometimes children are stressed by things that aren't problems, but simply challenges (such as a difficult test, an upcoming music recital, or meeting a new relative or friend). One way to deal with this kind of stress is to prepare for the event to the best of your ability, and then to let it go. Worrying about a test or recital won't be as bad if you know you've studied and prepared. If you're ready, and do your best, you can relax. Meeting and making new friends can be a nervous undertaking, but it's better if you think about how nervous the other person probably is, too.

Find out what kinds of worries your student deals with and talk through ways she can work through those stressful times in a healthy way. Holding problems, anxiety and fear inside ourselves is a very unhealthy way to live. It makes our bodies tense and our minds distracted. Depression and far more serious things can arise when we don't discuss our concerns.

Encourage your student to talk with people when she

starts to get worried or upset. Sometimes nipping a concern in the bud is the best way to handle it!

Chapter 9—The Chinese Dinner

Teacher Summary

Mario is worried that Chester might have eaten the $2 bill because he isn't getting the right kind of food. He's not sure what to feed him, but he knows Sai Fong will know. Mario takes Chester and heads back to Chinatown.

Sai Fong's shop is closed, but he hears Mario knocking and answers the door. He is delighted to see Mario and Chester and he invites them to eat a Chinese meal with him. After the delicious dinner, Sai Fong tells Mario that crickets need to eat mulberry leaves. He happens to have a mulberry tree in his backyard, so he gives Mario several leaves for Chester. Mario is grateful and returns home.

What we will cover in this chapter:

Science: Rice
Science: Ivory
Language Arts: Writing and Discussion Question
Fine Arts: Cooking - Two Chinese Dishes*
Life Skills: Special Occasions - Your Own Chinese Dinner

Science: Rice

Mario eats delectable foods with Sai Fong and his friend. One of the things they serve Mario is fried rice.

The most common food staple in China is rice. In fact, China and India are the two largest producers of rice in the world. Those two countries alone produce 50% of all the rice eaten on Earth. The United States produces less than 2% of the world's rice. In the United States, rice is grown mainly along the Mississippi River in Arkansas and Mississippi, as well as in California.

Rice is an interesting food and plant. The main parts of a mature rice plant include the roots, the stems, the leaves and the head. The head is what holds the kernels or grains of rice. Each plant head can hold nearly 100 grains of rice!

Rice grows in fields. Unlike other plants that would rot in similar conditions, rice does better if the field is covered in shallow pools of water. Farmers build low dirt walls called dikes to hold water in next to the plants. Each of these rows of water and plants is called a paddy. Rice paddies take a lot of work to maintain.

Traditionally, farmers in Asia have worked with horses and hand-pulled plows, working the mud and planting rice. When the rice is almost ready for harvest, the dikes have to be pushed down and the field drained. When the field is ready, farmers harvest rice by hand. They usually cut the stalks with sickles or knives and then leave them to dry in the sun. In industrialized countries, large machines harvest the rice and dry it with heated air.

If your student goes to the market and looks in the rice section, she will see many types of rice, including short-grain, long-grain, brown, white, basmati, jasmine, enriched and wild.

For marketing purposes (not a scientific classification), growers often call their rice by size-related names. Short grain is less than one-fifth of an inch long. Medium-grain rice ranges from one-fifth to one-fourth inch and long-grain rice is larger.

Brown rice has been hulled, but some of the layers called bran remain. Brown rice is more nutritious than white rice because the remaining bran layers contain most of the grain's vitamins and minerals.

When your student sees the name "wild rice," she isn't really looking at rice, at all. Although it's similar in appearance, wild rice is really a grain from a species of grass grown in Canada and the United States. It isn't related to rice, even though it is called rice.

Rice is such an important part of the Asian diet that in many Asian languages the word for "eat" means "eat rice!"

If your student is interested, perhaps you can purchase and cook several different kinds of rice. Look at the difference in grain length, taste, texture and smell. Rice is a nutritious and delicious grain to use in everyday cooking!

Science: Ivory

Mario looks at the Chinese book Sai Fong is poring through. Mario sees pictures of many things, including one of a princess sitting on an ivory throne. Ask your student if she knows what ivory is. Where does it come from?

Ivory is a hard substance that makes up the main part of the tusks and teeth of certain animals. The huge tusks of African elephants have been the most common source of ivory. Other animals that have ivory tusks are walruses, narwhals and hippopotamuses.

Ivory can be carved, polished and made beautiful. Sculptors in ancient Rome made many things from ivory including combs, buttons and even furniture. The Chinese were the first people to develop ivory carving as an art form around the year 1800 B.C. Chinese artists made intricate and beautiful ivory carvings. In North America, ivory carvings are called scrimshaw.

Unfortunately, because ivory became so popular, many hunters killed hundreds of thousands of elephants just for their tusks. Because of this, in 1989 all trade in ivory and other elephant products was banned by the Convention in Trade in Endangered Species. Now, finding real ivory to buy is rare, and many more animals are protected.

Locate a book on ivory carving or scrimshaw at your local library, or look for images online so your student can see pictures of carvings, just as Mario saw.

Language Arts: Writing and Discussion Question

When Chester sang, Sai Fong's old friend almost started crying. What do you think he was thinking of or missing?

Fine Arts: Cooking - Two Chinese Dishes*

Sai Fong and his friend make a delicious dinner for Mario and Chester. Chinese cooking is a fascinating cuisine to study. Your student may be familiar with the Chinese wok (if not, locate a picture or video online), but does she know why this method of cooking is so popular? A wok cooks food very hot, very fast. Chinese cooks have adapted themselves to an ever-present shortage of fuel. Because wood and other fuels are scarce, the Chinese have learned to spend a maximum amount of time in food preparation and a minimum of time in actual cooking. Isn't that smart? Most ingredients in Chinese cooking are diced, sliced or shredded. This is because small pieces of food cook more quickly than large pieces.

If your student is interested in cooking, she may wish to try her hand at Chinese cuisine. Here are two delicious recipes which are fairly easy to prepare and include easy-to-find ingredients. Enjoy!

Fried Rice

4 cups cooked rice, cold
3 Tbs. oil, divided
1/2 cup chopped onion
1 cup cooked chicken, pork or beef, diced
2 eggs, beaten
2 Tbs. soy sauce

Loosen and separate the grains of cold, cooked rice. Place a large skillet (or wok) over high heat. Add 2 Tbs. oil and heat the pan thoroughly (but don't scorch!). Fry onion quickly, stirring, until light golden. Add meat and cook for 2 minutes or until cooked, stirring constantly; remove meat from the pan. Pour remaining 1 Tbs. oil into the pan; add eggs and stir-fry until done. Add rice to eggs, stir in soy sauce and add the meat mixture back to the skillet. Stir and serve!

Wonton Soup

(Wonton means "swallowing a cloud." This soup really looks like a soup of clouds.)

1/2 lb. ground beef or pork
1 Tbs. finely chopped green onion
1 egg, beaten
1 tsp. salt
1 Tbs. soy sauce
1 Tbs. sugar
1 tsp. sesame or vegetable oil
1 Tbs. water
1 pkg. wonton skins*
5 cups chicken broth

Mix all ingredients except wonton skins and broth together. Put one teaspoon of the mixture in the center of a wonton skin. Moisten the edges of the skin with water and fold to form a triangle. Pinch the edges to seal. Fill and fold rest of skins.

Bring a large kettle of water to a boil. Add a few wontons at a time. Cook at a medium boil for 8-10 minutes. Add the cooked wontons to hot chicken broth and serve. (You may wish to garnish the soup with more green onion or diced cooked carrot.)

*Ready-made wonton skins are available at the supermarket in the produce section; leftovers can be frozen.

Chinese often drink hot tea with—or after—their meal. There are many kinds of Chinese tea, but perhaps the most delicious is called green tea. Almost any grocery store will offer green tea. If you live near an international grocery, find a box with Chinese writing on it. Purchase some and share it with your student during your meal!

Life Skills: Special Occasions - Your Own Chinese Dinner

Using the recipes in the previous lesson, or your own recipes (see the activity sheet for this chapter), let your student plan and execute her own Chinese meal celebration. With help, your student can decorate a table, fix food and present her meal to her family or a friend.

To know what kinds of decorations are authentic, your student can get a book or two from the library or look online. You will also need to find some inexpensive chopsticks (available at grocery stores or Asian markets). Using chopsticks is fun and memorable. Fortune cookies can also be bought at most stores, and make a delicious extra treat.

Finding ways to create memories through food and fun is a great way to help enrich your student's education. She'll always remember this dinner, and you will, too!

Chapter 10—The Dinner Party

Teacher Summary

Chester, Tucker and Harry are having a dinner party. They want to celebrate Chester's two-month anniversary of being in New York. The party will be held in the newsstand and Tucker is in charge of the refreshments.

The party is great fun. Tucker brings a buffet of foods and soda pop with ice! Chester learns to play a few new songs from the radio, and soon Harry is singing and Tucker is dancing. Unfortunately, Tucker dances a bit too freely and accidentally knocks a box of kitchen matches off the shelf. The matches scatter and one sparks. Soon, the newsstand is in flames. Paul, the conductor, hears the commotion and helps put the fire out. The three animals escape safely, but the Bellinis are devastated.

What we will cover in this chapter:

Social Studies: History - Vaudeville*
Social Studies: Career Path - Careers in Music
Science: Smoke
Language Arts: Writing and Discussion Question
Fine Arts: Types of Music
Fine Arts: "The Blue Danube"
Life Skills: How to React During an Emergency
Life Skills: Being a Polite Host

Social Studies: History - Vaudeville*

As Tucker dances breathlessly, he says to Harry and Chester, "Chester can play—I can dance... We should go into vaudeville." Vaudeville is a type of theatrical entertainment that includes a wide variety of acts. Although it is rare to see today, vaudeville was the most popular form of entertainment in America from the 1880s to 1930s.

Vaudeville was a fun and varied theater form. When people went to see an evening of vaudeville, they would be treated to 15 or more different acts. The acts might include jugglers, animal acts, skits, recitations, celebrity speeches, singers, comics and magicians.

The term vaudeville comes from a French word for "light play with music." People loved the action and entertainment, but by the 1920s a new form of entertainment was coming around—sound motion pictures. By the 1930s, vaudeville was declining greatly.

Your student can create her own evening of vaudeville quite easily. By including siblings or friends, your student can create a bill of different acts. Perhaps she plays a musical instrument or knows a magic trick. Maybe her friend likes to sing, or her brother can tell a great joke. With some imagination and creativity, your student can create a vaudeville program and posters promoting it. She can invite friends, grandparents and other relatives. Encourage your student to create a stage area, perhaps with a draped sheet for a curtain and a seating area for the audience. This activity could be a quick afternoon activity or a detailed, planned evening event. Have fun and enjoy this lost form of entertainment!

Social Studies: Career Path - Careers in Music

Chester is a great musician! In this chapter, Chester discovers he can play popular tunes by listening to the radio and memorizing the music. Is your student an aspiring musician? Is she interested in a profession in music? Career paths in music are numerous and varied. Almost all, however, involve natural talents and gifts and a great deal of work and dedication.

If your student is interested in a career in performing music (which could encompass orchestra, band or solo artist), then she needs to begin with lessons from a private teacher. After finishing high school, your student should apply, audition and attend a specialized music school called a conservatory. These intense formal lessons will strengthen your student's playing or singing abilities and give her important contacts in the music world. Beyond this formal training, however, your student should still expect to spend several hours a day in private practice and study.

If your student enjoys writing songs and wants to explore becoming a composer, she may be interested to know that many composers never set foot in an orchestra pit or at an opera rehearsal. Many composers enjoy successful, exciting careers writing and arranging music for TV shows, movies and commercials.

Some of the most practical and rewarding careers in music include the teaching professions. Your student can work toward and obtain a bachelor's degree in music and can teach music in schools or private lessons. Teaching someone how to play an instrument or sing more beautifully is an important and fulfilling career!

Other career paths your student may wish to explore in the area of music include: choir director; music critic; concert manager; making, selling or repairing musical instruments; and music therapy (working with patients in hospitals and nursing homes, using music to help the patients feel better).

If your student is interested in learning more about a career in music, she may wish to talk to a music/voice teacher or contact a local university.

Science: Smoke

As the fire builds in the newsstand, smoke also builds around Harry, Tucker and Chester. Does your student know what smoke actually is and why it is dangerous?

Smoke is made up of tiny solid and liquid particles suspended in gas. The little particles are mostly made up of carbon particles from burning fuel. Because smoke is made up of such small particles, it can easily penetrate the tissues in our lungs. Smoke can cause serious damage to lungs, just as it blackens and corrodes buildings, vegetation and logs in your fireplace.

Review with your student what she should do if she ever faces smoke and fire. Smoke rises. If your student is trapped in a smoke-filled room or hallway, it is vital that she remains close to the ground. Crawling on your stomach or hands and knees is much safer than walking upright!

Although smoke can be dangerous, it also has some beneficial uses when used properly. For example, in many areas where vineyards or orchards are located, farmers use smoke to help protect their plants during freezes. Containers with a burning, smoky substance in them (called smudge pots) are placed along the rows of trees or vines. The smoke billows around the plants and helps hold in warmth. Beekeepers also safely use smoke to keep bees calm during hive inspections.

Language Arts: Writing and Discussion Question

Tucker accidentally knocked the matches off the shelf in the newsstand. Even though it was just an accident, it caused major problems. Have you ever made a mistake or had an accident that caused serious problems? How did you feel? What happened?

Fine Arts: Types of Music

Chester and Tucker discuss musical styles—chamber, pop and classical. There are many different styles of music. Every country in the world has its own specific genre of music. For your student's information, however, the western world (including Western Europe and North America) has three major forms of music: (1) classical, (2) popular music and (3) folk music.

Classical music is composed with strict rules and performed by musicians from written sheets of music. Chamber music (what Tucker referred to) is included in this genre. Chamber music is a type of classical music written for small groups of musicians. These little groups, or ensembles, may perform in different sizes from two (duet), three (trio), four (quartet), five (quintet) or more. Chamber music is also classified by the type of instruments being played. For example, a string quartet typically includes two violins, a viola and a cello. A brass quintet typically includes two trumpets, a French horn, a trombone and a tuba. Other forms of classical music include symphonies and music for the ballet and opera.

Popular music is a large genre. This form includes music such as country, jazz, rock, video game and motion picture scores, bluegrass, hip-hop and more. Popular music is generally a bit simpler than classical music and tends to be more of a blending of styles.

Finally, folk music is the traditional music of a people. Most folk songs begin in rural towns or villages. Some folk songs have been passed down through many generations. A folk song is usually learned by listening, unlike classical music that is learned by reading a set of notes. Some folk songs your student may have heard include Ring-Around-the-Rosy, This Land Is Your Land, I've Been Working on the Railroad and Buffalo Gals.

Encourage your student to broaden her music listening. It is great fun (and educational) to listen to a variety of musical forms, appreciating each for its differences.

Fine Arts: "The Blue Danube"

Chester plays a perfect rendition of "The Blue Danube" waltz. Has your student ever heard this beautiful piece of music? It is very famous and played often by beginning music students.

Written by a famous Austrian composer, Johann Strauss, Jr., this waltz was only one of many he composed. Strauss, Jr. became known as the Waltz King during his day, having composed over 400 of these beautiful pieces. "The Blue Danube" is the one he is perhaps best known for, however. Listen to or learn to play it today!

Life Skills: How to React During an Emergency

After the fire begins, Harry and Tucker get nervous and begin to react wildly to the scene. But then we see Chester being very mature. "For a moment Chester got panicky. But he forced his thoughts back into order and took stock of the situation."

For your student, part of learning about safety and health is understanding how to react during an emergency. Talk with your student about how frightening and confusing an emergency can become. It can be difficult to remain calm and think. That, however, is the most important thing your student can do. Chester exhibits the perfect response in a situation—calming down and forcing his thoughts into order.

Teacher's Note: If your student has worked through the entire Five in a Row curriculum, she may remember a recurring lesson begun back in Vol. 1 with *Very Last First Time* called Crisis Thinking. If you have this manual, pull out the lesson and review the activity sheet to remind her of the steps to take in a crisis: Calm Down, Don't Panic, Be Quiet, Think Carefully, What Am I Supposed To Do?

Creating and practicing emergency drills for different situations can help your student remember what she needs to do and can help reduce some of the stress and fear. Tornado and fire drills can be reviewed in your student's home in a serious, but nonthreatening way. Also, basic first aid skills can be practiced, in case someone your student knows is injured.

Your student should also know where her doctor's number, an emergency police/fire number, and poison control number are. They should be clearly displayed somewhere in her home. Reviewing, discussing and practicing how to respond to emergency situations (including when and when not to call 911) can help your student be prepared to face future problems!

Life Skills: Being a Polite Host

Chester is getting the newsstand ready for a party. He carefully cleaned and put the shelf in order. When Harry arrives, Chester "hopped down, like a good host, to greet his new guest."

Five in Row Volume Seven

Take this opportunity to discuss with your student how we can be polite and gracious hosts to guests. Your student should understand how to kindly greet someone at the door (it could be a friend of hers, or a guest of someone else in her family). She should know how to offer a seat to the person and perhaps offer a beverage. Small talk, or polite conversation, should be practiced by your student as well. The goal of welcoming a guest into your home is to make that person feel comfortable, and get her to feel at ease. Even if the guest isn't coming to see you, it is still your responsibility to graciously welcome her if you answer the door.

If you know that a friend is coming over, then cleaning and straightening your room or play area is a kind way to welcome your guest. Learning these social rules and graces will help your student throughout her entire life—and her friends and guests will appreciate them as well!

Chapter 11—The Jinx

Teacher Summary

When Papa, Mama and Mario arrive at the burned newsstand, Mama becomes furious. She tells Mario that Chester set the fire and that all of the bad things that have happened recently are Chester's fault. She also tells Mario that Chester has to leave.

Later in the afternoon, Papa and Mario are selling papers and Mama is sitting in the newsstand feeling very angry. Suddenly, she hears the soft strains of her favorite Italian song. She begins to feel better, and even sings along. Soon, Mario and Papa hear, as well. Chester, the cricket, plays on and Mama is delighted. She decides that Chester can stay.

What we will cover in this chapter:

Social Studies: History and Geography - Naples, Italy * (two activity sheets)
Social Studies: History - Parts of a Newspaper
Language Arts: Writing and Discussion Question
Life Skills: Exaggeration - Sizing Up the Real Situation

Social Studies: History and Geography - Naples, Italy*

Throughout our story, we have discussed the fact that the Bellinis are from Italy. Your student may have completed previous lessons in this unit covering this country and its people. In this chapter, we discover that the Bellinis are from Naples, Italy. Take this opportunity to learn about Naples with your student.

Naples is the third-largest city in Italy. Rome and Milan are larger, but Naples is itself a big, bustling and growing city. Locate Naples on a map with your student. Point out that Naples is found at the foot of a mountain range on the west coast of southern Italy.

In Italian, Naples is called Napoli. Tourists and business people come from all over the world to explore Naples' important historic sites, scenic views, vibrant seaports and trade centers. Naples is a major center for manufacturing.

Naples is a city with greatly diverse economic areas. There are sections of great wealth and new buildings, as well as many impoverished areas. People living in both areas, however, are known throughout Europe as being quite lively, carefree and happy. Called Neapolitans, people from this city and the regions surrounding it enjoy annual music festivals, art galleries and delicious food. Does your student like pizza? Naples is the home of this delicious dish. It is believed that a baker in an Italian Royal court invented the pizza pie during the early 1700s.

Naples is home to many factories that produce items that include automobiles, cement, locomotives and textiles. Naples also produces many traditional wares including kidskin gloves, wine and jewelry.

Your student may wish to fix a pizza and listen to a little opera after doing this lesson!

Social Studies: History - Parts of a Newspaper

The Bellinis own a newsstand. Through out our story, your student has heard newspapers referred to and discussed. Even though much of today's news is found online, learning what is found in a newspaper and where to find it is a fun and important reference skill for your student.

To begin, purchase a local or national paper from a grocery store, convenience store, or gas station and sit down with your student to simply look it over. Point out the masthead or title bar of the paper. Show your student where the date, volume and issue information is located for each paper (on or under the masthead). Most newspapers include a small table of contents on the front page, showing readers where sections are located. Look with your student at what your paper includes—local and world news, editorials, comics, obituaries, weather and more.

Find an article that is continued on another page, and show your student how to find the continuation of the article.

Once your student is familiar with the newspaper, it may be fun and helpful to send her on a newspaper scavenger hunt. Below is a list of items you can give to your student.

- the name of her state
- a puzzle or game
- the name of another country
- a price over $50
- today's date
- the weather forecast
- a sports score
- a death notice (obituary)
- a comic strip
- a writer's byline (name of who wrote the article)
- a photographer's credit
- a letter to the editor

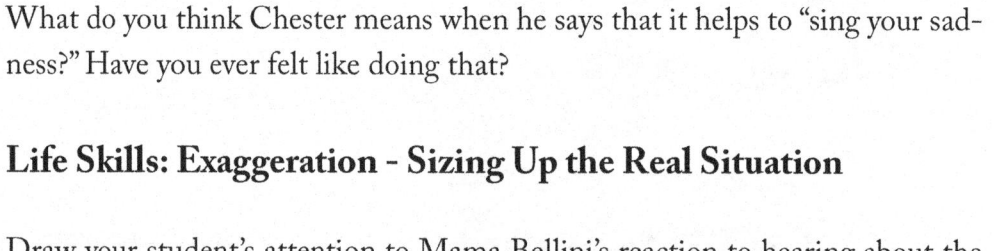

Your student can either circle or cut out the items she finds, or she can write out the information and where she found it. Your student will gain both knowledge and confidence by doing this enjoyable exercise.

Language Arts: Writing and Discussion Question

What do you think Chester means when he says that it helps to "sing your sadness?" Have you ever felt like doing that?

Life Skills: Exaggeration - Sizing Up the Real Situation

Draw your student's attention to Mama Bellini's reaction to hearing about the newsstand fire. As Papa and Mario look on, Mama wails, "Ruined—we're ruined!" Ask your student what she thinks. Are the Bellinis really ruined? Or is the fire merely a setback? After all, we read in the chapter that only the *Ladies' Home*

Journals had been burned, but Mama Bellini acts like the newsstand is completely gone.

Discuss with your student what exaggeration is and how some people don't look at the real situation, but instead blow it all out of proportion.

Mama is an excitable person and she can be quite dramatic. Remind your student about her reaction to Chester's arrival in chapter 2. She exaggerated there as well, didn't she?

When people exaggerate, they present a person or situation falsely. Instead of saying what really happened or what a person is actually like, a person who exaggerates may describe the situation in a way that makes it seem either worse or better than it really is. When you know someone who exaggerates, it makes you listen to what they say with caution. Even when they are really telling the truth, you wonder if they are stretching it a little.

Encourage your student to use exaggeration and drama in her fiction stories, but not in daily conversation. Being truthful and honest is the best way to relate to others and protect our character. People won't doubt what you say if they know they can trust your interpretation.

Chapters 12-15—Mr. Smedley, Fame, Orpheus and Grand Central Station

Teacher Summary

Mr. Smedley, a music lover and opera fan, is enchanted by Chester's newly discovered skills. He writes a letter to the musical editor of *The New York Times*, telling him all about Chester. Thousands of New Yorkers read the letter, which is printed in the musical page the next morning. Soon they flock to the Bellinis' newsstand to hear Chester for themselves.

The Bellinis love the crowds because they are both proud of Chester and enjoying selling more papers than ever. Chester works hard every night with Tucker, listening to the radio and learning new pieces to play. Every day, at 8 a.m. and 4:30 p.m., Chester enthralls large audiences in the subway station with his beautiful music.

Soon, however, Chester grows tired of the attention and the difficult job of playing every day. Playing was always a joy to him, but now it seems only like work. As autumn sets in, he longs to return to his beloved Connecticut and his old haunts. His owner, Mario, notices the change in Chester. Chester hears Mario telling his mother, "I almost wish he [Chester] hadn't come to New York—if he isn't going to be happy here."

Even though he knows the Bellinis will miss him, and he will miss them, along with Harry and Tucker, Chester knows he must leave New York and return home. After he is gone, Harry and Tucker discuss going to visit Chester the following summer.

Teacher's Note: Lessons for the four ending chapters of our book are being combined here. Why is that? You may wish to use this decision as a lesson for your student in how a fictional story works. In our book, *The Cricket in Times Square*, many topics and lesson ideas have been brought from the text. In all fiction stories, however, toward the end of the tale the author begins to wind things up. Instead of introducing new ideas and new characters, all the loose ends are tied together and very little new information is offered. For example, it would be odd if a brand new character was introduced in the final chapter of our story. It would also be strange if, for example, the Bellinis decided to suddenly sell their newsstand and begin an entirely new occupation. As always, Five in a Row works to extract and present learning skills and exercises for your student directly from the text. The lessons that follow are the final new and important topics your student can explore from our story, *The Cricket in Times Square*.

What we will cover in these chapters:

Social Studies: History - Mozart*
Social Studies: History - Tape Recorders
Science: Entomology - The Study of Insects
Language Arts: Creative Writing - Friendship
Language Arts: Completing a Story - Bringing the Tale Full Circle
Language Arts: Writing and Discussion Question
Life Skills: Fame - Positive and Negative Aspects

Social Studies: History - Mozart

Chester plays a piece of music by a man named Mozart. Is your student familiar with this famous composer and his music? Not every student will be a classical music enthusiast or expert, but every student should be introduced to this famous, talented and beloved composer—Mozart.

Born in Salzburg, Austria (January 27, 1756), Wolfgang Amadeus Mozart was the son of orchestra conductor and author, Leopold Mozart. Wolfgang showed amazing musical talent at a very early age. By the time he was only six years old, he was playing for the Austrian Empress in her court.

You may wish to discuss the word **prodigy** with your student. Mozart, perhaps more than any other person in history, exemplified this word in terms of music. His talents seemed to be far beyond his age, and he rapidly gained musical knowledge and success.

Leopold noticed his son's amazing gifts and devoted a lot of time to work with his son and help him learn more instruments. Although Mozart was a gifted musician, his true talents lay in the area of composition. By age 14, Mozart had already composed dozens of pieces for harpsichord, piano and violin, as well as other orchestral pieces.

Mozart married and worked in Vienna for several years. He was a prolific composer and made his living selling his compositions, giving public performances and giving music lessons. His money management was very poor, however, and he had difficulty supporting his family. His most famous opera, *The Marriage of Figaro*, was written during this time, and it gained widespread acclaim.

It wasn't enough, however, to keep Mozart popular. His critics were concerned that his musical style was too different. Mozart, like many artists (Monet, Van Gogh, etc.), suffered from being misunderstood. He was trying to do new things with music and composition, but often people are scared of what's new.

After *Figaro*, Mozart's popularity began to diminish. He continued to write many things including the famous opera *Don Giovanni* and a solemn piece called the *Requiem*. During his work on the *Requiem*, Mozart grew very ill, possibly from kidney failure, although there are many other theories as to his illness. Before the work was complete, Mozart died at age 35 on December 5, 1791. This man, whom we now recognize as one of the greatest composers of all time, died in poverty and was buried in an unmarked pauper's grave in Vienna.

Despite his short life, Mozart left the world over 600 breathtaking musical compositions! Take some time to let your student listen to a few of Mozart's pieces. Perhaps his most famous piece is the one that Chester learned, *A Little Night Music* (1787). Other excellent choices for your student's listening include *The Marriage of Figaro*, *The Magic Flute*, *Requiem*, *Symphony No. 41* and any of Mozart's sonatas. Your student should note that, although Mozart's life was often difficult, many of his compositions are intensely cheerful and vigorous. For this reason, Mozart is often a favorite composer of young music students.

As a lesson in musical appreciation, encourage your student to select one piece of music by Mozart that she especially enjoys or is drawn to. After she has listened to the piece several times, encourage her to either write a short essay or poem discussing how it makes her feel, or to paint or draw a picture of what the music reminds her of. Music can evoke strong feelings and Mozart's compositions can offer inspiring fodder for written and art pieces.

Social Studies: History – Tape Recorders

In chapter 12, we read that each day during Chester's concerts, Mr. Smedley "brought a tape recorder and made recordings of all the new pieces Chester learned." Has your student heard of a tape recorder? During most of the 20th century, tape recorders were used to record and play sound on a magnetic tape.

If your student used FIAR Vol. 6, she may remember that Thomas Edison invented the phonograph in 1877. (Chapter 8 of *Skylark*, in this volume, contains a lesson on the phonograph, as well.) Just a year later, American mechanic Oberlin Smith visited Edison's laboratory because he wanted to find a way to record telephone signals with a steel wire. Later, in 1928, tape recorders were invented, which used a new and improved means of recording sound with magnetic tape. By the 1940s and 1950s, tape recordings had revolutionized the fields of sound recording and sound playback, greatly affecting the movie, television, and music industries for decades to come.

Your student's parents or grandparents probably owned a small, portable tape recorder of some kind. In the 1970s–1990s, portable stereos called "boom boxes" were extremely popular. If your student is interested, show her pictures of tape recorders and audiocassettes online. If a family member or friend still has a tape recorder and/or an audiocassette, take the opportunity to demonstrate them in person!

Today, digital recording has replaced most analog methods such as the tape recorder. Your student could use any electronic device with a microphone (cell phone, laptop, etc.) and record herself playing music (like Chester), or perhaps reading a book for a younger sibling, giving a short speech, or singing.

Science: Entomology - The Study of Insects

As Chester grows increasingly unhappy at the newsstand, Mario and Mama notice it, as well. Mama thinks he might be sick and encourages Mario to take him to a "bug doctor"—an entomologist.

Has your student ever heard of entomology? Here is a great opportunity to share a few brief basics on what this study involves and how it helps us. Entomology (ehn tuh MAHL uh jee) is a part of zoology. Entomology is the study of insects. People who conduct research and study in this area are called entomologists. Although people have been interested in insects for centuries, entomology wasn't developed until the late 1700s. It was during the 1750s that an important Swedish naturalist, Carolus Linnaeus, developed a useful, comprehensive system of classifying plants and animals. Linnaeus' work is still vital to animal and plant science. He developed ways of naming and organizing all plants and animals by assigning each two different names. The first name refers to the creature's genus. The second name refers to the creature's species.

Teacher's Note: Animal and plant classification have been covered at various times in the *Five in a Row* curriculum—even as early as in *Before Five in a Row*! You can use this lesson as a springboard to continue your study or to begin learning about classification and scientific names. Locate library books or online information or videos that are at your student's level.

Entomologists study the insects of the world—and there are 1 1/2 million species of insects! The study of insects is very important. Besides wanting to learn more about them for their beauty and diversity, scientists know that insects are quite competitive with humans for food. Farmers, in particular, fight with insects every day and often lose the battle. Each year, up to 40% of global crop production is lost to pests such as insects. Entomologists who work studying insects which endanger crops and humans practice a branch of science called economic or applied entomology.

Students who enjoy insects and wish to pursue a career in entomology must have at least a bachelor's degree in entomology or biology. Teaching or research positions require a master's or doctoral degree in entomology from an agricultural university. Entomologists can work for the government, universities, cultural institutions and museums.

Language Arts: Creative Writing - Friendship

Think back with your student over our entire story, *The Cricket in Times Square*. Selden's masterful tale covers many topics and themes, including a powerful theme of friendship.

Mario and Chester are good, faithful friends. Chester, Harry and Tucker are also close friends. Talk a little with your student about what makes someone a good friend, and how these characters helped and supported each other.

After your discussion, encourage your student to write a short story that uses friendship as a main theme. She can develop two or more characters, and involve them in different situations. Her story can either show a good friendship, or one that needs work.

If your student is having trouble thinking of a plot or characters, then remind her that many writers get their ideas from personal experiences. This doesn't mean she should write a biographical story, but instead that she should think back on her own friendships. What made certain friends dear? Why did other friendships fade? By first listing or clustering these ideas, your student can then compile certain ones and use them to develop her own story.

Language Arts: Completing a Story - Bringing the Tale Full Circle

After your student has completed *The Cricket in Times Square*, talk with her about the ending George Selden chose. Chester returns to the place where he came from—the country. Other loose ends are tied up as well. At the beginning, the Bellinis were poor and their newsstand was struggling. Through Chester's talent and fame, the newsstand is now successful and famous. Tucker and Harry have made a new and dear friend as well.

Encourage your student to examine and explore the endings to stories that she reads and writes. Does the author wrap up all the loose ends of the plot? Does she leave something to the imagination? By practicing different endings for her stories and by looking at other authors' choices, your student can develop her writing skills and create wonderful endings.

Language Arts: Writing and Discussion Question

In the end, Chester Cricket decides to return to his home in the country. What do you think of his decision? What are the pros and cons? What would you have done?

Life Skills: Fame - The Positive and Negative Aspects

The Cricket in Times Square presents a great examination of what fame is and how it affects people. Discuss with your student how fame affected Chester, Tucker and the Bellinis and their business.

Many people who are famous describe their success as bittersweet. They say that although it is nice to be known by lots of people and be wealthy, the trade-offs are difficult. Privacy is often lost—it becomes harder and harder to be alone or out in public without being bothered by the public. For Chester, the fame brought both happiness and heartache. He enjoyed the success and money that the Bellinis received, but he grew tired of being forced to play and he didn't like the crowds of people staring at him.

Often, people are jealous of others who are famous and wish that they were famous, as well. It is important to remember, however, that all things—even fame and fortune—have positive and negative sides.

Teacher's Notes

Use this page to jot down relevant info you've found for this *Five in a Row* chapter book, including favorite lessons, go-along resources, field trips, and family memories.

THE CRICKET IN TIMES SQUARE

Dates studied:

Student:

Favorite Lesson Topics:

Social Studies:

Science:

Language Arts:

Fine Arts:

Life Skills:

Relevant Library Resources: Books, DVDs, Audio Books

Websites or Video Links:

Related Field Trip Opportunities:

Favorite Quote or Memory During Study:

The Cricket in Times Square - Chapter 1

Name:
Date:
Geography: **New York, NY Landmark**

Virtual FIELD TRIP

The lessons on **New York State** and **New York City** introduce general information about New York ... the city and the state. Choose a famous landmark in New York City (seach "landmarks in New York" online and take a *virtual tour* of that location. Take notes below of any information you learn about it. Print and paste an image of the landmark into the frame above. Write any notes or information that you learn into the space provided below.

_____
_____
_____
_____
_____
_____

The Cricket in Times Square

The Cricket in Times Square - Chapter 2

Name:
Date:
Science: **Label A Field Cricket**

After completing the **Science: Crickets** lesson, use the page below to label the parts of a cricket. Search online for "field cricket anatomy" or "parts of a cricket." The parts to label are listed below.

Antennae	Walking Legs	Ovipositor
Head	Fore & Hind Wings	Cerci
Thorax	Jumping Leg	Compound & Simple Eye
Abdomen	Spiracles	Palpi

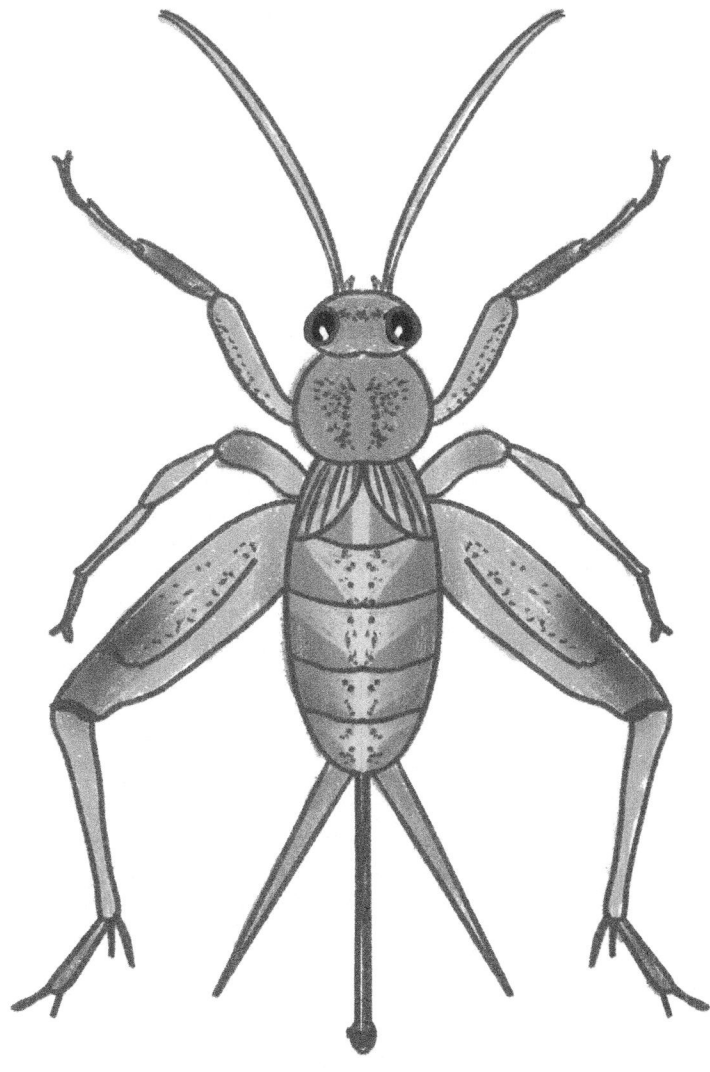

The Cricket in Times Square - Chapter 3

Name:

Date:

Science: **Migration**

The **Science: Bird Migration** lesson introduces animal migration. Below you'll find several resources (books and movies) that you can use to dive in and learn more about animal migration.

A couple of go-along books that you could use for research are:
Going Home: The Mystery of Animal Migration by Marianne Berkes
Fly Away Home (Medallion Editions for Young Readers) by Patricia Hermes

The novel *Fly Away Home* was based on the screenplay for the film, *Fly Away Home*. The film was inspired by the life of Bill Lishman, a Canadian artist who actually taught geese to fly. You could read the book, watch the movie, or do both!

Another movie about animal migration is *Flight of the Butterflies*. In it you learn about monarch butterflies and the immense, multi-thousand mile journey they embark on during their yearly migration.

Title of Book or Film: _____

Summary or Notes of Special Interest: _____

_____

_____

_____

_____

_____

_____

_____

The Cricket in Times Square - Chapter 4

Name:
Date:
Science: **Chemical Elements - Noble Gases**

You learned about Neon in the lesson **Science: Chemical Element - Neon.** Neon is a noble gas; there are six noble gases that make up group 18 of the periodic table of elements. Search online for "what are the noble gases," then list them below in the blank spaces provided. Use a highlighter or light-hued, colored pencil on the table of elements below to color in all of the noble gases in group 18.

_____   _____   _____

_____   _____   _____

Fun Fact: In 1898, German chemist Hugo Erdmann coined the phrase "noble gases" to describe these six gases. Like a nobleman who might consider it undignified to associate with commoners, noble gases tend not to react with other elements.

The Cricket in Times Square - Chapter 5

Name:
Date:
Language Arts: **Vocabulary Words**

Use the crossword puzzle below to review the vocabulary words covered in **chapters 1-4**. The clues and answers are provided for you on the following page.

Language Arts: **Vocabulary Words - Crossword Continued**

The crossword clues and answers for the vocabulary words covered in **chapters 1-4** are provided below to be used with the crossword on the previous page.

Across

3. (ch. 4) the study of personal space and how much separation people maintain between each other in social situations

4. (ch. 4) the study of body and facial movements, in conjunction with language

6. (ch. 3) alone and sad

8. (ch. 4) shots which help prevent certain illnesses

10. (ch. 3) a sausage made from liver

12. (ch. 3) a small bunch of weeds or grass; a little mound

13. (ch. 3) listening secretly to a private conversation

Down

1. (ch. 2) garbage or trash

2. (ch. 2) a palette using only one color

5. (ch. 3) the hindquarters of an animal; back legs

7. (ch. 4) a type of microscopic, single-celled organism that can be either helpful or harmful in our bodies

9. (ch. 3) searching about for what you can find

11. (ch. 4) a type of germ which invades a cell and multiplies within the cell

flip for vocab words: immunizations | virus | bacteria | proxemics | kinesics | forlorn | tuffet | liverwurst | haunches | eavesdropping | scrounging | refuse | monochromatic palette

The Cricket in Times Square - Chapter 6

Name:
Date:
Geography: **China - Cultural Study Through** _____

After completing the **History and Geography: China** lesson, choose one element below to learn more about China's culture. Fill in the blank above with the subject you choose to study. Take notes, print off images or draw items you want to include in your research and presentation. Finally, create a presentation of the information you find during your research, such as a piece of artwork, a written paragraph or two, or any other method of sharing what you learned.

- **Music** — "Music of China Wikipedia" is a good online source that mentions common types of Chinese music, including specific features and instruments.
- **Artists** — Who are the most famous Chinese artists? Whoever you choose, Qi Baishi's Twelve Landscape Screens from 1925 are beautiful and worth viewing online! He is a more contemporary artist than many of China's famous painters but was not influenced by western art. His paintings stayed true to early Chinese painting styles while infusing them with his own whimsical flair.
- **Food** — What are some traditional Chinese foods? Find recipes and determine which ones you might be able to make at home.
- **Architecture** — Research pagodas or common features of Chinese architecture such as curved roofs (and why they are curved).
- **Travel** — "11-Day Classic Wonders Tour" and Yangtze River cruises could provide two China-specific travel searches.
- **Astronomy** — What constellations are visiable in China?
- **Flora or Fauna** — What plants and/or animals are specific to China?
- **Landmarks** — What landmarks is China known for?

The Cricket in Times Square - Chapter 7

Name:
Date:
Language Arts: **Dictionary Entry Page**

After completing the **Language Arts: Dictionary Skills** lesson, use the sheet below to list the information that you discover in the dictionary when you look up the three assigned words: **soufflé**, **admiration** and **rumble**. You can create multiple photocopies of this page and cut along the dotted lines to produce many printable dictionary entry pages that you can use whenever you encounter a new word. Keep the completed entries in a file folder and review occasionally.

Word: _____

Pronunciation: _____

Definition: _____

_____

Use this word in a sentence: _____

_____

_____

The Cricket in Times Square - Chapter 8

Name:
Date:
Language Arts: **Vocabulary Words**

Use the crossword puzzle below to review the vocabulary words covered in **chapters 6-7**.

Language Arts: **Vocabulary Words - Crossword Continued**

The crossword clues and answers for the vocabulary words covered in **chapters 6-7** are provided below to be used with the crossword on the previous page.

Across

2. (ch. 6) the top part of a steeple or tower which narrows to a point

4. (ch. 7) a country's money

6. (ch. 6) small, unusual items such as toys and cheap jewelry

8. (ch. 7) a deep, heavy, continuous sound

9. (ch. 6) a temple or other sacred building with many stories forming a tower

10. (ch. 6) a pair of long, slender sticks used by many Asian people to raise food to their mouths

13. (ch. 7) a frothy, baked dish made light by including beaten egg whites and baked in a hot oven

Down

1. (ch. 6) a fast, joyful solo dance, usually done in a folk style

3. (ch. 7) a disk which detects electric activity

5. (ch. 7) a feeling of pleasure and approval of something fine or well done

7. (ch. 7) (electroencephalograph) a machine used to monitor brain waves

11. (ch. 6) a substance which gives off a sweet smell when burned

12. (ch. 6) a silk robe held together by a wide sash

flip for vocab words: jig | spire | pagoda | incense | kimono | chopsticks | novelties | electrode | EEG | currency | admiration | rumble | soufflé

The Cricket in Times Square - Chapter 9

Name:

Date:

Fine Arts: Cooking - Rice for Breakfast and Dessert

After completing the lessons for chapter 9, you will have learned many things about rice, including that it is a main staple in the Chinese diet. You will have seen two recipes and discussed creating your own Chinese-inspired dinner.

To dive further into recipes and ways in which rice plays a frequent role in Chinese meals, search the following two suggestions online and record the answers below with an explanation of the dishes. Print and paste an image of the dish into the frame next to the recipe title and description. You might choose to print off any recipes you find and try them out if they interest you.

Search online: "Chinese rice for breakfast" and "Chinese rice for dessert," then fill in the blanks.

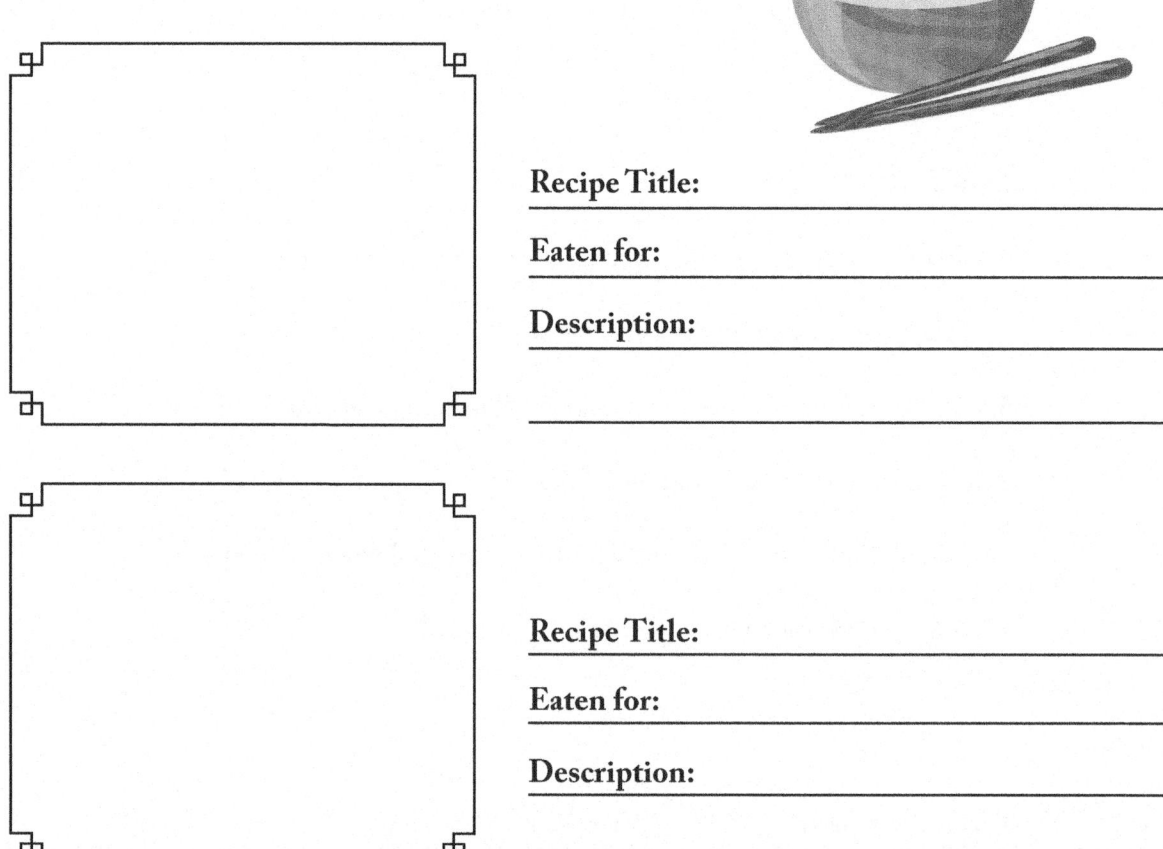

Recipe Title:

Eaten for:

Description:

Recipe Title:

Eaten for:

Description:

The Cricket in Times Square - Chapter 10

Name:
Date:
Fine Arts: **Vaudeville - Research a Famous Vaudeville Act**

After completing the **History: Vaudeville** lesson, you will have had a general introduction to the theatrical entertainment known as vaudeville, which encompassed a wide variety of acts, including singing, dancing, magic tricks, joke telling, etc.

Research a specific vaudeville act by searching "most influential vaudeville acts" online.

Jenny Lind, Charlie Chaplin (who started out in vaudeville as a child) or Williams and Walker would be interesting vaudeville acts to research. Williams and Walker were responsible for many "firsts" in vaudeville and are a fascinating pair to learn more about.

A go-along book that you could use for research is: *Who Was Charlie Chaplin?* by Patricia Brennan Demuth

Print and paste an image of the vaudevillian performer(s) into the frame. Write information gathered through your research into the spaces below.

Name(s) _____

Lived: _____

Known for: _____

_____

_____

The Cricket in Times Square - Chapter 11

Name:
Date:
Geography: **Naples, Italy**

Virtual FIELD TRIP

The **History and Geography: Naples, Italy** lesson introduces general information about this Italian city. Search online to find a virtual field trip to watch or use resource books from your library to learn more about Naples, Italy. Print and paste an image from your research into the frame above. Write any notes or information that you learn about this city into the space provided below.

The Cricket in Times Square

The Cricket in Times Square - Chapter 11

Name:

Date:

Geography: **Naples, Italy - Neapolitan Foods**

In the **History and Geography: Naples, Italy** lesson, you learned a bit about the history of pizza, specifically Neapolitan pizza, and its ties to Naples, Italy. Research Neapolitan pizza; print and paste an image into the frame below and write the traditional ingredients into the space provided to the right.

A fun go-along book to pair with learning about Naples, Italy is: *Naples!* (Recipe for Adventure #1) by Giada De Laurentiis

Neapolitan Pizza

Ingredients: _____

_____

_____

Next, search online "history of Neapolitan ice cream." Learn about the origins of this tasty, triple ice cream combination and then include the typical flavors below. Print and paste an image of Neapolitan ice cream into the frame or color it in yourself using the classic colors associated with each flavor.

Neapolitan Ice Cream

Three flavors: _____

_____

_____

The Cricket in Times Square - Chapter 12-15

Name:

Date:

History: **Biography - Who Am I?**

In the **History and Geography: Mozart** lesson, you learned about Wolfgang Amadeus Mozart. Search online or use the two recommended books below to dig deeper and learn more about this famous composer.

Go-along books that you could use for research are:
Wolfgang Amadeus Mozart: Getting to Know the World's Greatest Composers by Mike Venezia
Who Was Wolfgang Amadeus Mozart? by Yona Zeldis McDonough

Another fun go-along book that ties to this lesson without qualifying as a research book is:
A Mouse Called Wolf by Dick King-Smith

Print and paste an image of Mozart into the frame. Write information gathered through your research into the spaces below.

Name: _____

Lived: _____

Known for: _____

_____

_____

Connections to story: _____

_____

_____

Chapter Book
Sample **Lesson Planning Sheet**

Helen Keller has more suggested lessons per chapter than you will probably want to (or be able to) cover. The sample planning sheets below and on the following pages show ideas that *could* be chosen for the first two weeks of this study. You are free to choose any of the lesson ideas and keep track of your choices by noting them on the reproducible, blank Lesson Planning Sheet (following these pages). For more ideas on making the best use of your Five in a Row curriculum, be sure to read the *Tips and Advice for Five in a Row Chapter Book Studies* section as well as *How to Use Five in a Row Volume 7* earlier in this volume.

Week 1

Title:
Helen Keller

Author:
Margaret Davidson

Monday

Read Chapter 1 together, then:

Social Studies

Discuss timeframe of story (do the math mentioned in lesson)

Language Arts

Remember Mary Ingalls and scarlet fever from Little House books? Read excerpt from manual

Tuesday

Science

Anatomy – the eye
Discuss parts of eye, and do activity sheet (use library book or a diagram online for reference)

Chapter Book Sample Lesson Planning Sheet Week 1

Wednesday	Thursday	Friday
Read Chapter 2 together, then: **Social Studies** Mention some facts about Perkins Institute, look it up online **Language Arts** "Deaf and dumb" – explain the term and what it used to mean (and why we no longer use it)	**Science** Do the sensory deprivation exercise, followed by: **Language Arts: Writing** Write 5 sentences about this exercise using the prompts	**Life Skills** Discuss hope and determination and then do the activity sheet

Chapter Book

Sample Lesson Planning Sheet: Week 2

Week 2

Title:
Helen Keller

Author:
Margaret Davidson

Monday

Read Chapter 3 together, then:

Language Arts

Discuss who slept well that night, and why

Science

Sound/vibration and the experiment with bowl and plastic wrap

Tuesday

Science

Exploring the five senses (need to reread chapter for this), then do the activity sheet

Chapter Book Sample Lesson Planning Sheet Week 2

Wednesday	Thursday	Friday
Read Chapter 4 together, then: **Science** How good is your sense of smell? Do activity sheet on other senses being heightened	**Language Arts** First, discuss writing a persuasive argument **Language Arts: Writing** (Use the ideas discussed above to do this) Pretend you are Miss Annie and you want to convince the Kellers to allow you to take Helen away from the family for a while. Write a letter that Miss Annie might have given to the Kellers to persuade them to let her do this.	Read Chapter 5 and 6 together, then: **Language Arts** Laughing and sobbing at the same time – discuss how/why **Life Skills** Anticipation for each new day, optimism, and pessimism Watch *The Miracle Worker* movie from 1962 (mentioned in chapter 3 lessons) for family movie night!

Chapter Book Lesson Planning Sheet:

Week ___

Title:

Author:

Monday

Tuesday

Chapter Book Lesson Planning Sheet

Wednesday	Thursday	Friday

Index

Social Studies

Geography
Boston, MA, 18
China, 220
Coney Island, 229
Connecticut, 204
Diamond, MO, 128
Iowa, 148
Italy, 215
Kansas, 142
Long Island, 198
Maine, 94
Mass transit, 194
Missouri, 142
Naples, Italy, 241
New York, 191
New York City, 193
Plymouth Rock, 33
Prairie Notebook, 104
Sea Notebook, 104
Yangtze River, 222

History
African Methodist Church, 140
Automobile, 95
Braille, Louis, 28
China, 220
Circus, 27
Civil War, 128
Coney Island, 229
Drought, 56, 67
Du Bois, W.E.B., 151
Edison, Thomas, 140
Family portraits, 55
Flood, 67
Fulton, Robert, 32
Geneology, 127
Great Chicago Fire, 73
Harvard University, 36
Hauling water, 83
Homestead Act of 1862, 146
Italy, 215
Julius Caesar, 97
Kansas, 142
King Jr., Dr. Martin Luther, 166
Last names, 139
Mass transit, 194
Missouri, 142
Mozart, 244
Mythology, 217
Naples, Italy, 241
New York, 191
New York City, 193
Newspaper, 241
Orpheus, 217
Perkins Institute, 18
Phonograph, 86
Plymouth Rock, 33
Postal service, 143
President Benjamin Harrison, 35
Radcliffe College, 36
Royal society, 166
Scarlet fever, 15
Segregation, 134
Shellac, 86
Steamboats, 32
Sullivan, Anne, 33
Tape recorders, 245
Tuskegee Normal School, 151
U.S. currency, 225
U.S. legal system, 230
Vaudeville, 236
Washington, Booker T., 151

Wells, 90
World War II, 39

Career Path
Astronaut, 63
Astronomer, 63
Firefighter, 75
Illustrator, 149
Music careers, 237
Speech therapist, 33
Teacher, 158

Science

Animal gestation, 59
Bacteria, 210
Barometer, 68
Bird migration, 205
Birds, 152
Botanist, 164
Buoy, 101
Carnivores, 65
Chlorophyll, 131
Chloroplast, 131
Combustion, 77
Composting, 155
Cows, 65
Crickets, 198
Disease, 199
Entomology, 246
Eye, 15
Film photography, 57
Fire, 76
Five senses, 21
Garden, 165
Genetics, 104
Germs, 210
Heat exhaustion, 71
Herbivores, 65
Insects, 158
Ivory, 233
Legumes, 155
Loon, 102
LORAN, 102
Matches, 200
Mice, 195
Neon, 211
Nitrogen, 154
Oceans, 96
Ornithology, 152
Oxidation, 77
Parts of a flower, 164
Pathogen, 199
Peanuts, 167
Photosynthesis, 131
Primates, 29
Rain gauge, 68
Reservoir, 91
Rice, 232
Sensory deprivation, 18
Shade, 87
Sleep, 226
Smell, 23
Smoke, 237
Soil, 154
Sweet potatoes, 161, 167
Synthetics, 169
Thermometer, 68
Tides, 96
Traits, dominant and recessive, 105
Vibration, 21
Viruses, 210
Water safety, 101
Water table, 91
Weather station, 68

Language Arts

Analogy, 84
Author's license
Black Beauty, 37
Book organization, 201
Completing a story, 247
Creative writing, 22, 26, 30, 105, 207, 247
Dictionary skills, 227
Editing, 207
Etymology, 25
Fantasy stories, 196
"Humbug", 159
Imagery, 84
Ingalls, Mary, 16
Interviewing, 77
"Jabberwocky", 25
Nonverbal communication, 212
Opening line, 196
Pamphlets, 161
Persuasive writing, 23
Proofreading, 207
Reading out loud, 212
Selden, George, 218
Symmetry in writing, 99
The Secret Garden, 135
Vocabulary, 26, 31, 37, 58, 60, 67, 72, 78, 85, 89, 93, 97, 99, 103, 106, 130, 131, 137, 153, 156, 202, 209, 213, 223, 228
What You Know First, 87
Writing accents, 222
Writing and discussion questions, 17, 19, 22, 25, 26, 30, 34, 37, 41, 58, 60, 66, 69, 72, 78, 85, 89, 92, 97, 99, 103, 105, 130, 131, 135, 137, 141, 143, 144, 147, 149, 153, 156, 159, 162, 165, 168, 169, 197, 202, 209, 213, 219, 223, 227, 231, 234, 238, 242, 247
Writing style, 57

Title index

Helen Keller, Margaret Davidson, 14
Skylark, Patricia MacLachlan, 54
The Story of George Washington Carver, Eva Moore, 126
The Cricket in Times Square, George Selden, 190

Author index

Margaret Davidson, *Helen Keller*, 14
Patricia MacLachlan, *Skylark*, 54
Eva Moore, *The Story of George Washington Carver*, 126
George Selden, *The Cricket in Times Square*, 190

Fine Arts

Accordian, 145
Analogous colors, 61
Brick making, 157
Charcoal rubbing, 132
Choirs, 137
Color mixing, 61
Colors of drought, 73
Complementary colors, 61
Designing currency, 228
Juggling, 31
Juice paint, 136
Julius Caesar, 97
Making toys, 17
Music types, 238
Opera, 219
Perspective, 214
Primary colors, 61
Secondary colors, 61
Singing, 137
Special occasions, 103
Tertiary colors, 61

The Miracle Worker, 22
"The Tyger", 79
Vegetable stains, 136
Williams, Garth, 202
Wind chimes, 223

Cooking
Corn dodgers, 138
Fried rice, 234
Helen Keller's Roasted Apples, 38
Sarah's Biscuits, 85
Sweet potato recipes, 162
Wonton soup, 235

Music
"Hush Little Baby", 99
"The Blue Danube", 239

Life Skills

Adoption, 141
Anticipation, 27
Anxiety, 231
College applications, 145
Commitment, 82
Determination, 20, 138
Developing expertise, 133
Emergencies, 239
Fame, 247
Finding silver linings, 214
Fire safety, 81
First aid for burns, 82
Honesty, 231
Hope, 69
Hosting, 239
Ingenuity, 147
Making gifts, 89
Making hard choices, 93

Making new friends, 209
Optimism, 69
Pet ownership, 165
Self-directed study, 150
Service, 170
Stress, 231
Stuttering, 133
Working through fears, 106

Supplemental Book List

Helen Keller

The Little House Series by Laura Ingalls Wilder
Out of the Darkness: The Story of Louis Braille by Russell Freedman
Helen Keller's Teacher by Margaret Davidson
Black Beauty by Anna Sewell
Who Is Stevie Wonder? by Jim Gigliotti
Who Was Freda Kahlo? by Sarah Fabiny
Who Was Louis Braille? by Margaret Frith
Six Dots: A Story of Louis Braille by Jen Bryant
The Word Collector by Peter H. Reynolds
The Right Word: Roget and His Thesaurus by Jen Bryant
The Word Snoop by Ursula Dubosarsky
The Watcher by Jeanette Winter
Who Is Jane Goodall? by Roberta Edwards
I Talk Like a River by Jordan Scott
The Buck Stops Here: The Presidents of the United States by Alice Provensen

Skylark

Three Names by Patricia MacLachlan
Word After Word After Word by Patricia MacLachlan
White Fur Flying by Patricia MacLachlan
Kindred Souls by Patricia MacLachlan
The Poet's Dog by Patricia MacLachlan
Fly Away by Patricia MacLachlan
The True Gift by Patricia MacLachlan
Cat Talk by Patricia MacLachlan
Once I Ate a Pie by Patricia MacLachlan
Snowflakes Fall by Patricia MacLachlan
All the Places to Love by Patricia MacLachlan
We Didn't Mean to Go to Sea by Arthur Ransome
Caleb's Story by Patricia MacLachlan
More Perfect Than the Moon by Patricia MacLachlan
Grandfather's Dance by Patricia MacLachlan
Meet Kit: An American Girl by Valerie Tripp

The Story of George Washington Carver

A Separate Battle: Women and the Civil War by Ina Chang
Between Two Fires by Joyce Hansen
The Secret Garden by Frances Hodgson Burnett
Who Was Rosa Parks? by Yona Zeldis McDonough
Who Was Albert Einstein? by Jess Brallier
Who Was Booker T. Washington? by James Buckley, Jr.
With Books and Bricks: How Booker T. Washington Built a School by Suzanne Slade
Martin's Big Words: The Life of Dr. Martin Luther King, Jr. by Doreen Rapaport
Who Was Martin Luther King, Jr.? by Bonnie Bader

The Cricket in Times Square

Accidents May Happen by Charlotte Foltz Jones
Mistakes That Worked: 40 Familiar Inventions & How They Came to Be by Charlotte Foltz Jones
Stuart Little by E.B. White
Charlotte's Web by E.B. White
d'Aulaire's Book of Greek Myths by Ingri and Edgar d'Aulaire
The Name Jar by Yangsook Choi
Going Home: The Mystery of Animal Migration by Marianne Berkes
Fly Away Home (Medallion Editions for Young Readers) by Patricia Hermes
Who Was Charlie Chaplin? by Patricia Brennan Demuth
Naples! (Recipe for Adventure #1) by Giada De Laurentiis
Wolfgang Amadeus Mozart: Getting to Know the World's Greatest Composers by Mike Venezia
Who Was Wolfgang Amadeus Mozart? by Yona Zeldis McDonough
A Mouse Called Wolf by Dick King-Smith

Scope of Topics

Helen Keller

History
Late 1800s America
Early 1900s America
Vice President Chester A. Arthur
President James A. Garfield
Scarlet fever
Penicillin
Perkins Institute
Circus
Louis Braille
Braille
Robert Fulton
Steamboats
Plymouth Rock
Anne Sullivan
President Benjamin Harrison
Harvard University
Radcliffe College
World War II

Geography
Boston, Massachusetts
Plymouth Rock

Career Path
Teacher
Speech therapist

Science
Eye
Sensory deprivation
Sound
Five senses
Primates

Language Arts
Mary Ingalls
Archaic terminology
Persuasive writing
Etymology
Creative writing
Writing and discussion questions (every chapter)
Black Beauty

Vocabulary Words
etymology
etymon
braille
Louis Braille
primate
tandem

Fine Arts
Toy making
Juggling
Cooking

Life Skills
Determination
Anticipation

Skylark

History
Family portraits
Drought
1930s America
Dust Bowl
Floods
Land reclamation

Great Chicago Fire
Hauling water
Wells
Henry Ford
Ford Motor Company
Early 1900s America
President William Howard Taft
Ragtime music
Great Depression

Geography
Your state's history
Fire risk
Wells
Maine

Science
Film photography
Animal gestation periods
Cows
Herbivores
Carnivores
Weather station
Thermometer
Barometer
Rain gauge
Heat exhaustion
Fire
Oxidation
Combustion
Shade
Water table
Reservoir
Tides
Oceans
Water saftey
Loons
Genetics
Dominant traits
Recessive traits

Language Arts
Writing and discussion questions (every chapter)
Writing styles
Learning to interview
Analogies
Imagery
Vocabulary
Personal inspiration
Author's license
e. e. cummings
Developing symmetry
Creative writing

Vocabulary Words
motif
gestation
premature
primary colors
secondary colors
tertiary colors
analogous
complementary
rumen
regurgitate
cud
reticulum
omasum
abomasum
land reclamation
heatstroke
heat exhaustion
oxidation
combustion
kindling temperature
analogy
shellac
license
well
groundwater
reservoir
watertable
global ocean
tides
symmetry

bouy
chart
LORAN/LORAN-C
trait
genetics
dominant
recessive

Fine Arts
Watercolor painting
Color mixing
Colors of drought
Theatrical "fire"
Cooking
Julius Caesar
"Hush Little Baby"
Special occasions

Life Skills
Optimism
Fire precautions
First aid for burns
Commitment
Making gifts
Hard choices
Family relationships
Working through fear

The Story of George Washington Carver

History
Geneology
Personal portfolio
Diamond, Missouri
The Civil War
Union Army
Confederate Army
Frederick Douglass
Segregation
Last names
African Methodist Church

Thomas Edison
Kansas
Missouri
U.S. Postal Service
Zip codes
Homestead Act of 1862
Tuskegee Normal School
Booker T. Washington
W. E. B. Du Bois
Royal society
Dr. Martin Luther King, Jr.
"I Have a Dream" speech
Civil rights
Rosa Parks
Albert Einstein

Geography
Diamond, Missouri
The Civil War
Kansas
Missouri
Homestead Act of 1862
Iowa

Career Path
Illustrator
Teacher

Science
Photosynthesis
Birds
Ornithology
Soil
Composting
Nitrogen
Legumes
Insects
Sweet potatoes
Parts of a flower
Gardening
Botanists
Peanuts
Synthetics

Scope of Topics

Language Arts
Writing and discussion questions (every chapter)
The Secret Garden
"Humbug"
Folios
Pamphlets

Vocabulary Words
geneology
chloroplasts
chlorophyll
photosynthesis
glucose
expertise
vocal cords
larynx
contralto
mezzo-soprano
soprano
tenor
baritone
bass
determination
ornithology
W. E. B. Du Bois
legume
refractory brick
building brick
composting

Fine Arts
Cooking
Charcoal rubbings
Juice paints
Vegetable dyes
Choirs
Singing
Accordian
Finger painting
Brick making
Crayons

Life Skills
Understanding stuttering
Developing expertise
Determination
Learning about adoption
College applications
Ingenuity
Self-directed study
Pet ownership
Service

The Cricket in Times Square

History
New York
Central Park
Boroughs
New York City
Mass transit
Italy
Michelangelo
Leonardo da Vinci
Mythology
Orpheus
China
U.S. currency
Federal Reserve
Coney Island
U.S. legal system
Vaudeville
Naples, Italy
Parts of a newspaper
Mozart
Tape recorders

Geography
New York
Central Park
Boroughs
New York City
Mass transit
Long Island

Connecticut
Italy
China
Mandarin
Yangtze River
Coney Island
Naples, Italy

Career Path
Careers in music
Music perfomance
Songwriter
Composer
Music teacher
Music therapy

Science
Mice
Crickets
Insects spreading disease
Matches
Pathogen
Bird migration
Germs
Bacteria
Viruses
Imunizations
Neon
Sleep
EEG
Rice
Ivory
Entomology

Language Arts
Writing and discussion questions (every chapter)
Organization of a book
Fantasy story writing
Opening lines
Drafts
Revising
Editing
Proofreading
Reading out loud

Nonverbal communication
Kinesics
Proxemics
George Selden
Dictionary skills
Creative writing
Completing a story

Vocabulary Words
monochromatic palette
refuse
scrounging
eavesdropping
haunches
liverwurst
tuffet
forlorn
kinesics
proxemics
bacteria
viruses
immunizations
jig
spire
pagoda
incense
kimono
chopsticks
novelties
soufflé
rumble
admiration
currency
EEG (electroencephalograph)
electrode

Fine Arts
Garth Williams
Perspective
Opera
Create your own wind chimes
Create your own currency
Cooking
Music types
"The Blue Danube"

Scope of Topics

Life Skills
Personal perspective
Making new friends
Optimism
Honesty
Dealing with stress and anxiety
Special occasions
Dealing with an emergency
Hosting
Fame

Inspired learning through great books.

Five in a Row is a complete,* well-rounded, literature-based curriculum that takes your child from pre-K through middle school.

For ages 2-4

For ages 3-5

Before Five in a Row is a rich treasury of creative ideas that help you gently, consistently prepare your children for the lifelong adventure of learning. Now in a revised second edition, this bestselling volume is the foundation for inspired learning through great books and future studies with the entire Five in a Row curriculum.

More Before Five in a Row inspires your child's learning through extraordinary children's picture books while nurturing your relationship with them and making memories to last a lifetime! Designed for ages 3 through 5, this preschool and kindergarten curriculum is filled with lessons for you and your child to enjoy together and prepare your child for the lifelong adventure of learning.

For ages 5-12

Five in a Row is an easy-to-follow, highly effective instructional guide for teaching Social Studies, Language Arts, Art, Applied Math and Science using outstanding children's literature as the basis for each weekly unit study. Lessons are designed for children ages 5 through 12, and include discussion guide and questions, teacher answers, hands-on activities and suggestions for further study. Visit www.fiveinarow.com to view suggested age ranges for each volume.

Volume 8 Coming Soon!

Five in a Row Bible Supplement (for Vols. 1-4)

The *Five in a Row Bible Supplement, 2nd Edition* provides hundreds of lessons in character development with accompanying Bible references. Each story has numerous lessons to choose from, all in an easy-to-use format.

Full-Color, Laminated Story Disks

Available for *Before FIAR*, *More Before FIAR*, and *FIAR Volumes 1-5*.
Storybook Maps are also available for *Before FIAR* and *More Before FIAR*.

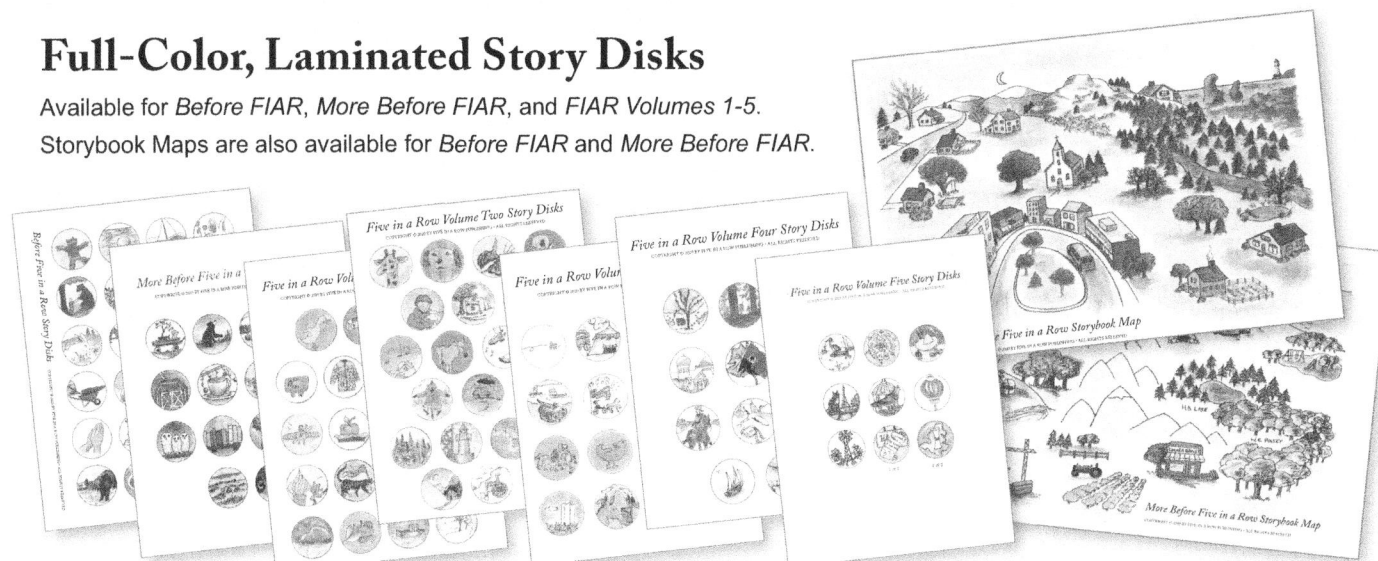

Digital Resources
Available from fiveinarow.com

FIAR Mini Units

Five in a Row Mini Units are digital unit studies based on children's picture books that include lessons for ages 2-12, designed to be used for one week.

FIAR Planner

The *Five in a Row Combined Family and Academic Planner* was created to give you access to school planning pages specific to the Five in a Row curriculum.

Notebook Builder

More than 120 pages of notebooking templates for all ages, appropriate for any topic or unit of study.

FIAR Nature Studies
(Spring, Summer, Fall, Winter)

FIAR Nature Studies encourage your entire family to enjoy and explore the outdoors in all four seasons. It is a true unit study approach to nature studies; suggestions introduce you and your child to poetry, music, and art that tie in to the season.

You will need to add math and phonics/reading instruction to **Five in a Row.*

www.fiveinarow.com

Made in the USA
Monee, IL
07 September 2022

13481265R00157